...

RETURN

OF THE

SWALLOWS

The Memoir of
Dorothy, Countess Praschma

as compiled and edited by Ilona Praschma Balfour

ISBN-10: 171883392X

ISBN-13: 978-1718833920

BISAC: History / Europe / Germany

Ilona Praschma Balfour

Prologue

Dorothy Eva Ferreira, my mother, was born in South Africa to Adriena and Peter Carlisle Ferreira, a family with deep roots in the country. Her father was a descendant of Commodore Ignatius Leopold Ferreira, a 17th-century Portuguese explorer who was shipwrecked near a colony of French Huguenots and converted from Catholicism in order to take a wife, Countess Almine du Pre, and settle there.

Dorothy's uncle, also called Ignatius Ferreira, joined with British forces to fight in the Anglo-Zulu wars against the Zulu leader, King Cetshwayo. For his effort in the campaign he was awarded the Most Distinguished Order of Saint Michael and Saint George.

He was one of the pioneers of the gold rush in Johannesburg and established a mining camp where the first diggers initially settled. Their tents, wagons, reed huts and wood-iron building were gathered around Ferreira's position and he laid out what came to be called Ferreira's Camp.

But the discovery of gold and diamonds brought speculators and investors to South Africa and finally their greed led to the Anglo-Boer war.

Near Duivelskloof, in the Northern Transvaal, is the *kraal* or village of the mystical rain queen, Modjadji, in a sacred forest of unique cycads. In this same area, a place of green mountains and verdant fields, Dorothy's family had a farm, Mooiplaats.

It was 1900, during the height of the Anglo-Boer War, a time when the mighty British army realized they were unable to win on the battlefield. While the Boers, most of them farmers, were off fighting, orders were given to "sweep the veld clean." Farms were looted and burned, livestock killed and Boer women and children taken to "concentration" camps, where they died by the thousands of starvation and typhoid.

When the British soldiers came to Mooiplaats, Adriena knew that her newborn infant would not survive in the camp so she entrusted her baby to an African woman, a member of Modjadji's tribe, hiding in a hut in the bushveld. There, she nursed Dorothy until the war was over and her mother came back to claim her.

Dorothy and her sisters had a carefree childhood. They spoke Sotho in addition to English and played with the African children on the farm. An aunt taught them to read and write, play the piano, flower arranging and all the necessary social graces. Dorothy would ride on horseback to the nearest mission station to borrow books and thus acquired a broad general knowledge.

A number of German immigrants had settled in the Northern Transvaal including a family from Upper Silesia, seeking a new life in a new country far away from the financial depression which was sweeping through Europe. At the request of their previous employer from Germany, Johannes Count Praschma, one of these families offered to take his wayward son under their wing.

In 1929 Engelbert Count Praschma, Baron von Bilkau, the handsome, adventuring young German aristocrat, deemed a profligate by his family, arrived in South Africa.

Sadly he had a history of unrestrained behavior, unpaid debts and legal problems, even imprisonment. Dorothy would learn this only much later.

On hand during a welcoming party for the visiting count the guests heard a commotion and rushed outside to hear one of the maids shouting: "*Mokopa,*

mokopa! Snake, snake! A mamba!" This brought the guests, including Engelbert, out of the house.

Speaking in Sotho, Dorothy called out: "Where is it? Where did you see it?" Grabbing a broom from the maid's hands, Dorothy flailed at the snake until a gardener arrived with a spade and mercifully finished it off.

He dragged the snake toward a heap of leaves while the two maids ran off screaming. They were far more terrified of the dead snake's spirit than the live snake. Dorothy returned to the front of the house and the count immediately stepped toward her, bowed deeply, took her hand and kissed it gently. "You are a hero," he said. She smiled, said nothing and went back into the home and exhaled. She was rattled. No one said he was so handsome — and had such unbelievable manners.

The count also could not get Dorothy out of his mind and began riding the five miles to the Ferreira farm several times each week. On each visit she'd receive the same bow and a kiss on the hand.

One evening he came up and was surprised to hear the farm girl at the piano, playing one of his favorites, Dvorak's "Humoresque." She could easily blend into European society. How many countesses did he know who could kill a mamba?

Dorothy and Engelbert fell in love, and, in an echo of her Portuguese ancestor, she converted to Catholicism in order to marry him.

His older brother, Joseph, had married famous Russian actress, Erna Thiele, renounced all claims on his inheritance and, disenchanted with the growing influence of that ambitious Austrian, Adolf Hitler, left Germany for America and Hollywood.

The family castles, estates and properties, including the family seat at Falkenberg, were held in a *fideicommiss*, a legal entailment which stated that the oldest son would be the sole heir. Now it was Engelbert's turn. As the second in line, he stood to inherit everything.

But in the light of his irresponsible behavior and the fact that his wife, an African "peasant," would not be a suitable countess and deal with the traditions of centuries, his siblings maneuvered to have him disinherited. Meanwhile the third son, Friedrich, sensibly married a princess which helped to restore the family honor. It was decided to install him as the owner of Falkenberg. This made Engelbert resolve to return to claim his rightful inheritance as soon as possible.

After Dorothy and Engelbert's baby daughter, Ria, died in infancy, Johannes, Engelbert's father, wrote a harsh letter to Dorothy stating that she should remain in Africa as there was nothing for her in Germany. But he was growing old and feeble. It was 1935. Adolf Hitler, had just abolished the office of president and declared himself Führer und Reichskanzler, promising a new age of German prosperity.

Engelbert, with his pregnant wife and two sons, booked passage to Hamburg, where he would work as a journalist while sorting out his family affairs.

It had been on Dorothy's mind for some time. Years before, as a young girl, she was on a hunting and fishing trip in Portuguese East Africa with several neighbors and family members. One night they camped near a village by the Limpopo River. The hunt was successful and an impala was shared with the local chief. After they had eaten, the witchdoctor threw a handful of bones onto the ground and began to tell their fortunes. When it came to Dorothy's turn, he told her that she would meet a man from far away, he would give her two white presents and they would have four children, two of them good and two bad. He continued that one day she would return to Africa again.

Before leaving Cape Town to board the ship to Hamburg, Engelbert presented Dorothy with a pair of beautifully carved white ivory earrings. Were they fulfilling the witchdoctor's predictions?

— IPB

###

CHAPTER ONE
A NEW FAMILY, A NEW COUNTRY, A NEW HOME

Hamburg
Autumn, 1935

The voyage on the good ship *Wangoni*, of the Hamburg
Woerman Line, sailing from Cape Town, was pleasant. There
were many amenities, much music and singing; dancing and
sport. I won the *Wangoni* Derby. The highlight of this game is
the betting and the winning pool, causing much hilarity and
goodwill all round. It was, however, when we docked at
Walfish Bay some flamboyant women came aboard — all well
and good, but their advice given to Engelbert on how I should
manage my children! — my little Peter, 15 months old,
teething and suffering from fever should have been potty
trained, the children must eat more and sleep more, etc., etc.
The advice was well meant, but not wanted. Perhaps it would
have been acceptable if I could have spoken German. But now
I wondered if all German women were so insufferable and I
wished to see the last of them. Instead, we docked in
Southampton and the English speaking people left.
Tomorrow, we dock in Hamburg and I have cold feet. Can I
face Germany after my father-in-law's bitter letter? Will I ever
understand these alien people?

Yes, tomorrow afternoon we dock in Hamburg. Then,
somehow, the name seemed to lose some of its
apprehensiveness because there appeared in my mind's eye —
away in the past — a number of people who had become real
friends, people with strange sounding names, like Ambrosaat,
Pfeffer, Bombol! They had all come from Hamburg. They had
joined my parents' musical evenings — "with violin, oboe, and
with clarinet!" There was also our neighbour Johann Dicke,
with his clear tenor voice and with tricks of his violin — all
had come from Hamburg.... I said a little prayer and I spoke

with Engelbert. I did not acknowledge that I had cold feet, but "let us stay in Hamburg," I said.

On the quay-side Engelbert spotted his cousin Arthur. Arthur was solicitous and gentle, and of course he won my heart when he said, "Your little boys look like real Praschmas." We spent the evening together discussing matters. He explained why I was not to be taken to Falkenberg until after his father's death. Soon it was agreed, with much relief on both sides, that we remain in Hamburg. Engelbert remarked about the many excellent schools. I said, "That must not be overlooked, especially as I am expecting a baby."

We lived in a street called Ellenbusch. The name sounds nicer than the street appeared to be. If it had dreams, I could not read them, but then I could not read German either. The dark three-story buildings came down solidly, or branched off from the pavement. I found, especially in Hamburg, that by autumn the streets are scarcely a place in which to weave dreams; however, there was just one bright spot that became my Port of Call, and that was the butcher's shop. The local butcher was a man somewhat after my own heart, because between meats and sausages — inviting enough for a *braai* (cookout) — he also understood how to arrange pots of homely cacti and succulents that could only have had their origin on the sunny side of an African *kopjie* (hill). So we hope that our butcher has sweet dreams and that Ellenbusch sometimes chuckles and whispers nice things to him about African *kopjies* out in the sunshine.

Our Landlady was a *Frau* Goebbels, related to the Reichs Minister; the meals she served us were mostly made up of "Brat-Kartoffel and Sauer Kraut." The people of Hamburg like substantial food. She said it was beyond her comprehension that I did not like "Kartoffel and Kraut!" It was also beyond her comprehension that I could be firm with my children about a little misdeed, but when they said, "Solly, Mammie," I could pick them up and kiss them. But *Frau* Goebbels took a definite dislike to me when she proudly brought out all her needle-work to show me and I said: "*Du bist schlimm.*" Instead, I should have said, "*Sie sind klug.*" Our Afrikaans word "slim" means "clever," but in German, "Schlim" means "bad, evil." This I only learned from Engelbert later, when I asked him why she had left me in high dudgeon. So our Afrikaans got me into hot water.

Engelbert was busy with his own affairs; he had started work with one of Hamburg's newspapers, *Die Illustrierte Zeitung*. He made light of the matter, but after some days, we both sat up in surprise at *Frau* Goebbels. I had drawn the curtains aside to allow the children to sit and look out into the street when, unceremoniously, a Gendarme came into our room. "What have you done with the lace curtains?" he asked. "*Frau* Goebbels has reported that you have destroyed them." He pulled them out and examined them, looked kindly at me, shook his head, and said, "She is a *Hexe*" — a "witch." I learned a new German word.

After some weeks, we managed to get a self-contained flat in Hamburg 43. Here, there was more open space, gardens and a children's park. We could expand.

Engelbert's work often took him away from home. He was now working as a journalist for the *Illustrierte* and the *Fremdenblatt*. I tried to accustom myself to my new environment — along the crooked path that a pitying Divinity rules for us to amble along — but I felt very small in the great Elbe Emporium. That mighty harbour, some 30 miles from the open sea, is annually visited by some 1,500 ships bringing in wealth and weighty cargoes — not only iron-ore, lead, and coal, but also High Diplomacy. Hamburg has always been a Free City, because when once you open up some sort of trade, you open up all sorts of channels. This is what Hamburg's Merchant Princes understood and followed down the ages. This is how culture came and Hamburg was rich in many things. She was not only a Free City but a Cosmopolitan State; here you can see people… some are strange-looking customers. Not only in the great hotels, not only in the cool, tree-lined Allees or in St. Pauli — you meet people from every call of life, from every part of the world. Hamburg is a city steeped in tradition. It is also full of sights and sounds and smells; principally the scent of the sea and Ooh! That ever delicious scent of coffee roasting!

I learned a lot in Hamburg — for a *backvelder*, there was much to learn; luckily, I did not know how much, for now began (isn't it Charles Dickens who mentions in the *Tale of Two Cities*, the best of times and the worst of times. My big stumbling block is the language, I must try to overcome my lack of vocabulary… meanwhile, by appropriate signs and expression I do my shopping. People are very sympathetic; this morning, for instance, I tried to buy some onions. "Uie," said in Afrikaans, produced eggs. Then, showing tears streaming down my face, the kindly shopkeeper brought out horseradish, and so it goes, until I am invited to come and look behind the counter. There is also the money question. I almost long to see a sixpence or a little "tickey" (three-pence coin), bless them! I have learned quite a lot about the Groschen; I have learned how to count them — carefully!

It is November — not a good time to arrive in Hamburg. No! No! Every day I wonder when the sun will shine, and every day I take my little boys for a walk, hoping to sit down in one of the many parks… all are dank and soggy, there is no sun.

Often I think of a poem by John Freeman:

> Than these November skies is no sky lovelier,
> The clouds are deep, into their grey the subtle
> spies
> of colour creep,
> Changing their high austerity to delight
> Till ev'n the leaden interfolds are bright.
> And, where the cloud breaks faint far azure
> peers
> Ere a thin flushing cloud again shuts up that
> loveliness,
> Or shares.
> The huge great clouds move slowly, gently, as
> reluctant
> the quick sun should shine in vain,
> Holding in bright caprice their rain.
> And when of colour none — nor rose, nor
> amber,
> Nor the scarce late green
> Is truly seen, in all the myriad grey,
> In silver bright and dusky deep, remain
> The loveliest

Faint purple flushes of the
Unconquerable sun.

And sometimes it comforts, and sometimes it does not.

It was on one of these dark days, when I saw (with a whole mixture of feelings) the moon for the first time in Hamburg, sailing out among the clouds. I looked and then I wondered why it seemed so blurred... until I found that my eyes were full of tears, then I said to myself: You are on the wrong side of Jordan, wipe your tears. It is your birthday! There will be better days.

*****

On another sombre day in November, we received the tragic news of Engelbert's father's death from a heart attack. Engelbert was deeply distressed — he repeated the Chinese proverb of how the bundle of sticks held together could not be broken, but... something was not in order, I sensed it in all his letters, something was not in order — and now he is gone.

It was a long journey with two small children. However, it was cosy and warm, travelling in the great blustering D-Zug that wore a heavy coat of ice and snow — from Hamburg over Berlin/Breslau to arrive at Brieg Station that winter evening in November.

Everywhere there was snow, snow, snow. I could never have imagined so much snow in a whole world as I saw on this journey. Ignatz (my youngest brother-in-law) met us at the station and we travelled by car to Falkenberg, the family estate in Upper Silesia. It was dark when we arrived, the castle was brightly lit up, but I felt that I was in a strange world, amongst strange people. All of them were dressed in black, including the servants, for we had come to attend the Requiem Mass for Engelbert's father.

Two of Engelbert's sisters, Pia and Antoinette, found pleasure in fussing over our little boys; they bathed them, fed them, declared them to be 90 percent Praschma and put them to bed.

Being weary after the long journey, I made no objection, although feeling an alien in a strange world and loath to see my own out of sight. I walked the long, icy corridors and up flights of stairs, wondering how one could ever become accustomed to such a huge castle and speak a strange language.

After dinner, we sat in the white salon, where many questions were asked and answered. This was also a family reunion, for Engelbert had been overseas for over seven years.

Among some visitors present, I met Friedrich Prince Salm-Salm (Uncle Friedrich) and his son Francois, two very charming gentlemen, who both speak fluent English. Sitting in the luxurious salon and learning to know everybody made me feel more comfortable, but when the long curtains were drawn aside and the double windows were opened wide for some moments to let in the clear frosty air, as I looked out into the night across the snow-lit silence of the garden, suddenly a bough of a tree, brittle and overladen with snow, broke with a startling crack. I felt drawn right away from reality into the mystical unknown — for could the shot not have been a vibrant salute from the guns of the Flying Dutchman's frigate? Will I presently see his ghostly ship with blood-red sails sailing over the vast white silent expanse of garden and park? An additional eerie note was struck when the ancient clock on the tower slowly and stridently toned the hour, seeming to dominate the silence with a deep vibrant pulse.

In that strange, snowy light, I now felt sure that I was somehow an earthbound spirit and not a person — a spirit, because, I questioned — What is that eerie singing? I can hear the poignant voice of Senta imploring the Flying Dutchman's return: Ahoy, ahoy, ahoy! Is it singing, or is it only the wind that has suddenly sprung up moaning and scuffing on the walls and towers and rattling the windows of the castle? I shivered and felt very far away from sunny South Africa. I took a last look at the frozen clouds, the windows were secured, and the heavy curtains drawn.

Never did I value my old motto more than this evening: "I am not afraid, I am only a little simple."

It did not take much more than a walk through the entranceway of the castle and onto the bridge that spanned the ancient moat to make the acquaintance of the *Haus-Heilige*, (saints of the house): St. Johannes Nepomuk, St. Donatius, St. Florian, St. Wendelin, and, of course, Our Lady. We leave them there: John and Dona, Flori and Wendel, where they have stood guarding the entrance to the castle for I don't know how many generations, through the portal under the tower that leads to the inner courtyard. We mount the broad shallow staircase to the proportionately wide corridor, where most of the family portraits have been thoughtfully hung with names and dates and here, like one can do in your own family gallery. I lingeringly spend quite a lot of time. To realize that the descendants of these people will stand up manfully, like their saints, to recite the Credo, through fire and sword ….

In the gallery, there are cardinals and crowned heads; there is a very old portrait of the Melancholy White Lady, the apparition, a girl clad in white, who is said to sometimes at night still glide to your bed and then disappear. There are later portraits; here is Johann Nepomuk Praschma, 1725 — 1804. He looks what he was — a prominent man amongst blue bloods and fearlessly outspoken, but, by the soft expression that lingers about his lips, his large eyes and his hair that is so carefully brushed and curled up above his ears — I would not say it to his face, but Johann is a bit egoistic. His wife, Maria Anna — nee Countess Zierotin, 1723-1786 — quite a lordly Dame and quite a spendthrift, or so her green and red parrot in the same portrait seems to say.

Their son, Jean-Charles Praschma, 1756 — 1822, immaculately dressed in dark velvet coat and white cravat. Maybe he rather disappointed his parents if they expected great things of him. For J.C. was a dreamer — he had fair hair, like my Peter, and blue eyes; his wife — another Zierotin, 1761 — 1793, holds her sari-veil timidly, with one hand — perhaps her mother-in-law was rather too candid for her to lead a happy married life. Their child, Marianne was only three years old when she was laid to rest in the family vault.

Friedrich Praschma I, 1786 — 1860, looks melancholy, for all that he wears a ribbon of distinction — maybe the ribbon of a Knight of Malta — around his shoulders. Friedrich has not inherited his grandparents' happy outlook on life; perhaps it was because he was a little lad of seven when his mother died. Friedrich was unhappy, and he was rather stubborn, so he consoled himself with Johanna Countess Schaffgotsch, 1797 — 1867. It took him quite a long time to persuade her to marry him (or perhaps, she convinced him to marry her?) as she was quite a beauty, and, quite likely, she did more for the Praschmas than the two preceding Czechs had done.

Friedrich II, 1833- 1909, was a lovable man; he was prepared for and ably carried out all the responsibilities that his birth and heritage required of his person. His wife, Elizabeth, Countess Stolberg-Stolberg, 1843-1918, was rather a hard nut to crack for all her fair curls and blue eyes. She could lay down the law, so it was just as well that her sensitive daughter-in-law, Marie, Baroness Landsberg-Velen, was clever enough to manage her own affairs and a large family in her own way and also my father-in-law, her husband, Johannes Nepomuk Praschma, 1867 — 1935, who, I believe, gave all his best interests and service to his country and his tenants. And now, the family and friends and retinue are assembled to pay their last respects to him.

*****

From the entrance hall, if you open the door directly under the largest stag antlers that I have ever seen, you come into one of the living rooms called *das Gelbe-Gewolbe* (the yellow arched vault). The ceiling is part of the architectural structure of the castle, but in this room it is a feature of beauty as it soars overhead in distinctive ribs. The yellow room — by its proximity to the large dining room — is a very practical sitting room — always smoke- and flower-filled with antique coppers and leather chairs. In the window niche stands a flower stand that takes my fancy. It is a sled that once sailed over snowy ways — now it is gilded and filled with begonias and bright leaved potted plants.

The 'small' library joins the *Gelbe-Gewolbe*. I have never opened one of the leather-bound volumes, in rows behind locked glass doors in heavily carved book-cases surmounted by family coats-of-arms. In the great library upstairs you can spend many hours among works of art and romance, — Duff Cooper and, I could not believe it, even Gertrude Page!

On the ground floor are also the large dining room, pantries and kitchen, and the chapel which is actually as large as a church, presided over by Our Lady, where the old people of the village, wrapped in their dark coats and shawls, come to say their rosaries. Under the chapel is the family vault where the family ancestors are buried.

The state rooms are all on the first floor, also the "spare rooms" and all the private rooms of the family. The second floor is almost entirely reserved for guests.

You can go on exploring through rooms and corridors and towers — on and on and you are always likely to find some new item of interest. Along the walls in the corridors, on the second floor, you can see many etchings and engravings — ancient *Kupfer-stiche* (copper engravings, plates) among others, the bear hunts and stag hunts which I find beautiful and "*interessant*."

As there did not seem anything interesting to do before lunch a day or two after our arrival, Francois Salm suggested we visit the family vault. This I was quite prepared to do, as I had never seen a vault. We dressed warmly, as the temperature was below zero. Francois said we must walk fast to keep warm. I found it hard work to walk fast on the slippery ice. When we got beyond the bridge, the wind seemed to hit our faces with little iron bars. The village children, on skates, were skimming happily along the icy streets. Peasants about their own business travelled hither and thither in sledges with bells ringing out in the frosty air. No one took notice of us. We walked a long distance, the wind seeming to become more boisterous, and it was difficult to talk. Still, we walked on. I thought it strange that the vault is such a long way from the castle. Then Francois bent down to ask me, "But where is the vault??"

"But this is funny," I answered. "We have lost the vault and I have no idea where it is!"

"Neither have I," said Francois. He took my icy, gloved hand in his and we retraced our steps.

After lunch, first having made diligent inquiries, we were told that the vault was on the tennis court side of the castle, under the chapel.

We found a heavy locked door. With some trepidation, I walked down the steps to enter a large cellar-like room where the coffins are placed upon cement blocks, sealed, and cemented over. Franois lit some tall wax candles in dark, heavy holders placed before a bench where you kneel and pray. I had always wondered at the waste of burning candles in churches, but it was in this crypt, with the coffins standing in solemn rows, that I came to understand that we light a candle to be mindful of God's presence among us. He who is the true Light which lighteneth every man coming into the world. So surely, it is not only the early Christian martyrs' right to walk forward with calm fortitude to meet their fate, but we, like them, have our marching orders in the *Gloria Tibi Patri* — and even if we are simple, we need not be afraid.

*****

Hamburg

I was glad when we returned to Hamburg after the funeral. Eastern Europe seemed to me to be on the outer crust of civilization, while Hamburg with the tall ships that sailed on the seven seas; lofty cathedral towers; old gabled houses, that stood not only roof on roof, but wall on wall — houses peculiar to the worthy people who had built them — of solid character and earnest dignity. To me it seemed that Hamburg was situated in the very center of civilization. There was also another reason that kept recurring to me, like the ebb and flow of the Elbe River itself. It was that the same breezes that fanned the great harbour could carry a swift message across the Atlantic, to Cape Town, to the very doors of the Transvaal; and therefore, when we returned, I was glad to feel so much nearer home again, and I could have sung with a scruffy old sailor, "Oh for a breeze that blissfully tickles the nostrils!"

Not long after this there was a breeze that blew with a vengeance, and it ended in a great gale that swept the water from the Elbe to the North Sea. The electric current failed — we did not know what to do, how to manage, and then I learned to know a friend in need; with a loden coat flapping over her shoulders, someone crossed the street and knocked at our door.

"I have just made this plum tart," she said, and from under a cover, she produced a plate of hot tart. "You may have eaten of our fresh plum tart and you like it? Yes?" Big purple plums strewn with sugar peeped out of the pastry. We did like it. Tante Walther was invited in and we also liked her. She had heard that we were strangers. She had also once been a stranger in England and therefore, on a day like this, when the storm-wind has driven the water from the Elbe to the sea and there was no electric current, she knew that our heaters were cold. Would I bring the children and spend the day with her? She had gas heaters and the children would be warm. We accepted gladly, and from that day on, we often spent an afternoon together.

Tante Walther had played in an orchestra when she was young — our mutual friend was Franz Schubert. We both loved the violin, she had many tales to tell, she knew many people and had many interests — but the Third Reich? "No!" she said, "We have all been ordered to hang out flags in honour of Goebbels' visit to Hamburg! Who are all these bureaucrats? Hitler is not a German. Are you putting out a flag?"

"We don't possess a flag."

"Well," she said, "I will not have that *Haken-Kreuz* (swastika) fluttering from my window to save my life!"

At this time, I could not understand why the people of Hamburg hated Hitler, so I said, "But here in Hamburg I see the poorer people with pots every morning going to the Welfare to fetch their dinner; for workers, holiday trips are provided. In Africa, you see children without shoes, here they all wear shoes."

"Yes, much is provided, but the *Partei* does not give the people time to think for themselves. Just look what is happening to the Jews! Do you listen to the radio?"

I did listen quite a lot, it is one way of getting my ear "tuned in" to the German language; I liked to hear Paul Linke conducting the Hamburg orchestra, I liked to hear his daily program, "*Morgen Gruss*," the morning greeting. However, it was Engelbert and Tante Walther who enlightened me as to how Hamburg had always been a free city, better administered than governed, but now the city was literally incorporated in the German Reich and had to heel to the Wilhelm Strasse in Berlin.

"I have a *Wut* (I learned a new word: 'rage') against the Third Reich," said Tante Walther. "Everywhere there are spies and informers, the children are being demoralized, our country will be involved in a dreadful war of bloodshed and destruction; Hitler is a coward, ultimately he will die for his country by calmly putting himself out!"

(At the time, I thought Tante Walther's words were very strong, but they proved themselves true).

*****

We did not always talk politics, and when Engelbert got me a servant, we did what most people did in our area... we went for long walks. Sometimes, as often, when it rained, we set out, like a little regiment, grown ups and children, with rain coats and umbrellas; it was fun!

Although the winter was long and dreary, with much hard work, there were many compensations. People truly have a marvelous sense of overcoming difficulties and amusing themselves. In Hamburg there are many theatres, there are concert houses in great variety, and where else in the world can you find a place of so much variety, of so much exuberance as St. Pauli in Hamburg?

It is not only the Merchant Princes that the people of Hamburg are proud of — there are the other great men, especially the older ones — those that, so to say, laid the good, firm stepping stones, those that, much in the same way as the Praschmas are proud of their "Haus-Heilige," the people of Hamburg are called upon to remember. Four of their great sons' names are commemorated and are placed with other adornments on the columns of the massive Kersten Miles Bridge. Kersten Miles (d.1420) was a hero who fought with hammer and tongs, or perhaps more truly with cutlass and fisticuffs, to ensure the place (against fearful odds) where now the great harbour of Hamburg stands.

There is Simon von Utrecht (d.1437), celebrated conqueror of the much-dreaded North Sea pirates and champion of many deeds of valour. Simon and his ship, *Bunte*

Kuh (piebald cow), are celebrated in many old ballads and *liedern*; a model of the *Bunte Kuh* hangs in the Great Hall of the Raths Wine Keller, which is called "Die Bunte Kuh." Simon was quite a character, and as colorful as his *Bunte Kuh*!

There is Dietmar Koel (d.1563), who captured and brought home the dreaded Danish seaman and pirate Claes Kniphof. Dietmar was a man of peace; he soon gave up fighting pirates and became a member of the Council. He was instrumental in bringing about the peaceful introduction of the Reformation to Hamburg.

There is Berend Jacobsen Karpfanger, one of Hamburg's most famous seamen, who in 1678 with his frigate *Kaiser Leopold*, captured five French privateers in the mouth of the river Elbe. Some years later, poor Berend went on an expedition against the Corsairs. When in the bay of Cadiz, he went down with his frigate on fire, having first brought his crew to safety. If Berend had stayed at home, this would not have happened, nevertheless, he was a valiant man, one of the best.

*****

No one having lived in Hamburg can forget the bright appearance of the Binnen Alster, the beautiful lake with a flotilla of proud white swans, hundreds of fishing vessels, and innumerable people. Many of them were like we were — just happy to sit in the sun on a fine spring day. The Alster is enclosed on three sides by handsome rows of buildings and tree-canopied streets. On the east there is the Alster dam, on the south, the Alster Jungfernsteig, on the west, the Neuer Jungfernsteig. The Inner Alster is separated from the Aussen Alster by part of the ancient Rampart Gardens and traversed by the railway uniting Hamburg with Altona. Crossing the lake is a beautiful bridge — the Lombard Bridge.

Like the great harbour of Hamburg, the Alster has been the labour of engineers and workmen over centuries of time — from being an insignificant little river, they have succeeded in creating the bright and beautiful *Kleinod*, "Jewel" of Hamburg.

In spring, the weather cleared. Overnight, catkins, lily-of-the-valley, mint, and wild violets appeared as if by magic.

They were a wonder and delight, but I looked in vain for the reputed sweet-scented flowers of Europe. There seemed to be nothing to surpass some of our indigenous flora, or the honey-suckle that my mother planted against our verandah pillars, and our cabbage roses with as sweet a scent as any of the lovely new hybrids.

And the song of the birds? Well, our own busy-bodies, the Cape weaver-birds, it will take a good bird to beat their songs. Actually, one cannot expect to hear birds singing in a city. But there is a far famed cuckoo. In spring, the windows were thrown open wide and one night I heard a cuckoo call in Hamburg. I hurried to the window, but to my disappointment, the bird had flown; at midnight I sat up in bed to hear: "Cuckoo! cuckoo!" — I counted 12 calls! ... merely our neighbour's clock. I was disappointed.

******

Sunday morning, 9 August, 1936

There were late roses blooming in the park.

I had never heard the bells of all the churches, far and near, issuing so clear and consistent a reminder to "Rejoice and be glad." To me it seemed as if each chime had a little gladsome echo in my heart. It was because a child was to be born to us; so it seemed not to matter that our little boys were in Falkenberg with their grandmother and I was missing them.

A few more turns around the park and then I was in Barnbeck, in a hospital where there were many new arrivals.

Almost the first words I heard in the hospital were: "Sunday's child is full of grace and fair of face." This has all along been the "signature tune" of our Ilona Maria Emma. Engelbert took notice of it when he saw her and added, "I am so glad it is a little girl."

*****

Yes, custom.... Not the way we talk about the Levy of Customs, but how the denizens of this world adapt themselves to circumstances that become customary; there are some that require a lot of imagination.

This was my experience when Ilsa, my little *Haushelferin* (house helper), told me that her mother was making cakes for her confirmation. I said, "I am sure they will look very pretty."

"No," said Ilsa, "my mother can only bake cakes, they don't look nice."

"Well Ilsa, bring me one and I'll frost it for you."

Ilsa brought me a cake and said, "This is the big one!" It was a big one! While Ilsa took the children for a walk, I mixed up some icing sugar, got out my icing tubes, and made some roses. The next day when Ilsa saw the cake, she was enthusiastic, but she said, "Can't you put just a little colour on it? Green and silver and gold?" I told her I could add some green leaves and also some silver balls, if we could obtain them. All were duly added and Ilsa carried the cake home. Shortly afterwards, she was back with her sisters carrying trays of cakes. "My mother is so happy! My confirmation will be beautiful! Will you please ice the others?"

It was a tall order, I haven't much imagination; my forte at home was attending to the farm work and the animals. I wished my sister Clem was at hand. However, seeing their eager faces, I said I'd do my best. I spent the rest of the day and evening icing cakes. This time I made pink roses, I dipped biscuits in cocoa mixture with cherries and nuts, browned coconut, lemon peel and silver balls. Eventually I had quite a display on my pantry table when all was cleaned up.

Now came a kind invitation from Ilsa's mother to join the confirmation party on the Sabbath afternoon. After feeding my baby and putting her to sleep, I shook out my black frock with the lace sleeves, got dressed, and walked over to the von Lous. Surprisingly, I was greeted by the sound of music and lusty singing. Before I realized what was happening, I found myself whirling around to the strains of the "Blue Danube Waltz" in the arms of a tall, young man. He bent down and said, "*Schwarzer Zigeuner* (black Gypsy), you waltz beautifully!"

"No," I said, "I'm just spinning 'round on my wooden leg."

"Ach, then I will clasp you to my heart and never let you fall," and he suited his words with the action.

I said, "I can't find my breath."

"*Schwarzer Zigeuner*, you take away my breath!" he said.

The music stopped, my cavalier led me to a seat. "I'll get us a drink," he said. "What will you have, a Kuemmel? Have a Kuemmel with me!" My only knowledge of caraway is its innocent use in buns and cakes, but I can assure anyone that German Kuemmel is no innocent drink; indeed, it can hold its place — breast to breast — anywhere, with Russian vodka.

After the first few sips, everything seemed to multiply before my sight while, with his endearing, "*Schwarzer Zigeuner*," my cavalier brought me a drink of another kind. I sat, or perhaps I fell back in my seat, and wished for nothing more than to lie under the table. I could not bear those kind eyes upon me, so I sent him off to dance with the pretty girls.

When my vision somewhat cleared, I made my way to my hostess, thanked her, and said I must see to my baby. "*Ach, nein*," she said, "You haven't even looked at your cakes! So beautiful!"

"Oh, yes." They seemed to multiply under my gaze. "I think I must go home."

When I got outside, I had to cling to a telephone post for some moments — and when I got home, Engelbert was back with the boys from their walk. Baby was still asleep. I undressed and went to bed. Engelbert brought me some coffee, then we heard an emphatic knocking at the door. There was my cavalier, repeatedly calling, "*Schwarzer Zigeuner! Schwarzer Zigeuner!*" Engelbert went to open the door. I do not know what my husband said to him. But I know what he said to me.

The next day when Ilsa came, she was very happy about her confirmation.

"But, Ilsa," I said, "Confirmation is serious. It is admitting a person to the full privileges of the Church." Ilsa was in agreement, but she said, "We have our customs."

Yes, Ilsa. Customs? Some are strange and require a lot of imagination. Like the baker who swept the glowing oven with his cat's tail: "Accustom yourself, tomcat, accustom yourself, everything depends only on custom." I think that Wilhelm Busch said that.

###

CHAPTER TWO
WE TRAVEL TO KYJOVICE

September, 1936

When a letter arrived from Czechoslovakia from
Antonia Countess zu Stolberg-Stolberg, my mother-in-law's
sister, inviting us to spend autumn with them in Kyjovice,
Engelbert said to me, "It will be a new experience for you. They
have a lovely home in the country, where I spent many happy
holidays, tramping about the forests and mountains." The
invitation was particularly welcome to me as we had come
from a healthy high-veldt South African climate, and in low-
lying, damp, and windy Hamburg, the children had developed
coughs that no amount of care and coaxing would stop. So I
eagerly looked forward to higher altitudes and the pine forests
of Czechoslovakia.

For the boys, we bought jerseys and two dark sailor
coats with gilt buttons that they are inordinately proud of.

While preparations were being made, I asked Engelbert
if Aunt Antonia was like his mother. "Oh, yes," he answered
enthusiastically, "She is just as beautiful!"

I therefore decided to add a little lustre to myself — to
buy a brown hat that I liked, with a blue curled feather and a
brown travelling costume with a blue blouse, and I felt as
elated as if I had been the recipient of a fond kiss, or had done
a great favour for myself!

We got ready.

Again, it was an autumn day that found us closely
packed in the Hamburg-Berlin Express on the first stage of our
journey to Czechoslovakia. Hitherto, I had only vaguely heard
of Aunt Toto. Therefore, on this journey I asked Engelbert,
"Who actually are the inhabitants of Kyjovice?" Yes, there was
also Uncle Fritz, Count zu Stolberg-Stolberg, and two
daughters, Christl and Regina.

From Berlin, we first spent a short time visiting Engelbert's two aunts, Countess Strachwitz and Countess Ballestrem, in their respective homes. From these two ladies, I already had overtures of friendship, so I did not feel quite a stranger in the castles of Boeckey and Glasersdorf. After spending about two weeks with them, Engelbert journeyed back to Hamburg while the children and I started on our way to Kyjovice.

Late in the afternoon we arrived at the Czech border, at Oderberg, an industrial, smoky-looking town, where the Vienna Express only stops a few minutes. With three small children I had to alight very quickly, and before I had time to look around, Franz the footman and Karl the chauffeur came forward to greet us courteously. They took our baggage before the customs and as soon as this procedure was over, Franz, with a ceremonious bow (which bow I later on learned to know very well), assisted us into the car, while Karl saw to the luggage. Thus, thankfully, we started on the last stage of our long journey. The great car was all that could be desired in comfort and as it spiralled along the different grades of the steep road with purring ease, we rested, and I found time to reflect. How curious it is to come into the lives of strange people in a strange country, at any particular time; like going to a play in the middle of an act, with no programme-notes to guide one. Well, I thought, I shall have to sort out the characters and find out what they are up to, but still I felt a little bewildered.

Soon I was lulled by the car singing a low note, like bees in a clover field, and by the air, sweet and fresh, from the newly mown fields that bordered the roadway, while the countryside around lay enveloped in a quiet air of peace and domesticity. As twilight deepened, the lights of little villages shone out like golden stars. We travelled through Ostrawa, what seemed a large city with many well-lit plate glass windows. Then further along roads that wound through pleasant valleys and up the steep hills, where dark pine trees stood outlined against the evening sky. By now, it was quite dark, and as I wondered when we would arrive at our destination, Franz kindly gave the information. "Directly, we will be passing through Count Stolberg's forest." And almost at once the great, dark, bold pine trees, scented and veiled, hand-in-glove with the wind and all the whispering elements of the night, came frostily down to skirt the road. Even in the dark, I enjoyed making this first fleeting acquaintance with real old deodars. Soon afterwards, we passed through the village of Kyjovice, and then— emerging from what seemed a very long, dark, avenue of chestnut trees — we stopped in front of the castle. From the interior, somewhere, a bell pealed. Franz opened the door of the car and, with one of his ceremonious bows, helped us to alight. From the great, well-lit, oaken doorway Aunt Antonia came forward to greet us; her blue eyes spoke the same welcome that she extended with her little white hands. Dressed in a soft pastel frock with lace, and with white hair, always a little unruly, to me she seemed much more beautiful than I could ever have pictured her.

"Now... come in, children... I want to see you all!" she said. "This is Anna and this is Zdenka, who will take charge of the children. Come up to your rooms first — and let me look at you. I have received many letters telling me about you all."

Anna took the baby, Ilona. "*Lieber Gott*," she said, "*wie suess*" (how sweet). We walked and talked along a long stone corridor, where I noticed on the walls, between quaintly embrasured and barred windows, hung beautiful old lithographs of Arab steeds, depicted against a background of desert scenes; then, up a flight of shallow, polished stairs surmounted by two colossal carved pillars, another corridor, and then — was it because we came from a strange outside world that the large room we entered seemed to me as if here is where cherished dreams come true? The furniture was of no particular date or period, but with richly carved and inlaid pieces, deep-tone colours and luminous white, was like the interior of an old masterpiece. Above the great bed hung a tapestry rug, woven with skill, made beautifully with figures and soft colouring. The embroidered curtains before the deep windows harmonized with the rug in more vivid colours. Over one corner of the room hung a large, antique cross; before it stood two little potted spruce trees, while a bowl of flaming flowers shed their fragrant incense before our thorn-crowned Lord.

A large bearskin rug lay between the bed and an inlaid cabinet containing valuable oddments of pewter and pottery, while on a dark walnut bureau a fair, white alabaster clock ticked away the hours, where doubtless some bygone ancestors have sat and kept their diaries. All this I fleetingly had time to notice while Aunt Toto coaxed up the fire into leaping flames — later, I often watched, and learned that she loved to perform this little rite, at which she excelled, especially for us.

Meanwhile, Anna and Zdenka were helping the boys to undress in the *"Jungherrenzimmer"* (the young gentlemen's room) next door. Distinctly, I heard how intrigued they were, when the boys proudly showed off the fine gilt buttons on their new, dark sailor overcoats.

As it was late, supper was served for us in the small dining room upstairs. Afterwards, I went to the library to meet Uncle Fritz and two other guests, Baron and Baroness Gemmel, a couple with an Old World courtesy of manner who looked as if they had closer affinity with the family portraits than the reality of life. Therefore, I was surprised when later I saw Baroness Gemmel puffing away at a long, dark, after-dinner cigar, in a long holder. An evil-smelling smoke, so I concluded that surely she can stand up to the vicissitudes of life. There were also two other inmates of the library; two sleek Doberman dogs, dozing near the fire, their intelligent heads on their paws: Ronnie and Roderick.

High above the engravings and the book cases is a beautiful molded ceiling. The same design is executed on the white double door. Among the engravings on the wall, I recognized the ugly, winsome face of Schubert, and the beautiful face of Schiller. Later, I learned that in this library, rich treasures were to be found — it is a collection of rare beauty. Here are early 14th-century calf-bound volumes and missals, written and illuminated in the best Benedictine Art, with opening words and texts in burnished gold; also rows of printed books; master drawings; autographed manuscripts; historical letters — Percival of the Holy Grail in the *Niebelungenlied*, in earliest manuscripts — classics, ancient and modern — here are all the queens and kings of England, arranged in a fat row, bound in royal blue, keeping good company with Chaucer and Shakespeare, Voltaire and Moliere — and here are children's books: *Alice in Wonderland* making her debut with *Little Lord Fauntleroy*. On the high shelf are the four-and-twenty volumes written by Christian zu Stolberg-Stolberg on the life of Our Lord (written after his conversion to Catholicism). Even before Franz came to the library with the small silver coffee service and a jug of cream, I felt that I did not need programme-notes to guide me among these likeable people, beautiful with a saintly goodness, and it was easy to imagine happy hours spent in this library — the friends sitting closely by.

On the first morning after our arrival, we were awakened by a medley of unexpected sounds. Far away, a clock toned an early hour, while — from the open window — came the soft, throaty cooings of turtle-doves. Now came a pattering of little feet along the corridor, then the hurried ringing of a bell. The melodious tinkling had scarcely died away when I heard the tuning-up strains of a violin — now, two violins, and forthwith, the gay music of a Strauss Waltz together with lively singing.

All this awakened the children who inquisitively burst into my room to ask what the bell-ring was for, and the music. "Is it a party?"

"May we run down immediately?"

I was not acquainted with the customs of the house, so I said: "No, it's too early — but we will ring and find out."

In answer to my ring came pretty Zdenka, but as she spoke even less German than I did, and I knew no Czech, it was more by signs and expression that I understood, while she hastily dressed the children, that the bell was rung every morning for the household to attend early Mass. And the music — just the *Zigeuners*, the Gypsies, playing in the servants' hall below. And now, while the children's toilette was being completed, I tried to find out from Zdenka what time Mass was said. "What time is the Mass, Zdenka?"

"*Viertel ein Siebeni, Frau Graefeni.*" (quarter-one-sevenish, Countess). The alabaster clock showed six forty-five.

So I said: "Is it Mass now?"

"*Nein, Frau Grafeni,*" said Zdenka patiently, "*Viertel ein Siebeni.*"

Meanwhile, the boys were clamoring to go down and see the Gypsies. "Well, Zdenka," I said, "We don't get beyond

Viertel ein Siebeni so you take the children down to the Gypsies and then you please will take me to the Chapel."

"Oh, no, *Frau* Grafeni, the Gypsies will steal the children!" said Zdenka in distress.

"Well, then, Zdenka, please take care of the children and I will follow." This I did leisurely, directed by the sound of the music, but with questioning thoughts. What can *"Viertel ein Siebeni"* mean? To this day, I don't know. And, I am sure, neither does Zdenka.

Where can the chapel be? The idea of Gypsy music and Holy Mass before breakfast — what alien people live in this country?! No, no, I thought, here can be no law, no order — but a long glance in the corridor assured me of order. Here was a safe, peaceful atmosphere. The walls of the corridor are adorned with 16th-century copperplate engravings; directly opposite my door is a quaintly carved old cabinet topped by a row of jugs with bright-hued hand-painted flower designs, mostly blues and reds, typical of Czech art. Wood for winter heating was piled very high and very neatly in two great baskets in a little niche. The shining mahogany rails of the stairway reflect genuine credit to the hands that polished them, while between the stairway and the wall, on a shelf flooded with soft morning sunlight from tall windows, stands a gleaming row of copper samovars. They differ in ages, sizes and styles. I was fascinated, because I thought, "Surely these are pots of gold collected from the foot of the rainbow."

In the servants' hall I found my two children clinging to Zdenka's hand, wide-eyed with admiration of the *Zigeuner*. These included some dark Gypsy women, quite an old man — he could easily have been mistaken for a Cape Coloured or mixed race man back in Africa — who was swaying and playing his violin (a Paganini of his art) with flashing flourishes and dashes. Beside him stood a youth, quite a boy, playing on a small violin: the little fellow ably seemed to follow the jubilant waves of "The Blue Danube."

In the kitchen next door, I espied the tall white cap of Rudolf the cook, nodding and swaying from side to side while the two kitchen maids, Blond Fanka and Black Fanka (as I learned to know them), sung and kept time to the music. Another gay tune, and the Gypsies were given a steaming mug of coffee and a much prized slab of bacon. Uncle Fritz passed along the corridor and gave them a coin. This, together with an appreciative audience, the children and myself, produced the real modicum of good form, so they played some of their old melodies. Now, so playfully exuberant that even the copper in the kitchen seemed to reflect sparkle and laughter, but soon the music trailed off into minor cadences, soul-moving and sad enough to fill the eyes with tears. Then, with bows working furiously, they ended with a fierce, triumphant finish, father and son voicing the soul of a people who had suffered much and conquered adversity. Zdenka tugged at my sleeve and whispered "*Frau* Graefeni, it is *Viertel ein Siebeni*."

While Anna and Zdenka attended to the children, I hurried to Mass. Afterward, I went to the white marble-flagged dining room, only a couple of doors away from the chapel. We are at liberty to help ourselves to breakfast. I found Uncle Fritz already busy preparing his own breakfast. The toaster was set, and the samovar was bubbling away. Uncle Fritz came over to speak to me when I saw a thin cloud of smoke rising from the toaster.

"Oh, your toast is burning." I ran to rescue it, and then chancing to look across to the samovar, I saw that the teapot set under the tap was running over — and there goes the tea! We both laughed merrily, and I believe a seal was set on our friendship.

So this is Czechoslovakia. To us it is a new land, but, in right, it is as old as its very hills — a land that has its roots receding into the dim ages of the past. Nevertheless, here we can form a new concept, take a new look, as it were, of many of the things that will interest us, and I can write down some of the things that will interest my children and also what they will be up to. A Magnificent Diary! — that in some future time we can look into through my monocle, a diary with my seal suspended on a purple ribbon, and sometimes we will be amused, and sometimes again, as life strides along, perhaps we will look through with a sigh (or a tear), or a smile.

*****

October, 1936

The Lion of Slovakia is thatching his hut and making provision against winter blizzards. This is what the country people say when, in autumn, the sun shines out, heartening and warm, and the air, like an elixir, is as stimulating as our own high-veld winter days can be. Aunt Antonia wanted us to take advantage of the late autumn sun; and as Ilona does not walk yet, she sent Anna and Zdenka and Franz up to the attic to fetch the perambulators. Soon they are brought down — the likes of which I had never seen before: the pram is a tall, high-wheeled, cryptic wicker contraption, lined and curtained in pale cretonne. The push cart, on slightly lower wheels, is a commodious counterpart of the former. I could picture such perambulators being handled in Queen Victoria's royal nursery!

Ilona cooed and enjoyed the outing; the boys looked very small as they trotted proudly alongside. Heaven forbid that my child should fall from this height, and I kept a strict eye on the high pram, but soon relaxed my vigilance as I saw how Zdenka, with her young strength, efficiently manipulated the "waggon," so I found time to look around — to admire the white, classic simplicity of the house. The architectural pattern is old and enduring; the only embellishments are the glass *Vorsprung* (a closed-in, square, glass porch), the deep, embrasured windows, and the great oaken doors, wide enough for a span-and-four to drive through easily — indeed they often do so, on the east wing, when bringing in loads of wood for winter heating. The house is situated in extensive, park-like grounds, and now in autumn — with the exception of a group of ancient, sombre fir trees — there is a perfect bonfire of colour in the park reminiscent of Leo Sowerby's Overture --

"Autumn coming with her sun-burnt caravan
Like a long Gypsy train
With trappings gay
And all the colours of the Orient."

Here, in the park, are stately green and red oaks, where gregarious birds halt their tuneful orchestra to dart over to the alley and gorge on the clustered, red berries of the *Ebereschen* (mountain ash) trees. In rich contrast to its affinities is a shrub I had never seen before: a purple-leaved smoke plant. It has elegant sprays of rich, claret coloured smoke that are "puffed" out to the colourful scene around. When I asked Aunt Toto, "And what are those two remarkable golden trees?" She answered, "They are tulip trees," and then, a little regretfully, she said, "But quite soon they will be losing their yellow leaves." The two gaunt-stemmed trees stand about six yards apart, with an astonishing wealth of golden leaves against a dark background of firs. The fruits are so brightly luminous as if the refulgent eye of the sun had been caught and held captive in their golden crowns. And then, with a sweet smile, Aunt Toto said almost mysteriously, "All must walk gently here, like Aladdin in his enchanted palace, so gently that you do not even hear your own footfalls — because in spring, a sea of crocuses will deck the ground under these trees."

Situated about a stone's throw from the tulip trees is the "theatre place" — an open air arena, where Komtessen Christl and Regina, daughters of the house, frequently staged plays. Only the week before our arrival, the young people with their friends had played *As You Like It* — two spirited horses were among the cast. In the theatre chest in the attic I believe there is a marvellous collection of Old World costumes, but for the last play, most of the costumes had been borrowed from the theatre in Opava. This open-air stage is artistically set between opportunely cut cypress hedges at the foot of a sloping hill. On the hillock, guests are advantageously seated. The seats are for anyone who cares to attend, and Aunt Toto told us that the play had been one of the festivities staged to celebrate Uncle Fritz's sixtieth birthday, and she added: "Next week we have invited our friends to a dinner party. It will be followed in the evening by fireworks and the local brass band playing in the park. Then later on, Uncle Fritz has invited his officials from the village to a formal dinner. So, you see, there is a lot that calls for my attention.

"Now, let us go down to the green house. I must instruct the gardeners about placing my choice chrysanthemums, and then I must run off and leave you."

In the hothouse, two gardeners were busy placing the chrysanthemums — they had been grown out in the open and now were ready to bloom — to save them from frost and have them handy for making wreaths. These beautiful white chrysanthemums have specially been grown to make floral tributes for All Souls' Day. The garden girls were bringing them in by wheelbarrow loads, while the gardeners bedded them out on the hothouse floor. There were also rows of other plants already potted, and I felt as happy as my boys when the chief gardener, Mr. Schubert, presented them each with a pot of chrysanthemums for their very own. Aunt Toto said we could remain in the hothouse, and, although eager to look around at all the plants in the three large rooms, I said we would return later when the people had tidied up. I felt we should not intrude while they were at work.

With Zdenka's help, the two little boys proudly took their flowers to the *Jungenherrenzimmer* and I took charge of Ilona in the high-wheeled pram. We followed the rather steep path leading to the *Lusthauschen* (summer house), where, Anna said, "It is very agreeable." There were children's toys, and if we cared, she would send up our tea. Komtesse Christl had only just arrived from Vienna, she would join us there. We found the *Lusthauschen* near the tennis court to be a very novel little house, solidly built, with a miniature chimney, and picturesquely finished off with many-coloured glass door panes. It is furnished with a table and high-back painted chairs, and a quaint green-tiled stove, where autumn chestnuts were ceremoniously roasted. One corner of the room is fairly taken up by a brightly papered and curtained doll's house, where the children are able to walk in and out. In it are many treasures; they include a rocking horse, and a bear and a cow on wheels. Zdenka joined us — she put Ilona in the sandbox and the boys entertained themselves for hours among the toys. Anna brought tea, and Christl came to make our acquaintance. She is a young girl, just about to finish college, in looks and manner quite opposite to her younger sister Regina. Christl has a soft, creamy complexion, rounded red cheeks, and brown eyes and brown hair that seems to curl up right from the roots. Christl is lovely, but her chief charm is the serene expression of her mouth.

Regina is much fairer, with thick braids of auburn — gold hair and golden eyes. Both girls have studied psychology and related subjects that I am barely familiar with. I think that both these cousins of Engelbert know as much of the human heart as old Shakespeare himself.

Regina, for all her attractiveness, is a born pedagogue and although I have not heard her say it, I can clearly hear her saying, "Right is right and wrong is wrong — and two wrongs do not make one right."

Christl, again, lives in imitation of Christ, with everything it involves of asceticism and self-negation. I can also hear her — with her lucid eyes, reciting the Beatitudes of the Mount, "Blessed are they who mourn... Blessed are they who thirst and hunger for justice sake... Blessed are the pure in heart for they shall see God... Blessed are they who suffer persecution... Blessed are the merciful for they shall obtain mercy...."

Aunt Toto went downstairs to the kitchen to write up the menu for the servants and Herrschaften. I accompanied her — she spoke for quite a while to Rudolf, then to Mrs. Shimmack, an extra hand from Opava, who knows how to arrange nice dishes, and whose assistance is needed for some expected guests, Engelbert's cousin Helene among them. I look forward with much expectation to meeting Helene because of the lively comraderie of her informative letters written to me in South Africa.

The birthday dinner for the following week was discussed, incidentally, in the peaceful atmosphere of the large, white-tiled kitchen, where St. Joseph is installed as House-father, where the copper gleams and the wooden spoons and utensils are arranged in their allotted places, where there are plenty of herbs, spices, honey, and butter always at hand. I felt a sudden desire to make a sphere of work for myself. I wanted to make a birthday cake. Fruit cakes are seldom, if ever, made in Germany. Instead, for very special occasions, there is the exalted Baumkuchen, while delicious buns are made in a great variety, and also the good old Streusel — and Apfelkuchen, tarts, and a beautiful hazelnut wreath. When I mentioned a fruit cake, Aunt Toto said: "But I will be glad, if you make one — the housekeeper must obtain raisins and citrus peel. The other ingredients, spices, etc., are all on hand." I asked *Frau* Schimmeck if there were any icing-tubes. "Yes, quite a variety, great and small," but the rose-tubes that I specially needed were not among them, so Karl Zusky was immediately called. Karl, the ingenious handyman, is also the first singer in the chapel choir. I explained the form of the icing tube to him, and not long afterwards, he had it ready.

As soon as the raisins arrived, Mrs. Schimmeck, eager to learn how to make an English cake, helped me to weigh out the ingredients, and after much mixing and stirring the batter was put in a good slow oven. It rose up level and baked beautifully. When it was baked, I poured a few tablespoons of brandy over it. It smelled very appetizing. Meanwhile, I had started making the pale-pink roses; the next day I iced the cake in the large pantry. The servants all came to admire it — it did not look too bad.

The formal dining room downstairs is generally only used when there is a large party of guests. It is one of the rooms with a beautiful, groined ceiling, from the centre of which hangs a golden chandelier with innumerable glass prisms. With a white marble floor, the room is done in yellow and white, with bleached furniture, except for the Bohemian coloured crystal vases, set before tall mirrors on each wall. The mirrors reflected a wealth of crystal light from one to the other, and together with the rich coloured lights of the cut-glass vases, the effect is bright and very beautiful. In the middle of the room is the large, oval dining table. Quite a special feature of the room is the spiral staircase — I had never seen such a narrow, winding, carved little staircase. Here, the guests come down, one by one, or go up to the red salon above. I can picture a young lady looking mischievously down to her waiting cavalier below.

This dining room is now prepared for the birthday dinner. Only Franz is allowed to touch the chandelier. Yesterday, I saw him with water and towels rubbing the glass prisms. And now they shine in lucid splendour. Franz has also "ground" the knives and polished the silver, including the two silver pheasants that make such a splash on the table. They were wedding presents given when Aunt Toto came as a bride from Westphalia.

Anna now brought in the basket of napery, the large linencloth was unfolded and put on the table. I say with regret that I shall never see another cloth like this one. The rich, soft folds hang almost to the floor; intricate designs are woven around the crown and family coat of arms. These are repeated around the cloth, in which the Stolberg stag — a rather fat stag

— stands prominent. There are dozens of serviettes, monogrammed to match the cloth. When the table was ready laid, with innumerable glasses, silver, and Dresden china, Mr. and Mrs. Schubert, the gardeners, came in to arrange the flowers. Roses in low silver vases, with the bloom of rich red velvet, very simply arranged; the silver pheasants were put into position. The whole effect was such that I was lost in admiration until, like my grandmother, "I could but softly breathe." Just lovely!

Joseph, the butler, pealed the bell — a sign that the guests were arriving. Uncle Fritz and Aunt Toto came down the stairs, in readiness to receive them. Cousin Helene and I took some of the older ladies to the Green Suite to remove their wraps. Christl and Regina took charge of the young people.

Uncle Fritz received many birthday gifts. I specially noted only two of them, the one for its size, and the other for its beauty. The heavy one is a grotesque, heavy inkstand, presented by the local fire brigade, and the other — that stole my heart — is a book of Chinese paintings (from the Princesses Wanda and Lulu Radziwill Bluecher) reproduced on beautiful art paper. The book contains exquisite flower paintings together with a short biography of the artists; in the book are pear blossoms and birds, flowering lilies and butterflies with delicately slanting wings that are the strokes of a master hand. It is said that "through subtle skills and poetry, Chinese artists succeed in suggesting the inner vitality of their subjects." I only have to open the book and look at the sensitive, crinkly, curved legs of the butterflies to see how true this is.

At the table sat the gentlemen of the old regime with all the gracious inheritance of speech and manner bequeathed to them by their royal forefathers. If perhaps some of the young people appear too dignified and aloof, it is not because of snobbishness, but rather due to the medium of a disciplined education. I learned to know that with most of the young blue-bloods, chivalry and charity wear a very lowly garb.

Among the guests was Aunt Emma Strachwitz, Aunt Toto's sister with her son Arthur, Ferdinand Wilczeck with his young handsome daughter Gina, who later married the reigning Prince Liechtenstein. Arthur married Prince Liechtenstein's sister, Sissi. Here sat the good Baron von Mattenkloit; the young couple Vetter von der Lilia, a pretty name, with three golden lilies on their family crest; the family Rozumovsky; Baroness Rhemon; the Gemmels; Kuhnberg; Wanda and Lulu Bluecher, with Prince Tony; Helene and my dear, dear Aunt Bertha, Uncle Fritz's sister, "*en petite compagne*."

I am not a connoisseur of wines — I don't know the least thing about them — but when Joseph carefully, in his snow-white gloves, opened a bottle and gave to Uncle Fritz to taste, who pronounced it good, I knew that it had been stored up for a great occasion.

Baron von Mattencloit, one of the last Teutonic knights, proposed Uncle Fritz's health. He spoke some glowing words of feeling and congratulation.

Uncle Fritz, responding, looked very slight and upright in his dark, tailor-made suit. In his response, he expressed a sincere welcome to all his friends present — many of life-long standing — then he added, "There are others," and then he looked kindly at me, and mentioned my name and all of Antonia's relatives. I felt that this was no formal expression of welcome, but a compliment and, in a sense, more than a compliment, because it was sincere and it gave the old back-velder an intimate feeling of unity and informality.

Fruit and liqueurs were served in the Red Salon. After dinner we walked up the spiral staircase to the Red Salon above — ladies first — where most of us remained. The men preferred to be with Uncle Fritz in the library, where, faintly veiled in cigar smoke, they enjoyed talking about hunting, Duff Cooper's book, biographies, histories, etc.

In the Red Salon, we chatted like ladies do all the world over, about cooks and books, children, and that always inspiring theme, the latest fashions: for are not life's little vanities the sauce *piquante* of our existence?

*****

When the weather permits, tea and coffee is usually served in the *Glass Vorsprung* (glassed porch), but this afternoon the samovar containing glowing coals and a shining brass hot water kettle was placed on a table in the large dining hall. The water in the samovar keeps boiling for a long time —

the finest China tea had been fetched from the storage cupboard — nothing was forgotten by Anna. Tea and coffee services replaced the blue and white *Zwiebel Muster* (onion pattern) that I had not seen before. These new sets are of finest Meissen China, lavishly patterned with hand-painted flowers and flying insects and just enough gold to give an authentic luxury look. When the guests were assembled for tea, Joseph came in carrying the cake I had made on a large silver salver: sixty slender, flickering candles lit it up and it did not require Aunt Toto to enjoin the guests to admire the cake with the faintly pink roses. I felt small, so very small I could have hidden my face in the rich folds of the table cloth. Fortunately, my face was saved, because the cake was good and the guests were enthusiastic, and also, while presiding at the silver tea service Aunt Toto looked smilingly — almost proudly — at me.

Some of the younger friends assisted Christl and Regina to hand out the cups and refreshments. Most of the guests spoke English, and they spoke it with great friendliness to me. I believe that Thomas Bluecher, a handsome young man, is more at home speaking English than German. The father of the three young men, General Prince Bluecher, was undoubtedly a provident man: he bought an estate on the island of Guernsey, thereby ensuring that his sons are British subjects. After tea a short walk was suggested in the forest. We walked along in twos and threes.

The park is extensive and, following the main path, you walk directly into quiet forest ways, where even at midday the sun scarcely penetrates. Here you can hear the call of forest birds that beckon you to even deeper solitude. You walk lightly on a carpet of pine needles and moss underfoot, into little green glades: mushrooms of many different varieties abound — but the pretty red-capped or pink-stemmed ones are strictly avoided: they are poisonous. Here, spruce trees grow among the green moss — perfect, perky little Christmas trees. There was not much time for me to admire the inexhaustible fount of delights that abound in the forest. The children must be bathed and we must get ready for a festive evening.

A number of guests stayed for supper. There was trout — butter and mustard — lovely!

After supper, there was a torchlight parade in the grounds. The brass band of the local fire brigade — in full regalia, Karl Zusky conducting — split the air with martial sounds, fireworks, music and singing until "good-nights" were said.

*****

Aunt Toto and Anna are busy arranging the chapel for tomorrow, 16 October, will be the feast of St. Hedwig of Silesia. The green and gold carpet has been brushed: the candlesticks polished, while on the altar a great many candles are arranged: presently we'll go to the hot-house for flowers. I have been in the sacristy for the first time and I am awed by the collection of vestments and fine linens: There are cross-stitch and embroidered scenes in colour upon fine silk and satin — gold and silver threads glitter — most of the work has been lovingly and handsomely stitched by family ancestors in far past and faded days, like the mellow faded lilies worked in minute petit-point on some of the garments. The most beautiful of all is the chasuble that Anna calls "Our Lady's," because it is only worn on very high feast days, principally for the Midnight Mass at Christmas. It is a rich cream satin that has an overall design of small embroidered pastel flowers — lovely. I believe the material is from Aunt Toto's wedding dress. There are cushions to kneel on — their covers are also embroidered in delicate cross stitch. I have such respect for the embroidery that I hardly dare kneel on them.

*****

In the hothouse, the large white chrysanthemums are in bloom — masses of flowers. They look like the white flowers of our dreams: the air is lovely with the acrid scent of the chrysanthemums and the sweet tang of apples — the apple cellar adjoins the glass house. The turtledoves have been brought from their cage in the garden, they fly around happily in the glass house and must feel as prisoners set free: their throaty cooings fill the air like a message of courage and deep peace to the heart. Aunt Toto says they will soon be building their nests in the tall palm tree — the one that tips the rafters — and they will know a winter home where pallid flowers bloom and golden stars gleam.

By meeting those who have won their spurs, or rather, their descendants, I have a chance of seeing quite a new side of society. Life is not easy for many of these people, especially the young people, but they face life in Hitler's *Dritten Reich* (third empire) with warm-hearted courage. What surprises me is how well informed and what a clear idea of what is actually transpiring people seem to have. Nobody seems particularly interested in the radio broadcasts, because they are biased and patterned with propaganda. Newspapers are avidly read. Someone has said, "We must read between the lines and be wide-awake because we live in a world of invisible eyes and ears."

I feel handicapped by not being able to speak German. I can follow a conversation almost clearly, but my replies are shaky and stumbling and my grammar is *arg schlimm* (very bad), and it is agreeable that most of the nobility speak two or three languages, some even more, like Baroness Rhemon, who speaks eight!

*****

When the official dinner for the village notables was announced, I felt somewhat diffident about meeting them. Dear, dear, I thought, now I must endeavour to give replies and express myself in German....

We all wore evening dress. The first to arrive were the four forest rangers. They greeted me as one man, *"Waidmanns Heil!"* (Huntsmans hail!). Then came the Priest and the Steward with a gracious *"Gruess Gott!"* (God's greeting!). The other men greeted *"Guten Abend"* (good evening). Lastly came Herr Lange, the secretary, with a gaffe: "Heil Hitler!"

The dinner was a success (in spite of him).

After dinner, we all sat in the library. Uncle Fritz passed his large cigar box around. The men spoke about timber, trees, hunting and game: they were very talkative and very humorous. These men are the true protectors of the forest and also of wildlife. They are usually wonderfully good shots,

but they are not the ones to be always killing — they know
that discriminate shooting is beneficial in their territories or
districts. Their conversation rang richly with adjectives and
exclamations: *Ausgezeichnet.... Fantastisch.... Grossartig....
Wunderbar!* They spoke of red game and black game. They
included a wily fox or two and the pheasants that would have
to be protected for another season or two. To me it seemed that
they brought a breath of forest air right into the room, and
what I appreciated was that these men of the forests have an
understanding of wild things, and understanding brings
compassion and love.... If they had been asked, I think they
would have sung a lusty "Huntsman's Chorus," especially
handsome young Gardringer, the Austrian.... They thanked
Uncle Fritz and Aunt Toto: bowed low and kissed the married
ladies' hands with *"Gute Nacht, Aufwiedersehen!"*

*****

There was Gypsy music on the green that seemed to
cause much undue excitement, until one of the servants
informed me, "They are strangers. They come from the Balkans
with a caravan, they have a lot of things: a donkey with bells
that runs around in circles with a monkey on its back." By this
time, I am accustomed to Gypsies. Among them are always the
beggars and the invariable fortune tellers: but to satisfy the
children, I must go to the green with a coin. Soon after I gave
it, a pretty woman came to beg for a blouse. She showed me
her breasts under her shawl — they were white and pink-
tipped and fair as two beautiful roses. I was so overcome that I
immediately went up to my room to fetch my shirt blouse.
Zdenka, divining my intention, came running after me and
met me on the stairs. Ruefully shaking her head, she took the
blouse out of my hands and said, "She is wicked. In her
caravan, she will have a whole trunk of blouses: you'll see,
she'll still steal something!" Zdenka has no faith in Gypsies; she
says they always get away with something.

Some little while after they had left, we looked for my
son, Engelbert — "Lekkie," as he calls himself. Zdenka
searched high and low and from attic to cellar called, in three
languages, *"Wo bist Du?"* (where are you?). There was no reply.

"Oh, don't worry," I said to Zdenka, "He'll turn up." But then Zdenka crossed herself, (this was something serious) and she was gone. She ran to the village, roused up the boys and soon, like red Indians, they were tracking the Gypsies. Ultimately, the caravan was overtaken in Prince Bluecher's Forest, with Lekkie running and skipping happily along with the woman wearing a shawl without a blouse: he explained to me, "She promised me the donkey with bells and a pretty little monkey..."

Oh little son of mine, I must leave no stone unturned in trying to teach you to avoid such women, who promise to lead you to the moon and all the stars, or perhaps only a donkey with bells and a pretty little monkey.

*****

It is getting cold, very cold. Outside, a thin film of ice is on the water. Zdenka dressed the children and took them down for breakfast, I lazed a while. Suddenly there was a stir at the door and Zdenka burst in carrying Lekkie against her breast, shivering violently — he looked like a drowned rat. Zdenka was white with fright and it took some time before she could tell me what had happened. The boys had each armed themselves with a piece of string and went out fishing while Zdenka prepared breakfast. They fished in one of the cement basins built at each of the four corners of the house to catch rain water. The water is about four feet deep: Lekkie slipped on the ice and tumbled into the basin, the water was over his head.... Peter, who is only three and a half, managed to catch him by his hair and held his head above water, meanwhile shouting lustily for help. It took some minutes before Zdenka heard him and ran to the rescue. Lekkie was dressed in warm pyjamas and put into my bed. Anna came hurrying in with a cup of hot milk and soon Lekkie's teeth stopped chattering. Peter came in sucking his thumb. "Come here, Peter," said Lekkie, "Let me look at you. Peter, you are my best friend and I'll love you all my life!"

Peter took the proffered hand, but he did not seem nearly as impressed with this brotherly overture as he might well have been.

It is a grey morning and low grey clouds fill the sky. At breakfast, Uncle Fritz said, "If it does not clear by 11 o'clock it will possibly start snowing."

For my part, I look forward, almost eagerly, to my first sight of snow in Czechoslovakia (even though my face grows long at the thought of how low the temperature may fall).

Zdenka brought a basket of wood to the *Lusthauschen* and lit a fire in the pretty, green-tiled stove. Then she started polishing the table and the high-backed peasant chairs. Together we dusted and washed the pictures. There are two plates of fruits and flowers, and two pictures of different varieties of fruits. And there is an old English print of the three little dogs, sitting up to ask for a meal, entitled "For What We Are About to Receive" — a homey touch in a far-away land!

Christl has joined us with the two Dobermans, Roderick and Ronnie, each on a leash: should they be left free, they bolt after game in the forest. I thought of how people of all nationalities are fond of dogs, and here we are pleased to agree that they are our best friends and protectors.

We'll take a walk in the forest… but not too far, as I am taking Ilona in the high pram.

Christl was not able to restrain the dogs alone and the pram was too heavy for the foot-path, so we left Ilona in a sheltered spot and walked on. I took Ronnie from Christl. Soon, large flakes of snow fell, alighting on the high branches of the trees: all was silent in the forest… not a bird note, not a rustling leaf, only the large snow flakes, interminably falling from the low grey heavens. Soon the scene was transformed by a carpet of snow: the dark glades looked mysterious and our pathway was converted into so many Christmas-like pictures… our faces were red. I exulted, I laughed. Ilona was almost forgotten when Lekkie reminded me, saying, "The snow will fall on our baby." We retraced our steps. Quite a lot of snow had already drifted into the pram and it lay white on the hood. Fortunately, Ilona was still sleeping soundly.

*****

When Aunt Toto and Zdenka heard that we had left the baby alone, they were distressed and said that I was very careless. "In future," they said, "you must beware of Gypsies and occasional wolves." I tried to excuse myself, by saying the snow had made me feel quite heady.

I think I am still a little heady, because I often think of a picture I would give a lot to paint; on pure white satin, a snowy carpet with shafts of light filtering through the deep purple shadows of the dark boled trees, touching them here and there with living gold.

*****

Aunt Toto has given me a present: one of her furs, a black fox. I am not fond of fox furs... too much bush and brush for my liking, but this poor beastie must have been slain when his soft fur had reached the first peak of rich bloom. It is featherweight, soft, luxurious, but his tail... his dark glory, his shadowy ornament is more than ornament, it is a singular adornment — because the children love to stroke the black, silky fur gently, only very gently with their little hands — it is a pure delight!

*****

Baron Gemmel has invited us for a musical afternoon. When Franz delivered the post this morning on his silver salver, Helene's eyes grew bright. "Surely there will also be musicians from the Opava theatre and that will be so interesting," said Helene.

To Baroness's musical evening I wore my grey satin blouse with the collar and reviers of lace, with my black skirt and the black fox fur: its light, furry tail cascaded over my blouse to tip my skirt. Helene thought that "it gives a stylish look" when she came to my room. "But," she added wistfully, "I don't know what to wear... I really don't know." "Is it because you have too many Paris frocks?" "No," said Helene, "but I do so especially want to look *charmant* this afternoon."

When she chose a green silk frock that suited her fresh colouring and auburn hair, I said, "Now you look really charming." It was fun to see with what pleasurable anticipation Helene looked forward to the evening. There are awfully interesting people to meet and perhaps also a little romance. There is a gentleman, Fritz Newzella....

We were ready to get into the car and now Helene was full of merriment. "Dory," she called out to me, "tell me, what is life without romance?"

"Isn't that what the Gypsies say?"

Aunt Toto joined us and asked, "What are you girls talking about?"

"Oh," said Helene, "Dory is trying to tell me the tragic story of life without romance."

"Aunt Toto," I said, "Helene is just weaving dreams."

"Yes," said Aunt Toto, "and sometimes she is plain silly."

It had been an enjoyable afternoon: the twenty-kilometer drive did not take long. The Gemmels live in a tall house in a quiet *"gasse"* (lane). The salon with the high ceiling and large windows is well suited for musical entertainment: with some of the guests I was acquainted, but not with the gentlemen from the theatre, or with Mr. Fritz Newzella. Helene has a happy knack of making friends, and soon we were all on good terms. Then, Greta Gemmel put down her long cigar holder and took up the bow of her violin. With the leader of the city's orchestra, she played Mendelssohn's Violin Concerto in E minor. As the rounded, mellow notes of the violins filled the lofty room, I wondered at the power of Greta's slender fingers holding the notes to send them rapidly from her bow "like a shower of pearls, with an inner gleam of tears." I felt I was lifted above the clouds, only to be brought back to earth again by the obnoxious smell of the smoke from her long black cigar.

It was late when we returned from Opava. I hastened to the children's room. Ilona was comfortable in the playing pen, but what is this? Lying in pieces in the playing pen was the white alabaster Viennese clock. In falling, it must have missed her head by inches.... *Deo Gratias*, her precious head is safe.... but the clock, and my Peter sitting on top of the writing bureau? Zdenka came in, she held my hand, I held hers. "What shall we do? I don't know."

"What must we do? I don't know."

Suddenly, Zdenka had an idea. "Karl," she said, and she ran to fetch him while I fetched Helene. Karl came and collected the pieces and said, "It is fortunate that the clock has fallen on the rug."

The next day the clock was set up in place again, without noticeable scars. And on that next day, Helene came to call me. I saw trouble on every feature.

"Your son Peter," she said. I went out to the entrance gate, and there stood my son Peter, with his little fat hands clasped around the throat of a large fowl. The bird's head reached up to his chest, the feet dangled just above the ground: obviously, the bird was dead. The servants had collected around.

"Peter," I said severely, "Have you done this?"

Without saying a word, he bobbed his blond head up and down. Joseph took the bird and I took Peter.

I said, "The cock is dead, did you see he can't walk anymore?"

Solemnly Peter bobbed his head.

I said, "The poor bird was so sore."

Now he repeated, "Poor bird so sore."

I covered my eyes with my hand. He thought that I wept, so he wept...we both wept.

*****

A day or two after Lekkie's disappearance, Zdenka took the boys for a walk in the village. Peter detached himself while she went to talk to her mother, and then, like a little fury, he dashed after some geese. Catching up with a peasant woman's fat St. Martin's goose, he managed to tie a loop of grass around its neck and then endeavoured to lead the struggling bird home — much to the annoyance of the owner. Now I felt it was absolutely necessary to speak seriously to Peter, but when he tried to explain, in his small way, "The cock is dead, so I tried to get another bird for Uncle Fritz," everybody tried not to smile.

*****

This morning, I sent the boys to play in the
Lusthauschen, the play house in the park. Afterwards, I
followed: Lekkie was riding the big bear: there was no sign of
Peter. "Where is your brother?" I asked. Lekkie said, "He's gone
for a walk." I walked through the park calling. We inquired
from the garden maids — from anybody who seemed likely to
have seen him but Peter was nowhere. Eventually, I got really
anxious, and when I was in the act of asking Zdenka to get in
touch with the village boys, Peter walked in, quite
unconcerned.

"I've been looking everywhere for you Peter, where
have you been?"

He looked up at me, his fair face as innocent as a
cherub's and said earnestly, "Mammie, I sat under the tree, by
the deep waters, where the ducks and the geese swim and
poor Cock-Robin died."

Nobody seemed to know where these deep waters
were located until I found a sequestered pond beyond the
stables, where snow white geese swim against a drift of golden
ripples, where an old prune tree thick-set with rich, purple
fruit dips branches into the deep waters.

A good place for meditation.

*****

Fraulein Auguste promptly lets it be known that "I am
Frau Graefin's Lady's Maid": she is quite the autocrat — not of
all the Russians, but of all the household servants. On the stove
you will find a separate pot of food boiling for *Fraulein*
Auguste and incidentally also for her hens. Auguste walks out
in a dark suit, taking the dogs for an outing. Because the
Fraulein cares for her nasturtiums, they have the best blooms
on the castle wall outside her window. Her room is a neat
bower, with freshly cut flowers and holy pictures galore. On a
cushion on her comfortable settee lies a lute with embroidered
ribbon streamers, one of which reads; *"Wo Man singt, da setzt
Dich nieder… Boese Munschen haben keine Lieder."* (Sit thee down
where songs are sung, for the wicked have no music). I have
not seen any of the servants sitting in Lady Auguste's room,

but I sat down on her sofa because she asked me to come to her room.

"*Frau Graefin,*" she said, "I must speak to you about your son Peter. He scares the living daylights out of my hens, and I get no more fresh eggs."

"Auguste," I said, feeling that I had somewhat paled, "that is bad, I'll have to take better care of Peter, but I think that after killing the cock, he has satisfied a natural curiosity. Peter has never seen birds in Hamburg and he wants to treat them as playmates. You see how he loves the dogs. I'll try to buy some fresh eggs for you in the village."

"I don't eat village eggs, I feed my hens myself and I like to know what I'm eating!"

"Well, then I must try to persuade your hens to return (I had a little vision of Zdenka assisting me), but how will I recognize them?"

"You will recognize them alright, *Frau Graefin,* because Peter has pulled out all of their tail feathers."

Sad to say, the hens did not return to their pen until the first heavy fall of snow, then as I chanced to walk past, I saw, sitting on the high perch in a row, the Lady Auguste's six dejected-looking hens, minus tail feathers.

*****

In Kyjovice, Sundays and feast days always stand out in sharp relief, and there are many feast days. On Sunday mornings, in the house chapel, there is always the solemn High Mass, with harmonious hymns sung beautifully by the Czech people of the village.

On weekdays, low Mass is always said at *"Viertel ein siebeni"* (quarter to seven) with its lovely atmosphere of peace whether in the cold grey light of winter or the bright summer mornings. Pots of flowers always bloom in the chapel in a mass of freshness, a little contrast to the tired voices of some of the old peasants who never seem to tire of singing age-old Slavonic songs of praise and glory to the Most High.

*****

Although Uncle Fritz does not encourage my children in their little escapades, I think sometimes they must cause him a quiet smile, because he has shown me, lying on his desk, an amusing collection of drawings that he has done of their adventures. They include Auguste's dejected, tailless hens. He said, "Dory, they are very much like Max and Moritz." (William Busch's wicked, childish characters).

Uncle Fritz is a busy gentleman. Every morning after Mass and breakfast, he spends some hours with his secretary in his office, and then, arming himself with shears and saws and other garden tools, you can see him in the park where he saws and trims... sometimes just to give his plants a little light, which he says is very essential. Then again, he loosens the ground with a trowel. Yesterday, he tirelessly scattered a top dressing of leaves and moss over his pet cyclamen and rose trees, pruning and pinning some of them down to the ground to keep them protected and cosy through the winter. Uncle Fritz knows his shrubs and trees, not only by their names, German, English, and Latin, but also by their families and habits. When he was called the other day for lunch, there he was at the extreme end of the park, shading his eyes with his hand, viewing his labours from afar off, before all the world, like men of old viewing the Promised Land!

Usually, in the afternoons, Uncle Fritz's spirited horse, Pomerance, is saddled and brought around and he rides out to his fields or to some of his farming enterprises. He has a considerable stud of horses, a dairy farm, and piggery.... Sometimes he takes his rifle and goes stalking for a lone deer or some other denizen of the forest. Usually he returns with his kill when we have already had supper.

What I enjoy seeing is when Christl rides with her father. She sits on her horse, side-saddle, in a tailor-made habit, wearing a black velvet peaked cap, and when she gives her horse the rein and they canter down the chestnut avenue, I almost feel a little envious.

###

CHAPTER THREE
FAREWELL, HAMBURG

December, 1937

    I am feeling sorry for myself because we are not going back to live in Hamburg, that great city with the salt tang of the sea in the air, where gulls fly around in readiness to snatch anything you may wish to throw from your window. Hamburg, where I made good friends, where I learned to speak German, where from many of the shops there emanates that homely aroma of roasting coffee. In Hamburg, with ships sailing out on the Elbe, I never felt very far from home... from South Africa. True — as I said to Aunt Toto (when she asked me, "But how did you manage? You had to economize? You all look so well.") — it was not all plain sailing... it was not all simple: I had to learn to act independently.

    But I could smile with friendly people like I did with the woman who owned one of the market stalls. On our first acquaintance, I held up one mark and said, "Now how much mixed fruit can you give me today? But please, not too many watermelons!"

    Instead of turning away from my childish request, "*Bitte, bitte,*" she said, "Look at these bananas, they are good: none better where you come from, but by tomorrow they will be over-ripe — good bananas. Apples, pears, all ripe and right for breakfast!"

    And the fish stalls? Oooh — the beautiful fish. With rows of mackerel: red bass: blue trout: purple fish: fat herrings, salt herrings, still more herrings, smoked, salted, dried or fresh... all good herrings and always cheap. I knew my friends like Uncle Fritz knows his trees.

*****

January, 1938

Christmas we spent in Falkenberg, which Engelbert felt that he should have inherited as the elder son but which now belongs to my brother-in-law Fritz. Fritz, who did not marry a South African peasant but a Princess Ratibor. My dear mother-in-law, Mammie, has passed away; and two of Engelbert's sisters have left to join a hospital as Red Cross nurses.

Falkenberg was not the same. The old castle in Upper Silesia had lost its patina; it would never be the same again.

Engelbert's work took us to Gorlitz, a town on the river Neisse. We questioned as to whether we should take a flat or live in the Otto-Stift, a hospice run by nuns. As I have never been an enterprising housekeeper and I missed my dear Hamburg, let us try the hospice.

Now I began my first acquaintance with nuns. I learned that convents are divisible into two general classes, Contemplative and Working Orders.

In the strict sense, only the women living in an Order with solemn vows are "nuns," while the term "Sister" is rightly applied to the religious with simple vows. The chief object of the Contemplative is prayer, but Contemplatives are not idle: they live chiefly from the fruits of their garden, they bake the hosts for the churches, do translations which are among their major intellectual efforts, and like other women, they attend to their house-hold chores, and efforts that do not interfere with their Rule.

An old aunt, Tante Janka, Sister of my father-in-law, the Mother Superior of a Carmelite convent, told me; "One order contemplates the heavens, that the others may cross the seas with safety." Scripture tells us that the earnest, fervent prayer of the just availeth much. The actual object of the Rule is to combine prayer with the practice of spiritual, corporal, and practical works of mercy. The essence of the religious state consists in the three perpetual vows of Poverty, Chastity, and Obedience. One becomes a Religious then to obtain religious perfection: the three vows take precedence in all things and in all ways, and there are many who feel the "Touch" on their shoulder and respond.

The Otto-Stift was a beautiful old house. We lived almost in state surrounded by kindness and consideration: however, I was quite unsettled... feeling like a trespasser,

feeling I was making too many demands on the nuns.
Engelbert insisted "If we don't occupy the apartment, someone
else will: it is the livelihood of the nuns. Just carry on like you
are doing, we'll decide after the new baby arrives."

It was a bitterly cold morning, when, in spite of the fact
that the snow-plow had just gone over the road, snow drifts
had piled up again. Several times our car stuck in the snow
and I feared we would not arrive in time at the St. Carolas
Hospital. I shall always remember the cozy room we entered
and the warmth of the good sisters' greeting.

*****

"And now," said Aunt Toto, with a world of love in her
eyes and not a little satisfaction, handing me back my precious
bundle, "we have a little Christian boy." This happened when
little Fritz was three days old. Uncle Fritz and Aunt Toto came
to visit me in Gorlitz — a long way from Kyjovice in the
middle of winter. Their visit was taken advantage of by
Engelbert to have the baby baptized. They arranged with the
priest to baptize him in the Nun's Chapel; a most important,
but quiet sacrament. Afterwards, we had tea in my room,
where among other flowers, the pot of lovely flowering azalea
that Engelbert had given me held first place.

"Now, let me see," said Engelbert, taking a slip of
paper from his pocket, and he read the names out: Friedrich,
Theodor, Maria (the Praschmas are all called Maria), Antonius,
Thaddeus, — here he took a deep breath and quietly added the
rest (his private collection) — Joseph, Leopold, Johannes-
Nepomuk, Ignatius Loyola, and if he had thought of it, he
would have added *Et Omni Sancti* (and all the saints), an old
custom of many aristocratic families. Such a lot of names for
such a little boy. Meanwhile he lies unconcerned about them
all, unconcerned even that today he has entered a new chapter
of his little life... his vocation of being, as Auntie Mother —
Aunt Toto — says, "A little Christian boy: I shall feel it right at
all times and especially at times of stress to call upon his
patron saints." Quite a litany. That they pray for many
blessings and much inspiration for him and to protect the

white soul of my child, who looks so beautiful in his christening robe.

I shall call him Fritzl.

*****

In the warm, charitable heart of Aunt Toto, there is a particularly warm spot for Engelbert.

On one of our visits to Kyjovice, when Peter was six, he was acting in one of the plays that Regina loves to stage. This time it was "Hans im Glueck," a little play that was arranged for Aunt Bertha's birthday. As Peter came on the stage, wearing the weather-worn leather cap on his fair hair and carrying the bag of gold on his shoulder, his smile was full of confidence, although he was minus two little front teeth. Aunt Toto said to me; "He is too sweet! Just like his father at that age, I remember well — he was the most charming of all of Marie's children and has always owned the most tender spot in my heart."

No doubt, our first memorable visit to Kyjovice was due to this same tender regard, because Engelbert, wishing me to become acquainted with his relatives, had written to Aunt Toto (as I learned years later) that he wished me to learn to know them, because my South African education qualified me principally to know only the difference between black and white: so to learn the right "tact" in my association with my fellow men that first visit was the prelude to many visits, both in the summer and the winter. Two events that are always eagerly anticipated and that have no strings attached are the early Mass and those pleasant walks in Uncle Fritz's spacious green-wood forests.

Aunt Toto and Uncle Fritz are both good tennis players, and the girls have a tennis coach. When guests are not present, tennis is sometimes the order of the afternoon. Czech boys come to pick up balls for us: it is funny that it comes naturally to me to want to speak Sesutho to them, like we did to our little maids at home.

Every morning I like to find a little sphere of work for myself from our patronizing Auguste in the sewing room or I help Fanka in the fowl runs where, with gloves on, the children also diligently help to collect nettles and are eager to chop them up for goslings and chickens. In winter, the potato and barley mash is heated for poultry and peacocks.

Regina came to my room, she stood hesitating and I gathered there was something she wanted to say to me. Eventually, she confided; "Aunt Hedwig is coming this afternoon."

"And who is this Aunt Hedwig?" I asked.

"Hedwig, Archduchess of Austria, who is married to Papa's cousin Bernhard. They live in the Tyrolean mountains in an old castle, inherited from her Grand-father, the Emperor Franz Joseph."

And still Regina lingered. Presently, she said, "Aunt Hedwig is so good, one can't be pretentious with her, but of course, there are set forms and rules of etiquette that we observe. When we visited some ladies in Troppau last time Aunt Hedwig was here, they were so correct, one good friend, quite an old lady, curtsied so low to kiss Aunt Hedwig's hand that I feared she would not be able to rise again." So while Regina lingered, I said, "If you show me the ropes, I'll do my best." I am learning the right tact.

The Archduchess Hedwig has arrived with two of her children; Franz-Joseph and Marie Elizabeth. Hedwig is a serious person with a good face and a good figure, dark eyes and dusky hair. Franz-Joseph is distinguished looking — no likeness to the portrait of his grandfather in Kyjovice. Marie is slight, almost skinny, promises to be pretty... lovely young people. At breakfast-table this morning, I had occasion to observe that, dressed in a tailor-made blouse and dark skirt, Hedwig is, as Regina has said, "wholesome." She does not expect rules and formalities at all times, so I think I'll keep to my own "tact."

*****

May, 1938
The Lobster Hunt

Last night, Uncle Fritz invited us to hunt *Hummer* (lobster). He told us that during the months that do not contain an "r" in the spelling, lobsters can be caught;

otherwise, they are soft-shelled. The children and I accepted the invitation along with Hedwig's children. I looked a lovely sight. For walking in the water, I put on the big Wellington boots that Uncle Fritz gave me for walking in the snow and slush, I wore my shortest tweed skirt and tied a handkerchief around my hair. We said so long to Aunt Toto and Aunt Hedwig, who stayed at home. Hedwig complemented me, saying, "Dory, you always look so suitably dressed."

We carried torches and baskets. Mr. Balhar, the hunter, led the way. He knows the best mountain streams. We thought it was quite an adventure. In the dark, the lobsters come out of their retreats under stones and branches to feed. We walked along narrow paths and climbed over boulders to shine our torches into pools of clear running water where we could discern trout, crabs, and lobsters. We had great fun pouncing on the lobsters and putting them in our baskets, in which we already had a supply of nettle leaves, for keeping them cool. Hunting the streams continued until we were several miles from home. By this time the moon had risen high over the dark wooded heights and we had caught enough lobsters for several meals.

It was a new experience. Uncle Fritz was giving the children an unprecedented feast, and when it was time to return home, they started singing softly, happily harmonizing Mathius Claudius' evening song, *"Der Mond ist aufgegangen"* (the moon has risen).

I do not think that in all the world there is an atmosphere better suited to the words and the tune, of this lovely song than in this valley, when the heavens are in deep repose and the faded moon makes a dim silver haze over the mountains curtained with hazy, lazy pine forests.

*****

15 October, 1938

Uncle Fritz has always been famed for his forest feasts and parties, but during this holiday, I think, it was to bring some light to relieve the seriousness of the present time (Hitler has invaded their beloved Austria and broken every promise he has made) that a number of homely feasts have been arranged in Kyjovice especially for Hedwig and family.

When Regina came to my room… this time, no hesitation. "Tomorrow," she said eagerly, "will be the 16th of October, Aunt Hedwig's feast day. We are having dinner in the large dining room downstairs. The table will be laid with the best silver and china, but as the Schuberts are away, Papali asks if you will arrange the flowers. After dinner we will have a little concert, the children will be in fancy dress and will recite and sing songs. Mother has asked me to sing, if you will play my accompaniments? We can go now and practice." Which we did, and then we went up to the attic to examine the contents of the "Theatre Box" for costumes for the children. After we had opened the box we sat among an assortment of old fashioned costumes and dresses mostly made from beautiful materials and laces.

In that dusty garret we sat and had a little chat. I said, "Regina, it is not only for your Aunt Hedwig, but also for the young people that you are doing a fine thing."

"As to that," said Regina, "We all have a job to get on with. If we don't — the fault, dear Brutus, is not with our stars, but with ourselves."

"That depends on the line we take. Look at our friends in the Wilhelm Strasse in Berlin."

"Friends? Dory, you are a little ironical. If they think they can sit at the top of the tree without God's guiding light, they will soon be cut off — one by one, snip, snip, snip." (She snipped with her fingers.)

On the great table downstairs, many candles cast a glow of festive light — on snow-white table cloth, on flowers, on silver cutlery and beautiful silver dishes — however, it was a somewhat subdued party, children and grown-ups, who sat down at that festive-looking table. Uncle Fritz said, "Let us be thankful for these and for all other mercies." After this Old World grace, and when Joseph served the wine, the war-cloud somewhat dispersed: there was talk and there were smiles. The dinner was excellent.

The young people sat in the yellow salon, each one a little impatient to take a turn in performing some special act for Aunt Hedwig's party. My children, in traditional Czech

costumes, were to sing Czech songs learned from Zdenka:
Marie-Elise, ready for a recitation, was taking up much space
in a wide crinoline: but it was Franz-Joseph who stole the show
— a dark Gypsy maid — like someone said, a first class
Carmen, who brought the house down. When he "tripped the
light fantastic toe," the children found it hilarious. Then there
was singing, Regina sang her Schubert songs. When she sang,
"Where is the land where the orange flowers bloom?" because I
know where that land is, where oranges and lemons and
citrons bud and bloom, I felt I had the right to end the
accompaniment with a fine flare and flourish.

*****

One thousand years ago, a duke of Bohemia was
converted to Christianity. He endeavoured to also make his
people Christians, and was assassinated by his brother (must
have been a very wicked man) in consequence.

Duke Wenceslaus is regarded as the Patron Saint of
Bohemia (Czechoslovakia). He is the Good (Saint) King
Wenceslaus of the Christmas carol. To commemorate the
thousandth anniversary of their good saint, the Czechs struck a
golden medal. On one side of the coin, King Wenceslaus is
depicted riding a charger. On the other side is the wild Lion of
Czechoslovakia.

To wind up the holiday, a tennis tournament was
arranged. The first prize was to be the Golden Medal of St.
Wenceslaus. Play was started immediately after Mass. It was a
mixed doubles handicap tournament, joined in by a number of
players from a neighboring estate. There were many exciting
games that continued until the late afternoon. I often had to
stop my children from shouting when it was my turn to play.
My Peter would then wave and show that he was holding
thumbs. When the tournament ended, the children took all the
credit upon themselves — it was because they held thumbs for
me that I won the golden coin.

*****

1940 — Year's End

I like to sit under the ancient Linden tree. Rosario
(Engelbert's cousin) is sitting in Titas Park writing letters and
watching our children having a "sun bath," while I am just
romancing. I fancy I can hear the melody of Schubert's song in
the rustling leaves... one can have many thoughts. I wonder
why a person as quiet and retiring as I am, who was brought
up on a lonely back-veld farm and who loves the things that I
have known from early childhood, should have moved across
a continent, to be received into the houses and castles of
noblemen. I am very fortunate in the things that constitute this
new pattern of my life. I am fortunate in many things and
especially in the fellowship of good people .... but suddenly
my heart rocks. I am homesick for my own people, for some of
the things from which I have been parted: they become
clarified and very lovely to that "inward eye." I recall those
early walks, how the gentle wind, perfumed with the scent of
mimosa and eucalyptus coming from afar swept the blue-gum
avenue, tentatively testing the sturdy strength of those tall,
white-boled trees that rustled and raised their lofty crowns to
loftier skies. Those trees could whisper tales as good as trees
ever told — they never blamed and they never complained
and when, to tell them a tale of woe, you leant your head
against the tall white trunk, where the rugged bark had dried
and fallen away, they candidly questioned, "So? So? And now
skip along, my dear, and catch as you follow a falling leaf,
t'will bring you great good luck."

The Bush Crows

    I recall, how in summertime, when the rain clouds
cleared and you flung aside the bed clothes early enough, you
could catch the morning star... pure white, where it set, while
the low-veld still slumbered under a billowing blanket of snow
white mist. Far away on the horizon, the blue hills seemed to
rock and the *"randjies"* (ridges) skipped playfully like young
rams in the rise and fall of the mist, while the bastions of the
mountains stood aloof, silent, dark and sombre.

    In the east, the primrose light brightened and spread,
till suddenly, sunbeams touched the dew-drops and flung a
casket of living jewels over leaf and blade and spray. Soon, the
sun dispersed the mist clouds, and like poor banished spirits,

they arose and ambled away over the deep valleys and mountains.

Over all was a deep hush and the heart stopped to listen. Till the bush crows, flying low over the humble roof, called out to me, "Hi, hi. Wake up. You deserve to be shot, if your soul is not radiant and pure and calm!"

The Oriole

I recall an afternoon late, when we watched the herd of cattle leisurely return from grazing, how an oriole piped from the branch of a tall gum-tree. Dad puffed away at his pipe and then said to me, "A magnificent bird, piping his message every evening from the same old tree. What does that oriole say?"

A golden oriole piped from the old gum tree: "I eschew your shadow, your long, grey, wavering shadow, I sing my song to the Giver of Light and the beautiful human soul: *'Magnificat anima mea Dominum!'* You people... look at my coat, look at my vest, the band on my throat, I'm dressed in my best.

"You people... with a soul like a jewel, your very own human soul, you say, when you finally fall like a leaf from the tree and your soul flies on wings through cloudlit blue — what will the Giver, the Father of Light, find engraved on your human soul? *Magnificat anima mea Dominum*?

"You people... look at my coat, look at my vest, the band on my throat: I am dressed for the Blessed."

It was like this that my thoughts wandered under the linden tree, and when Lekkie looked into my face and said, "You are so sad, Mammie?"

I said, "I am not sad, I have been thinking of a sweet yellow bird...."

The thought of our last Christmas together gives me much consolation, chiefly because I recall how Engelbert took each of our children upon his knee, to each one he read a little homily about Christmas. To our little Fritzl, he only said, "*Sei Brav*, be good, so that you make the little Christ-Child happy."

Of all the words that man has collected from, "God's good web of loveliness," one that is very precious to me is the little word *"Brav,"* because of many warm connotations. You tell a person (in German): "*Sei Brav,*" meaning: "Be good, be obedient, be gentle, be calm," and if he be faint-hearted: "*Sei brav*," — "You must be brave."

It was to be our last Christmas together: we did not know it, but afterwards we knew we would all have to be very brave, and when I look back over my shoulder, along the way we have come, I see that Engelbert was rich…. inestimably rich, because: "By thy words, thou shalt be condemned," and because the only things a man can take with him are the things he has given away… and there along the way I see good, kind words.

We must be brave. After the end of all things.

###

CHAPTER FOUR
"I HEAR YOU CALLING ME"

31 January, 1941
Leubus Institution

It is dreary, bleak and cold outside.

Weakly, Engelbert asked me, "Is there much snow?"

I answered, "It has topped the high hedge and the snow storm is still piling on high mountains and deep valleys."

And now he is dead, *Herr Graf* is dead: his soul is freed. After I had lifted him to straighten the pillows, I bathed his temples: quite suddenly he looked at me appealingly... despairingly. Simultaneously, we realized that the reveille had sounded — he lay back, cushioned on the white pillows, but his soul... so infinitely dear to me... was freed from his earthly fetters — free to fly with the angel, away , silently away... beyond the troubled grey sky. I flung the windows open wide — free to fly to aeons of blue. I knelt in front of the open window, the cold struck out at me. "Go forth, O Christian Soul — out of the world to the Father Almighty, who created thee — in the name of Jesus Christ, son of the living God who suffered for thee — in the name of the Holy Ghost who sanctified thee — in the name of Holy Mary, mother of God: in the name of all the Saints of God." These kind human words I prayed. My eyes were clouded, I did not see the snowy landscape — not the hedge that I had lately said the snow had topped. My clouded eyes looked up to the sky, I knew that even now his soul was in contact with the beauty of it all — not a vague glimpse, a shadowy reflection, but the whole sweep of eternity! He would not wish to return.

Go forth O Christian soul. Why should I weep? Only a great weariness of soul possessed me... a great dire weariness. And now I longed, ardently, to be a small child again, sitting on my mother's knee — her arms about me. With this little comfort, I said, "I shall arise and go to my father's house, only to be a small child again... to go home."

Aunt Toto and Uncle Fritz met me on the stairs. "Dory," said Aunt Toto, "where are you going?"

I think my voice answered, "I am going to buy a coffin and then I am going home." Auntie Mother put an arm around me and then with a world of sympathy in her voice, she said, "Yes, you are coming home with us." Uncle Fritz kissed my fingertips and then seeing the utter misery in my face, he put an arm around my shoulders, stooped and kissed my forehead and said, "I'll see about the casket and make arrangements, and then you must come home with us."

Uncle Fritz walked out into the snow, down the street, I was sorry to see him walking through the deep snow. There was snow in my heart. I will arise and go home... not back to Breslau, like Papali and Auntie Mother thought. *Herr Graf* is dead, the snow can never melt. It is the *Daemmerung*, the twilight, the darkness, that is so close round us, and yet I must have other thoughts, my children: the sea that is so restless and wild that we must cross.... Together we had watched the moon's track fall in a column of silver across the waves and no matter, whether the sea was bathed in sunshine or cloud, whether the moon rose or the sun set, the path was set for me. I had thought that I was clever and brave and kind; I am neither. I will arise and go.

"Dory," said Auntie Mother, "do you want him to rest in Kyjovice? We will bring him there, you must say."

"Auntie Mother, no, thank you, he will wish to rest in the crypt in Falkenberg."

My thoughts wandered to where the coffins of his forefathers stand in hallowed line, where darkened wax candles burn.... Stay for me there, I will not fail thee in that hallowed vale. In Kyjovice, on the edge of the Czech village, it is light and fair: even now, over the graves, the snow spreads a deep maternal cloak, while the pine forest sings in retarded notes. On feast days and holy days the "lowly laid" are not forgotten. Flowers and lighted candles are put on every grave. In springtime color comes and stays, peonies burst into opulent bloom, uninvited wild primroses bloom and lilies lie like pale snow and birds sing sweetly. How can they sing sweetly? Because the love of God passeth all understanding: because Uncle Fritz and Auntie Mother bear His light of mercy and loving kindness.

"I will not fail thee: stay for me there in that hallowed vale till every valley is exulted."

But now it is dreary, dark and cold outside.

Why did they have to do this? Why did the family let this happen? Ever since Mammie died they have shown only unkindness and hostility. Why did they have to kill him?

I know that Engelbert got into financial trouble. He is accused of arms dealing and the family said he was a difficult case but why did they let him be taken to Leubus, this so-called sanatorium where people who are not useful to "the magnificent Third Reich" are sent.

Is it possible that the family actually handed him over to the Nazis because he was such a thorn in their sides?

Why did his sister Elisabeth who works for the military tell me, ten days ago, heartlessly, that as Engelbert is going to die soon the only thing for me is to go back to Africa and leave the children here to be adopted by suitable families?

Leave my children? Never.

*****

My mother never spoke of my father's death or the reason for his confinement in a sanatorium. From talking with relatives I gather that since childhood he was a difficult case, highly intelligent but unrestrained with no boundaries or scruples. His lack of inhibitions and dishonest tendencies created problems for him and the family which led to him being condemned and admitted to Leubus, an institution with a reputation as a place where enemies of the Reich were disposed of.

Leubus, a medieval monastery, had been occupied by the Nazis as a so-called *Nerven Anstalt*, a sanatorium. Actually, it is well known today that it was also used as a facility for developing and manufacturing engines for V1 and V2 rockets (using prisoners for labor). At the end of the war, the former abbey also housed radar components, and secret research.

People considered undesirable and not fitting for the pure Aryan race were confined there and medical experiments performed on the "patients." When deemed no longer necessary these laboratory animals were simply exterminated, usually poisoned.

This was during the time when *Aktion T4* was in effect, an official program in which mental patients and others deemed *"Lebensunwerten Lebens"* — "life unworthy of life" — were euthanized. The program was first put into effect in Occupied Poland and eventually claimed more than 70,000 lives throughout the Reich. Many T4 specialists went on to work in death camps; other doctors were later responsible for "wild euthanasia," or killing of social *ballast* without official directives but with government encouragement. — IPB

###

CHAPTER FIVE
AFTER THE *DAEMMERUNG*

Kyjovice, Czechoslovakia
3 February, 1941

It is night: the barometer has fallen again. It is so cold that tomorrow, extravagant ice flowers will pattern the window panes. My room is cozy with a fire cheerfully crackling in the tiled oven. The servants have solicitously brought me a tub of hot water and a jug of hot milk.

As I sit in the large bed draped in a canopy of many colors and the large, soft pillows about me and the swan's-down plumeau spread over my feet, I should feel as comfortable as a fairy princess, or perhaps a ripe apple must feel... when autumn tints are in the sky... all mellow.

A picture of the Madonna with the Holy Babe, painted on wood and framed in gold, is let into the carved framework of the bed. Now, her eyes, dark and a little sad, looked directly at me, as if, gently reproving: it would be grossly wrong to say we measured each other. I did not even, like Bernadette, "gaze at the Lady as hard as I could," I only tried to meet her look. "Mother," I faltered, "Mary, Help of Christians, I have extended both my hands to accept all the good gifts from the Hand of Our Lord: help me now, Mary, Help of Christians, to carry my cross over the dark and stony stretches. The snows will not melt...." I could say no more.

"You are very foolish," she seemed to answer me, "It is when we have lost that we have the greatest gain. When you have learned to pray your *Kyrie eleison* the snows will melt and a light shall rise up in the darkness and thy darkness shall be as the noon-day clear, and then you shall have the right to see the autumn-tints lingering in the sky and the afterglow will live with you, my child, to eternity where shines the crown incorruptible."

Now the Holy Child was pleased: he smiled and extended both his little hands in benediction.

*****

Breslau
Spring, 1943

For the past two years, I have been earning my keep as a companion-helper to Aunt Sophie, Countess Henckel von Donnersmarck except for the school holidays which I spend with my children. Lekkie and Peter are in Maria-Hilf, a convent school in Breslau; Fritzl is in Kyjovice with Aunt Toto; and Ilona is in Teltsch with the family Podstatzky-Lichtenstein. She and Ali, their daughter, are being educated by *Fraulein* Schmidt, a very stern governess. The children are happy but they miss me and I miss them intensely, but we must be brave; we all have to be brave.

I was able to spend a few weeks helping our Carmelite aunts, when the Gestapo took possession of their convent. The sisters had harbored Edith Stein, a Jewish convert to Catholicism who became a Carmelite nun under the tutelage of Tante Janka, Mother Superior of the convent.

*****

Tante Janka was Marianne Graefin Praschma, sister of my grandfather Johannes. She, together with her cousin Elisabeth Graefin zu Stolberg-Stolberg, endowed a Carmelite convent using their dowries, their inheritance. Carmelites are a very strict contemplative order. This attracted Edith Stein, a highly thought of, widely published German philosopher.

Today, schools, libraries, community centers and streets in Germany are named for Edith Stein. A postage stamp was issued with her likeness in 1983.

When discovered at the convent, she was forced to flee to Holland but perished in Auschwitz in 1942. Pope John Paul II proclaimed her a saint and martyr in 1998. — IPB

*****

Aunt Sophie, a sister of one of our Carmel nuns, is a strict pedagogue to all and sundry (myself included) — except to her son Alfred's dog, Susi — and I have had to be a pedagogue to the dog. Aunt Sophie is not an easy person to work for. I have learned a lot during these years; to be diplomatic, to write German, and to balance the bank books.

My days here at Kaulwitz are spent attending early Mass, breakfast, and at 9 sharp, sitting at the desk answering letters which Aunt Sophie dictates to her various Mission Societies. Aunt Sophie receives many contributions for the Mission either in money or materials to make vestments for church use (praise the Lord, the Gestapo — so far — have not fallen foul of her work). I spend most afternoons in the sewing room, which I like, especially when there is a lovely piece of satin or silk and I make either a Roman or Medieval Chasuble. There are also cassocks for the altar boys and other priestly vestments. The sewing is left entirely to me because Aunt Sophie says she can't thread a needle.... But, alas, what she did not leave to me are my hens and pigeons. When I invested in some chicks, I thought to have eggs and perhaps an occasional roast to take to my boys during the holidays (which you can't buy now for love or money). After Aunt Sophie had considered, she said, "Dory, you can't have hens here, I'll buy them from you." I then thought of ducks, but they are so messy.

Meanwhile, we visited Effie von Walhofen. She gave me some pigeon pairs. They are quite happy in a deserted dovecote. Again, Aunt Sophie considered; "Dory, you can't have pigeons here. I'll pay you for them." (Occasionally now she has a nice fat pigeon). I considered the possibility of turkeys, but they are difficult to come by. So, after careful consideration, I thought, aha, rabbits! I knew at the farm where I bought my chicks they could sell me a pair of rabbits. This time, I asked the estate manager's wife (very nice people) if she would keep my rabbit hutches. She agreed. On my return from our next visit to Breslau, I came back in triumph, with two large Belgium hares, a buck and a doe. The villagers vie with each other in borrowing the buck. They say I have brought new blood to the village and when they see me, they greet me respectfully.

I don't know what Aunt Sophie thinks.

*****

Breslau
Easter Sunday, 1943

We sat at Aunt Bertha's (Uncle Fritz's sister) dining table, and it was while the boys were sucking their rabbit bones that Aunt Bertha said, "Dory, we have had a lovely Sunday dinner. The potato dumplings that you showed Anna how to make with chives and parsley were as sweet and as soft as butter, and with the rabbit ragout, the dinner was just out of this world. How do you manage? You always have something to give, even in these sad days, and yet you have no broad lands... no estates?"

"You see, Aunt Bertha, it's like this: my parents said, 'Cast thy bread upon the waters, and after many days thou shalt find....' I constantly think of the blessings I have and when people are kind to me," I said with Aunt Bertha in mind and I looked specifically at her, "it is the bread, the blessing I have inherited from my parents."

"Yes," said Aunt Bertha, "that is how blessings are conferred to us. Only just the other evening I read that passage in the Bible."

"I have never read it," I said, wondering. "I don't even know where to find it."

"You will find it in both the Old and the New Testaments, just look up Ecclesiastes, Chapter XI, verse one."

And so I learned something again... and if anyone would like to learn how to make ragout and also potato dumplings with chives or onions and parsley, I'll give them the recipe — gladly.

Quietly, I thought of how sometimes blessings come to us in a strange guise, like when Aunt Sophie "bought" my hens, I did not know that soon, the owner must deliver 60 eggs per hen to the Nationalist Party per annum: I also do not know how the peasants manage to sell me as many eggs as I need. I am thankful that, at present, rabbits are still scot-free.

*****

September, 1944

The war draws to a close. The Russians are fighting in Vienna.

I feel tough and lean and scared as if I have all but escaped a veld fire. I know that there are going to be ugly patches to negotiate, and therefore — in a measure to meet culminating events, when the Red Army sweeps over the border — I have packed my belongings and have told Aunt Sophie that I am taking my children to a quiet peasant village called Piltsch, near Kyjovice, on the Czechoslovakian border. To this announcement, Aunt Sophie vigorously protested and said, in that sure way of hers, "Dory, you are a coward, you are running away! You hate the Germans."

"Aunt Sophie," I answered, "I don't hate the Germans, I don't hate you, I don't hate my own children, but I think the time has come when we must each act according to our lights."

I understand Aunt Sophie, and I sympathize with her because she has so very much to lose. Besides her life's work, the Mission Society, there is the beautiful church that she prizes like the apple of her eye, designed and built on their estate by her husband, Edgar Henckel. There are the three estates, Grambschutz, Reichen, and Kaulwitz with castle and country houses. There are treasures and riches — so much that has been handed down over the centuries: the Family Embellishments... the old family escutcheon, with the Henckel lions, can be carried away to other lands, with some threads from their old home, but not the rich lands of Upper Silesia. Why even Maid, her daughter-in-law, is on the eve of departure, with her children.

In quiet custom, we spent the last evening together. First, we prayed the rosary and then Aunt Sophie said, "I'll read this evening." She unlocked the glass doors of one of her book-cases and selected a volume — Longfellow — soon she found what she wanted: "The Children."

She read the poem without a break in her voice, then for a long time she sat thinking and her eyes filled with tears — thinking — her beautiful daughter Anne-Marie (the fair Henckel rose) lies buried in Rome. Alfred, her darling, whose belongings no-one is allowed to touch in his smoking room that still smells of smoke and pipes and leather: while over the mantle hangs the *ikon* that came back with his soldier's trunk from Asov. Alfred lies buried far, far away in Russia, on the shores of the Sea of Asov, in a soldier's grave. There are still Mai-Leonore, who is about to enter a convent, and George on the fighting front. May St. George, mighty in battle, protect him. May he protect us all.

*****

Kyjovice.
17 October, 1944

Black Fanka and Blond Fanka, Olga and her sisters came rushing in, out of breath. They all spoke together in excitement... all trying to say the same thing. We understood. "A *Pan Graf* (Mr. Count) has fallen from the skies. Dead. Yes. Two planes collided together. He lies on the hillside meadow!"

"This is dreadful!" we say. "But who says he is a *Pan Graf*?" The melancholy eyes of Black Fanka are full of tears.... Softly, she says, "He looks as if he is sleeping... lying small on the big meadow. The Gendarmerie will take him away on a stretcher." We ask again "But who says he is a Count?" They look pityingly at us and repeat, "We have seen him." Then they say; "His nails are clean, he wears two gold rings and he wears clean underclothes. The Gendarmerie did not let us see more, so he is a Count."

The young man was an American pilot: Howard Schmidt. He lies in the Cemetery of Kyjovice, and the Fankas and Olga and her sisters place flowers on the grave in the evenings, which the gendarmes remove in the morning. On the Feast of All Saints, in spite of the threatening S.S., fresh flowers and a little cushion and many candles are lit on the grave of Howard Schmidt, whose grave is far from his home in Verona, Wisconsin, U.S.A.

(Poor young Schmidt rested peacefully in the cemetery in Kyjovice, where he was buried on the 19th of October, 1944. Later, on the 27th of August, 1946, his remains were removed to a soldier's grave near Paris, as told to me by two of his compatriots, when I was asked to interpret for them at the exhumation. The people in Kyjovice regretted to part with him — not so the Russians.)

*****

Piltsch-Opava

Piltsch was a pleasant peasant village, like numerous villages scattered over the good lands of Eastern Europe. Here Fritz Newzella had bought a little villa for his bride, our cousin Helene, and set up his dental practice. It had been a quiet village and here, at Helene's invitation, I took refuge with my children, while the Russians were fighting their way through Vienna and into Germany.

In Piltsch, men lived as nearly as God meant them to live, by the sweat of their brow and very near to the good Mother Earth, and as you get the best results from the fields with a plentiful supply of manure, in Piltsch, manure was almost the order of the day! In winter, who wants to walk any distance to attend to your animals? So you keep your stock in the village, under your own roof. It keeps you warm — or does their body heat keep your house warm? And then also, as on a certain midnight, your animals whisper to you like they did to Mary and Joseph and the Babe. You walk directly out of the byre into your living room with your pails of rich milk, and you are quite familiar with the smell of dung in your parlour, and oh, dear yes, also in your bedroom; not the almost pleasant herbal odor of veld-grazing cattle manure, no, these great, soft-eyed, red and white *Sieben Taler* cows are born and bred in the byre and mostly fed on silage. The milk is rich and good, so just avoid the manure heap at your front door. The peasants would be surprised if you told them that in South Africa, even today, there are farm houses and school and church floors that are regularly "smeared" by hand with dung. "Disgusting," they would say, "and what a waste!"

Notwithstanding the smell of manure, Piltsch was a pleasant village, homely, snug, and in some respects oddly beautiful. Many of the stout white-washed houses were two-storied, with a closed-in entrance porch, some quite beautiful. Generally, a little stairway led to a couple of bedrooms where the slow clock ticked; where peasant embroideries and crochet-work mats were prized though generations; where beds were inordinately puffed up with finest goose down quilts and pillows. Oh, those important feather beds and great pillows! These, together with walls fancifully painted, mostly with pastoral scenes, all contributed to the makings of home, sweet home.

Quite a feature of Piltsch were the neat flag-stone pathways, said to have been laid down by French P.O.W.s during the Franco-Prussian War. There was the sluice, where dark water swept along in summer, or was iced over in winter; the hazelnut hedges; the little front gardens; a hoary pear tree or two; sweet scented honey-suckle vines trailing over fences, and lilacs in the spring; but most important was the white church, big and clean, with well worn pews, where old women with shawls about their shoulders contentedly sat counting their beads, and where Hans and Peter and Dieter and Hubert solemnly responded at Mass.

Helene with her four children, together with my two youngest, formed a close little family; here it was still possible to obtain eggs, milk and fresh vegetables, commodities almost unobtainable in the cities, even on ration cards, and so vital for the health and development of children. Except for my anxiety about my two boys away at Juliasberg in school and Helene's anxiety about her Fritz, we all felt that we could breathe in deeply. Fritz had been ordered to join the dental staff of an Army Unit. On the rare occasions when he returned on leave, Helene's eyes were so happy and so kind, especially when she said, "Dory, please take the children over to your place this afternoon." I readily agreed.

I knew that in Helene's "Blue Salon" there would be fresh flowers, or autumn leaves depending on the season; the table will have been laid for two with the best china and silver, there are honey-cakes with some of our homemade golden syrup on the silver cake salvers.... And Fritz? Yes, of course, in the Blue Salon, standing under the arresting engraving of

Paganini, Fritz, like the maestro, plays a little cascade of pearly notes on his violin, but when he catches sight of me, he waves his bow and says, "Come in! Come!" and almost in the same breath, he says "How are your teeth? Have some lunch with us, we've got some fresh horse liver; that Army vet is dependable."

"Thank you, no, Fritz, I've only come to say welcome home! I don't eat horse liver." Quietly, I thought to myself, mmm — that vet dependable? Not if you know that it is the nearest that Helene and I have ever come to having words.

After Fritz leaves, we stick to our butcher who only has an occasional ox foot for us. I take it outside to save a general mess in the kitchen. I scrape, I struggle, I chop and I cook — with a great amount of general and quiet coaxing the children have jelly and meat and marrow and soup.

The vet has found other *Frauleins* to honour with his horse liver.

I love all Helene's little boys, but Christian is a gorgeously endearing little fellow. Dressed in his sheepskin coat, he came across to me this morning. "Christian," I said, "it's bitterly cold, what are you doing here?"

"I'm not cold, Aunt Dory." Then, bringing his bright face close to mine, he said, "I am strong! So strong! I can fight like a bear!" And he stroked my face with a hot little hand.

I took the little hand in mine. "But why is your hand so warm, Christian? Are you sick?"

"No," he answered, "it is because I've got warm eggs in my pocket." Suddenly he looked very guilty. "Please," he said, "you won't tell *Frau* Paula (the cook) that I took the eggs from the pot on the stove, just to warm my hands?"

When I took him home, the eggs were returned to the pot without being missed by *Frau* Paula.

Aunt Toto has sent Black Fanka, the kitchen maid, to Helene for a "change of scene and sound." Fanka is brokenhearted because her boyfriend volunteered to work in a factory in Germany. "No more contact," said Fanka, "not even a Christmas message."

"But Fanka," I said, "send him a message, or a German *Fraulein* will comfort him."

"He is welcome," said Fanka.

Now Ferdie is engaged to a *Fraulein* and Fanka only wants to lie down and die.

Many people come and inquire from us what they should do. They affirm that the broadcasts announce that the Fuehrer is as sure of victory as he has ever been. From us they learn the truth.... as far as we dare give it to them; we try to tell the peasants that the Russians will show no mercy, and because we must consider our children, we are cowardly and therefore we think that the best thing will be to get across to the English or American lines, at least for a while. Here in Piltsch we will be completely cut off. It will be impossible to get either food supplies, wood, coal, or electricity. I fear that our presence does not give anyone the fortitude that is expected. It is an inherent belief that the *Herrschaften*, the nobility, are expected to set an example for the people to follow — but two poor women with a bunch of children in the face of the Russian advance.

Helene has already scored quite a triumph, but has gotten herself into serious trouble. She had to appear before the Gestapo on a charge of inciting the village youths against joining the S.S. But when I went to the local Burgermeister to intercede for Helene, he did not realize the irony of what he said: "If you *Herrschaften* still think you can take the initiative and not keep your mouths shut, after what has happened to Claus von Stauffenberg, Erwin von Witzleben, Peter Yorck von Wartenburg and all the rest of them, then we shall make an example of you all!" An example, yes! These friends and relatives of ours are a shining example for all time for the German Nation.

Daily broadcasts announce the number of British planes destroyed, of American convoys sunk; there is hardly a mention of German losses, but the poor peasants on the roads pass along in ever increasing numbers, together with *Panzers*, soldiers, and miserably exhausted looking people. We have tried to organize the women of Piltsch to help the refugees — mostly women, children, and old men travelling on the ice-bound roads — and while bomber planes pass overhead, these poor people are only too eager to accept a bowl of soup.

On a different note we hear that the castle of Drensteinfurt in Westfalia, ancestral home of Aunt Toto, has been bombed by the allies. Staid Baron von Landsberg, the owner, would not go down to the cellar during the air raid but sat stoically in his world famous library while bombs splashed into the moat surrounding the castle. After the raid ended the butler came rushing in, "Sir, sir, the windows are all broken, are the books alright?"

"What?" replied the Baron. "What, here I sit with the shit of centuries dripping off me and all you ask about are the books?"

(In years gone by the moat would serve as a sewer for the castle.)

Russian planes now frequently dart over the streets, strafing the waggons of the hapless travellers and all is confusion.

It is only our children who seem to be without fear and are always bright-eyed and light-hearted, providing little happy interludes for us, and are grateful for any little gesture we are able to make them. Above all, they still live in a world of their own bright imaginations that can, with the wave of a little hand, take the funniest quirks and twists.

This morning, I found Christian struggling to fasten up his pants. He was in a great hurry to be out, so for once, he allowed me to assist him, after which he found he still had time to impart a little confidence. With his curly head very close to mine, he looked at me with pert blue eyes. "Aunt Dory," he said, and the words came spluttering out, "I love so many things, don't you? I love to sit on the lavatory. It is so like a war, the bomb explodes with a bang and a crash! It is coal raven black and then the stink! F-u-u! You'll run!" Then, seeing my shocked expression, he added, "But it's not at all dangerous."

"No," he repeated, "*Gar nicht gefaehrlich!*"

Alas, alas! What is "*ganz und gar gefaehrlich*" and inexpressibly sad is that the Russians have entered Upper Silesia. They have crossed over the border in a broad offensive and have reached Juliasberg; this is heart-rendering. Only one week since I took my boys, Lekkie and Peter, back to their convent. Christmas, we had all been together, Helene's four — my four — and although my four are older, they all fitted in and agreed well, but we had to keep them all occupied. Reading was not enough, so Lekkie and Peter spent a lot of

time skating on the sluice pond with the village boys. We had
to devise meals — ox foot was a boon! — while for a special
treat, dumplings with a spoonful of butter and my golden
syrup, liberally strewn with poppy seeds called for a second
helping. We made homemade *nudeln* (noodles), adding a little
butter, syrup, and a spoonful of cocoa from a secret store — a
wonderful dessert! Luckily we have apples and carrots and
that good old stand-by, sauerkraut. Helene often arranged an
afternoon around the fire where Ilona sat entranced, the only
little girl among seven boys, listening to the Christmas story.
And it became very real, with the star shining on top of the
Christmas tree, with the Christ-child and the entrance of the
Magi. The holidays sped by peacefully (almost) and soon it
was time for the boys to return to school. Lekkie is a brave lad,
he faced to journey on the overcrowded trains with cheerful
equanimity. He shouldered the suitcases and urged Peter on. I
was distressed to part from them, especially my Peter, who
still needs a little mothering, but Lekkie will take care of him
and Reverend Mother has promised to send me a telegram or
send the boys to me should things become really serious, but
she said: "We feel so safe in our little corner." I returned,
however, with not a few misgivings and now, alas, the worst
has happened!

     With my rucksack on my back, I was at the station to
catch the first train this morning when Reverend Father met
me. "Where are you going?" he asked me.

     "To Juliasberg to fetch my boys!"

     "No, no," he said, "You know that the Russians have
crossed the border and because the nuns have had to
accommodate over a thousand wounded soldiers, Juliasberg
will be one of the first places to be evacuated. Your boys will
have fled with the nuns. If you travel now to Juliasberg, you
will run into the Russians. Take my advice and remain here
until you hear from them."

     I seemed to walk back from the station enveloped in a
black cloud. I fetched Ilona from Helene and together we went
to early mass and I started a thirty days Novena. I hope soon
to hear from my boys.

     Mail does not function any more.... I'll try to send a
broadcast message to the nuns from Opava, asking them to try

and get in touch with our relatives in Germany. The English and Americans should soon be in Germany — surely, surely, they will not allow the Russians to occupy Europe!

*****

Judging by the stream of fugitives on the roads, we are likely to be cut off by the Russians at any time now. I must hurry with my message.

*****

I persuaded a peasant to let me have his sleigh and horses to take me to Opava. At Broadcast House, they agreed to send a repeat message for me, I only hope they do so.

After I took a short walk around the shops — where there is nothing to buy, only empty shelves — I hurried back to where I had left the man sitting in his fur bags in the sleigh. I found a woman sitting in my seat, who unceremoniously informed us that she was also travelling home to Piltsch. Not liking the looks of her, but half-fearing she may be connected with the Gestapo, I said, "So! Shift up, there is room for us both." In the sleigh, at my feet, she had already deposited two parcels and two loaves of bread. The cold was intense, so I did not mind her sitting up against me. The peasant took the blankets from the horses — but instead of starting them up, as I expected, we sat delaying for some moments.

Then I perceived that our way was blocked by what appeared to be an army of people marching up the bleak street. As they came opposite us, I saw that they were gaunt, dirty, starved-looking men. All were dressed in thin striped prison suits. Some had blankets tied around, some had their heads muffled in rags or caps; between formations, they pulled hand waggons on which were loaded odd bundles — or a half-expiring comrade, too weak to drag himself any further. The sight of these pitiful looking people struggling past completely staggered me, and I questioned myself wildly: Who are they? Where are they going? Then, coming opposite to us, I saw two youths, young, like my boys, toiling up the street. Now I concluded they were Jews from one of the prison camps being evacuated before the Russian advance.

"Give me your bread," I begged the woman, "Please, please.... I have a loaf of bread at home and I'll give you all my ration cards." Snatching up the loaves, I stood up and endeavoured to throw them out to the youths.

"No. No!" shouted the woman, and she roughly grabbed the bread out of my hands and replaced the loaves at my feet. Unfortunately, the starving men had seen the bread — "*Brot!*" they imploringly called out, "*Brot, brot...*" and slipping and falling on the icy street, they surged over to us. Cruelly, the guards pushed them off — one lean fellow from the back of the sleigh fell over my shoulder — a guard tried to strike him with the butt of his rifle — I grabbed the gun. "Don't hit him, please don't hit him," I said, clinging to the gun until the unfortunate man had recovered himself.

Clop, clop... sounded their wooden shoes on the frozen street as they slowly moved forward. Some passers-by gathered around our sleigh. Seeing the tears streaming down my face, a young soldier came up to me: "Cheer up," he whispered. "We cannot help them." No, I could not help them and no strength was left in me. All the way home the tears streamed down my cheeks. The woman remarked: "You have a soft heart." I only say: "May the dear God grant that my heart must never be too small for a woman — that the measure I give to man and beast must never be diluted, then, perhaps, the storm that I raised on the frozen street of Opava will not have been quite in vain."

*****

15 March, 1945

This morning, I was loath to open my eyes and face the world, but my Novena must be prayed, Ilona must have breakfast (my little Fritzl is in Kyjovice). No matter how bad the night may have been, we cannot close our eyes to the realities of the day. We had breakfast, we tidied up, then came Helene's two boys running excitedly up to me. Mario called out, "Mammie's goats have gone to church!"

"What good goats they are," I said.

"Yes, but Auntie Dory, don't you see that the church gets cleaned on Saturday? Come quick, let us fetch the goats!"

As Ilona and I hurried along with them, I said to Mario (who is particular about ownership) "Are they not also your goats?"

"Yes, but now, you see, Herr Pfarrer, the priest, will be so angry with us!"

"Never mind, Mario," said Christian, "I'll chase them out of the church." and with a little whip he carried, he clapped to left and right, until, inadvertently, he struck Mario on the head: Mario shouted with pain, Ilona spoke some words of comfort, but Mario's good humor was only restored by the sight of the goats strolling up the aisle, like three American tourists, inspecting the old Baroque church. As we chased the goats home along the flag-stone side path we heard the siren sounding: soon, *Frau* Paula ran out to look for the children.

Helene was very much relieved to see us all safely back: already we could hear the loud droning of the approaching bombers….. Helene collected all the children around the little table in the dark corner of the hall. They all sat obediently, even baby Gottfried, with hands folded, feeling secure in Helene's presence and her prayers. I stood in the front garden with Fanka, under the old pear tree. We watched the bombers as they flew overhead at a very great height, like so many silver crosses glinting against the sunlight. By the long vapor trails they left, I concluded they were American planes.

Suddenly, a flashing streak descended from the planes and a resounding explosion followed. The planes had already passed over the village, so I started off with speed to tell Helene not to fear, when Fanka made a sudden lunge at me. With her eyes wild with fear, she sobbed, "Now we must die!" I shook her off but again she collapsed on my shoulder with such force that I staggered backwards. "Stupid!" I shouted angrily, "Can't you see that the planes have passed and I want to tell the Baroness that there is no danger! Anyway, you want to die, so now is your chance." Poor Fanka mournfully went to the kitchen to join *Frau* Paula.

This evening, Fanka still had her "hang dog" look, so I sent her off to bed, while Helene put the children to bed. I wanted to sit in the kitchen and listen to the foreign broadcast. And then it came….very softly, all the way from South Africa.

"After the war," said the voice of General Jan Smuts, "England will be very poor, Russia will be the colossus that will roll over everything...." The radio clouded over. I heard no more. And now, I also have that hang dog look. If only statesmen can see what looms ahead, if only they can put a finger on the trouble spots of the world, then our Fanka can put her head on my shoulder with pleasure and weep her woes.

Helene thinks she is very diplomatic in the way she tries to persuade me to take a trip to Kyjovice to ask Uncle Fritz and Aunt Toto if they will harbor us. I shall have to brave the muddy roads and the Russian fighter planes, there is no one else, and hitch-hike the 28 kilometers to Kyjovice. Helene will look after the children, while I will have to brace up the courage and explain our position to Uncle Fritz and try to contrive to get a conveyance and a removal van for Helene's belongings and her milk goats.

Walking through slush and snow, like a grenadier, I found again what a boon the wellington boots are that Uncle Fritz had given me. I arrived safely at Kyjovice and back. Uncle Fritz said we must not lose any time, he will send his coach-man with carriage, and also the *Britzska* (a high wagon with pneumatic tires) to transport us to Kyjovice. We leave tomorrow.

On my way, I called in at Opava to see Greta Gemmel. The old Baroness is very seedy. Greta asked me if I would be prepared to take on a packet that Aunt Toto had entrusted to her. Greta said, "We can make no provision for it, as we are also on the verge of joining the refugees: the packet also includes a tiny parcel for Ilona."

"I am sorry, Greta, I can't accept Aunt Toto's packet. She has not entrusted it to me and if I accepted it, I would not be able to forgive myself — but you may give me Ilona's packet."

From the despairing look of the people, the general upheaval, the refugees on the roads, the chill of the rivulets and slush, I felt utterly miserable and dejected until I came within sight of the cultivated fields of Piltsch. There, I saw catkins had already pierced their fluffy, yellow buds, while the March Hares were disporting themselves over the muddy fields, where from underneath the snow the first green shoots are bountifully appearing. I saw the hares playfully chasing each other, then they sit up and box each other, then up leap these little grey acrobats, like balls tossed up into the air, then off they go and the game is repeated. I realize now that the proverbial mad March Hare is not mad. They are extremely intelligent animals, responding to the cycle of the seasons, the age old pattern of their race, which surely is to say: mud or no mud, why wait any longer? Why not step out of winter into the unreserved promise of spring? I thanked the hares for their preview of spring. We must march, like the March Hares, through sunshine and storm, on and on, trusting to the kindness of Providence — to the promise of spring, on and on. Tired, but with March Hare fortitude, I arrived back, to start on our packing.

*****

19th March, 1945

The Russians are said to be fighting only about nineteen kilometers from Piltsch. We are intensely relieved to see the conveyances sent to fetch us from Kyjovice. First came Krisel with the carriage drawn by two greys, after came Neuwert with the carriage drawn by two black stallions that are as large and strong as if sired by an African elephant. Consequently, they caused quite a stir in the village, the people thinking that the dreaded Cossack advance had begun. Our belongings were soon loaded: Helene's bed, chests, carpets, suitcases... all on the Britzka. Then came the milk goats and my suitcases, and then Fanka and our children, with much relief, if half-heartedly, we joined the stream of refugees on the road.

We have arrived safely in Kyjovice with and on the roads we seem to have found a haven of refuge. Alas, the peace was of short duration.

Early on the morning of the 24th came the first rude awakening: two German generals with staff and soldiers stood before the door and demanded accommodation. Hitherto, there have only been some refugees from Berlin and a company of meek Besserarabians. The castle is crowded to the gunwales, and everywhere an air of secrecy and conspiracy prevails that would not be out of place in a thriller novel: dispatch riders come in or leave in a flurry, sentries challenge. As I furtively looked into Uncle Fritz's office — that the generals are now in possession of — I saw new maps on the walls where the formidable fighting fronts are pinned and chalked out. The enemy is steadily encroaching and closing in on all fronts (while we are kept entirely in the dark).

A day or two after the arrival of the generals, we could detect the first faint detonations in the air. "The Russian guns," we said in awe. Soon the firing and detonations increased. At nights we see the heavens glow, reflections from burning buildings and columns of smoke are in the air. Almost simultaneously with the generals came a Panzer repair company. Eighty colossal tanks came thundering up the chestnut avenue: soldiers piled out and were immediately busy putting up repair sheds in the park. More tanks keep rolling in for repair. They have churned up the driveway and the roads and have smashed electric posts and trees: the park looks like a battlefield, and Uncle Fritz is deeply distressed. He has spent a lifetime tending each tree and shrub. We are agitated — in despair. "Never mind the park being smashed up," said one of the soldiers, "the Russians are smashing every resistance!"

30th March, 1945

The fighting creeps nearer. After eight days, the generals with their staffs, and also the Panzer Company have packed up camp and have fled. We hoped to breathe again, but early this morning an "*Oberstabsarzt*" Surgeon Major, or rather two doctors with medical staffs, with wounded soldiers, with cooks and company arrived. Very soon they made themselves at home by turning the castle into a *Feld Lazarett* (field hospital). The doctors selected and took charge of the best rooms, spreading themselves comfortably out: all very disconcerting, as we much fear we will be pushed out and sent packing with the refugees.

31st March, 1945

Deo Gratias, the *Oberstabsarzt* has allowed us to keep our rooms. He is a youthful, blond looking man who "wears a spyglass cocked beneath his arm and a cap cocked askew," both in and out of doors, and I think, both night and day, by way of being prepared — for anything.

We have listened to a radio broadcast; Goebbels telling the German people that the Fuehrer is as certain of victory now as always. "What a sheep," I said. There was no response, until Aunt Toto said, "What characters! Pride comes before the fall."

I have come to respect our youthful doctor. He promises to be reliable and humane. I have heard him say, "I attend to friend or foe, to good and bad, for only God knows who's the gent and who's the cad." This very busy doctor rides out to the "fronts" every morning and somehow he still finds time to take my Fritzl for rides on his motorcycle, to Fritzl's great delight.

For years, we have practically been living on ration cards (except during our sojourn in Piltsch) or simply on what we could get for love or money. Therefore, it surprised us to see how well these German officers are still catered for. For example, after an ample lunch, our *Oberstabsarzt* often has bacon and eggs with his afternoon coffee. And while we have long since learned to make shift with "ersatz" tea and coffee, the officers get served with real tea and coffee, and even cocoa. They also have other luxuries that we have practically forgotten. Therefore, it is no wonder that the doctor's orderlies who have charge of these commodities are much in the good graces of our castle servants, and they vie with each other for their favors. We don't mind, as they have also procured coffee, tea, cigarettes, and SOAP in small quantities for us, a happy contribution to our rucksacks. Each member of the family has a rucksack packed in readiness for flight and for the leaner days to come.

12 April, 1945

Almost a month has passed since we arrived here. My constant thoughts are with my boys. Where can they be travelling? They are so small to be on the long road. Unless I ask our Lord to link their smallness in His Greatness — their little hands in His Hand every day — I have no peace.

During these past weeks, there have been so many officers and men in the house, mostly convalescents, that we have ceased to take count of them. The *Lazarett* has the use of the large kitchen, but the tidtbits for the officers are arranged in our small kitchen by their orderlies. Soldiers constantly come to and fro: actually, they are very well disciplined and very agreeable. These poor fellows realize that the end is very near, they are terribly distressed, all are only too eager to do little odd jobs for us — in and about the house — they sit down for a brief respite and the maids give them some of our ersatz.

Unfortunately, they completely unnerve and excite the romantic Czech kitchen maids, who at all times seem to be very temperamental. It does not take much to bring tears to their eyes — however, with the steady approach of the Russians, planes buzzing overhead and sudden flares, we are all unnerved. Every sound seems to be intensified: the banging of a door is like a thunderbolt. At every alarm, Helene collects her four children and runs for the cellar, and now we have many alarms and suffer many trepidations.

I constantly inquire from the soldiers in which direction they are travelling, hoping that perhaps one will be able to deliver a letter in Germany to my relatives asking them to search for my children. I write many letters but receive no replies — and the months pass by!

Sunday, 15 April, 1945
The day has dawned with a tranquil blue sky. We are thankful. After a quiet early Mass and meager breakfast, we walked around visiting the village people, especially the German population who have decided to leave home and hearth. All are very depressed — everybody waits for a word of encouragement, which, alas, we cannot give them. It is astonishing that even at this closing stage of the war, people still have faith in a miraculous deliverance, believing that Hitler has the means of turning the tide. I said to someone, "Like hell" (which I think was appropriate). We must be silent, there are many tall trees that we can be hanged upon.

Sunday afternoon — and with the skies still clear and with an almost eerie silence prevailing, I decided to have a game of tennis, because it is my sister Clemence's birthday. How thankful I am for her to be far away in South Africa. To me, tennis has always been a lure of luxury, for no matter how fast the game is, or how it changes, there is usually leisure for longer thoughts and deeper comprehensions. There is no better opportunity of enjoying the serene depths of the azure sky. Yes, tennis is a lure of beauty and the sparkle thereof is better than Pommery.

Therefore, to have my Champagne (although the Lady Auguste and some of the other folks were shocked at my heartlessness) I asked *Fraulein* Glasner, Uncle Fritz's secretary, to join me. The children romped around and picked up the balls for us, thoroughly enjoying themselves while we played with, so to say, one eye on the ball and one on the sky, and as soon as the Russian planes came overhead, we fled to the friendly shade of the large pine tree. We were childishly bold and we childishly enjoyed this first game of the season, although the gloomy thought persisted that, perhaps, this would be the last game for a long time.

Indeed, it was the last I ever played in Czechoslovakia. It was later when I came into the castle that the *Oberstabsarzt* met me. With a very solemn look on his young face, he said, "Have you got your belongings packed?" Then he added that he had just made a return tour of all the front lines per motorcycle; "It looks very serious, I think it likely that by tomorrow the castle will not be standing anymore." Forthwith, the good young doctor collected all his staff. They started striking camp and all left the same evening.

I was not slow to take advantage of their untimely departure. Hastily, I called Anna, Regina, *Fraulein* Glasner, and with them sped to the *Lazarett*'s apothecary, where we asked for medicines. We were each given what we asked for: a good supply of tranquilizers, lint, Togal powder, etc. We regret their departure.

16 April, 1945
The castle is still standing.

Early this morning came a new *Einquartierung* (billeting of hospital staff), this time for badly wounded cases from the front lines, and now we have a real insight of the misery and the suffering of the unfortunate soldiers: the seriousness of the hour is written on each face — young and old — each one realizes the grim fact that there can be no retreat, (the S.S. and the *Partei* see to that) and there is no question of surrender which, at best, will only mean miserable years of suffering and slavery in Russia. So they march, starve, struggle and fight in their heavy mud-caked boots. These gloomy soldiers tell us how the Red Army is leaping across rivers, encircling — always encircling and capturing village after village — living on American supplies and pillage. Russian woman soldiers are usually the first to swim across rivers and push their *Panzers* across icy fields.

The cannonading draws nearer. The firing sometimes follows in rapid succession, like one long shock wave of sound. We hear the "Stalin-organ," rocket launchers, whistling and the house vibrates on its massive foundations, with the thunder of Panzers and planes droning overhead. Cold fear is in everybody's heart. Again, quite suddenly, the firing stops, noise subsides, and all seems eerily still, and we have time to collect ourselves and see to the animals. This morning I went out to feed and milk the goats (I am considering giving them to the Czech gardener to care for), the fowls, and the rabbits. As planes are constantly overhead, I endeavored to walk in the shade of the house and trees. I saw the ambulances come in convoys, and realized only too well the pitiful suffering on all sides. One of the servant's houses has been converted into a Field Hospital. The wounded are brought here, hurriedly bandaged, and then transported further away from the firing lines. I heard the groans of the wounded. We suffer intimately with them, we suffer with our friends and relations and acquaintances: and I saw discarded on the road a blood-stained scarf and two heavy boots that looked as if still animated by the life of their late owner, but too weary worn to take another footstep away from this sorrowful scene where pools of blood lie on the road. Where the ambulances stop, my heart also seems to stop. We suffer intimately with the young lives that are cut off and will never see their homes and those dear to them again — and we pray earnestly for all... Alas, we have so little to eat that it is not possible to supply any sustenance to the wounded, although we know that most of them have been on the fighting front for days on end, without food.

*****

This afternoon Ilona was with me in the small kitchen. I was baking *harde beskuit* (hard-tack), and she was feeding some goslings when we heard planes circling overhead, then the rapid drumming of machine gun fire. I pulled Ilona away from the window and pressed her up against the inner wall and trembling, waited for the worst..... Shock upon shock, a few moments of utter silence, and once again rapid firing. Ilona appeared quite unafraid. I had to restrain her from going to the rescue of a gosling that had inquisitively run to investigate a burning stick that had fallen from the stove. Fortunately, the attack did not last long. I was frightfully anxious about Fritzl and as soon as the planes wheeled off, I darted out to see where he was. He has the knack of disappearing, in a wink, every time the danger signal is out. I have already found him in a tall tree observing the planes. I rushed along the corridor and met a lot of scared people hurrying to the cellar — Fritzl among them, with, for once, a look of real fright on his face.

The smell of powder was everywhere. Uncle Fritz came along and ordered us to the cellar, but as the planes seemed to have left, I said, "I think the attack is over and I will just see what damage has been done." I sent the children with Uncle Fritz to the cellar, then ran out to the Glass Porch and was relieved to see that only one of the large windows was shattered. From the village I saw clouds of lurid smoke arising. Soon the German soldiers were running to extinguish the flames that were rapidly spreading in the direction of the castle. The *Neubau* (new building) windows were shattered, including the kitchen windows. The high stone garden wall was in ruins. Luckily, the shell hit the garden wall instead of the castle. The glass house for grapes is flattened. In the park, a young officer has been killed. Near the garden wall, Franska, the harmless chicken maid who has spent faithful years of service in the poultry yard, lay dead, a victim of the attack.

Poor meek Franska. We carried her into the castle. She had many wounds on her head and legs. She had been gathering nettles for the goslings. Among the leaves in her basket I found the keys of the fowl houses. Planes were circling overhead again. We all sat silent and subdued in the cellar, while soldiers solemnly whittled away at some crosses for their fallen comrades. One bore the inscription "Carl-Heins Winter R.I.P." for the young officer only just killed on the lawn.

In the village there were more dead and wounded. Owing to the alarming cannon thunder, the burning houses, and the aeroplanes buzzing overhead, the villagers are all in a state of panic. Except for the German soldiers, not a soul ventured to quell the conflagration. Regina, with the courage and precision of a general, walked courageously about with the doctor and priest tending to the wounded and dying. After this attack, Helene hardly has the courage to leave the cellar with her boys. There is nobody to attend to Helene's goats and to feed the fowls and rabbits. Therefore, I persuaded Aunt Toto to sell the fowls, or rather, to barter them to the officers of the hospital staff. She asked me to approach them. I am keeping a pen of six Rhode Island Red hens and also the geese, ducks, and turkeys, and, of course, the peacocks. I approached the general, he sent me to the officer in charge of the commissariat. I have bargained with the officer for rice, sugar, and tinned meats..... Perhaps it is horse meat. We must be thankful. He wanted to know how many eggs the hens will lay. I said, "It depends on how well you feed them — but I will advise you to slaughter them all before the Russians arrive!" (Can I get into hot water for saying that?) I would be very prepared to have a turkey or two killed, but I think Aunt Toto would be rather adverse to this.

Wednesday, 16 April, 1945

Troops continue to pour into the village. From the road we hear the continual approach of heavy trucks grinding their way up the hill. To our dismay, we hear that heavy artillery has been set up on the hill bordering the village.

The Front has arrived at our door. The village is practically empty of peasants. They have all sought shelter in the forest. Uncle Fritz has also had a small bunker made in the forest where under the leafy flooring we have concealed potatoes and a small quantity of food.

Aunt Toto has prepared an altar in the cellar recess, where the priest comes to celebrate Mass in our catacomb as in the days of the early Christians. The children bring little offerings of flowers... firstlings of the infant year. Here the tiny red light of the votive lamp flickers like a beacon, where the censer swings and in the darkest night, the angels' wings rustle very near.

The Litany for the Dying is often on our lips: "Go forth, O Christian soul, out of this world, in the Name of the Father Almighty, who created thee, in the Name of Jesus Christ, the Son of the Living God who suffered for thee, in the Name of the Holy Ghost who sanctified thee, in the Name of Holy Mary, Virgin and Mother of God, in the name of all the angels and Archangels, and in the name of all the Saints of God." Gracious and kind human words, spoken for a soul winging its way with the grey angel... away, away... across aeons of sunlit blue.

###

CHAPTER SIX
DREAMS DURING WARTIME

My bedroom is almost directly below the stone stairway next to the chapel with massive arched ceiling and walls about four feet in breadth. In the bedroom I feel pretty safe with the children, cautioning them only to keep away from the windows. I can also communicate very well with Helene, who has similar rooms on the opposite side of the corridor. Yes, I feel safe, but I have dreams like Joseph and as colorful as his coat. Usually, they are precious and comforting, like when I dreamed I was standing on the seashore. The water was green and dark and troubled. As I looked, I discerned a large object welling through the water. It was too dark for me to see whether it was a whale or a train — but I knew it was connected with my children and that they were in mortal danger. So there and then I knelt down, cringing like a wounded animal at the feet of the Lord. I awoke calling out, "My Lord and my God.... Mercy!" For a while I still knelt beside the bed, repeating the beautiful words, spoken by a saint. And then I seemed to see a light. I sat down on my bed and knew that the danger, whatever it was, was past. My children are safe.

Last night we had an April storm. Wind and hail beat on the windows, and we were thankful still to be under a sheltering roof... but the refugees, the soldiers, the animals. My boys. Oh, I think we prayed for all, like the doctor has said, for friend and foe. Intermittent cannon blasts, wind, and hail continued through the night. How could one relax? Sleep?

But it was during this night that I had a wonderfully comforting dream; I entered a room where there were two beds. On one of them, my baby, little Ria (who died so long ago in Africa) was lying. She had grown bigger — her sweet face was like a fair beautiful rose. Reproaching myself for not having made up her bed earlier, I tenderly picked her up, intending to put her in the other bed as I did so, she opened her eyes and said, "Mother, do not fear, do not cry, the dear God is so good... so good. Mother, only pray a lot... so good." And she closed her eyes and slept softly on my breast.

I woke up. It was light and the shells were shrieking in the forest. I dressed the children without fear, repeating, "The dear God is so good... I know that He has given us an angel in heaven to look after my boys on their flight — after us all."

It is not only the low-flying Russian fighter planes that we have learned to detect and fear. Often we hear the droning of bomber planes — they are reported to be English or American squadrons flying at a high altitude, leaving long vapor trails. We are only able to detect them clearly when they fly directly against the sunshine, then we see them glint like miniature silver crosses, far, far up in the heavens. I do not run for the cellar, because I think, "in life, we are in the midst of death."

It is only from danger that we feel like fleeing (like the old song says, one thousand miles), but this morning, I could have fled ten thousand miles and more. Instead, I could only bow my head in sorrow, lying on the cold bare ground of the back yard of the *Neubau*. I saw, as I went around to feed the animals, row upon row of dead soldiers. One fair haired boy was wrapped in his military coat, heavy wooden splints still attached to his broken legs. *Requiescat in pace.* May they rest in peace.

As I retraced my steps, after feeding the animals, I did not have the courage to look upon the pitiful dead — that fair lovely boy. Instead, I looked up at the tree where a little bird sang a cascade of sad, sad notes, a requiem service for the early dead. What better song of praise and peace? And as the little bird had already sung for their repose, I found it good and well to pray for the living and I said my prayer for my boys: Link their little hands in Thy Hand.

Again, I had a realistic dream. I was travelling through a desolate region in Russia. After struggling through some wire entanglements, I found myself in front of a row of lonely barracks. There were no lights. Not a living thing seemed to breathe in that dreary place. Suddenly I was confronted by Stalin himself. Terrified, I knelt in the snow and said, "Excellency, I am looking for my children."

"Begone," he thundered. "You are trespassing in a forbidden realm of the Supreme Soviets!" His eyes were closed to mere slits, his face like a great charcoal drawing. Dead, only his militant moustaches were bristling, terrible. I trembled with fear as once more he shouted at me; "Begone. Your children are not in Soviet Russia." The snow crunched under his heavy nailed boots as he walked away. Trembling, I picked myself up from the snow. As his footsteps echoed away the full import of his words came to me, and I seemed to be lifted up on the wings of a passionate hymn of praise and carried far away from that desolate place. As I awoke, my heart was singing, "My children are not in Soviet Russia." (It is strange that I should have called Stalin "Excellency" in my dream — I have never heard him spoken of as such.)

Friday, 20 April, 1945

As I happen to take events more or less calmly, the kitchen maids have begged of me to let them sleep in my room. They tried to compliment me, saying, "You walk so surely, we feel safe with you. Because of the black-outs at night, we do not dare to put on a light." So, it was quite uncanny when I turned in late last night to find dusky forms spread out over my floor, and I had to grope my way over the sleepers to find my bed.

Saturday, 21 April, 1945

Helene with her babies and all the German people have fled. I ardently wished for Helene to remain with us. I did not try to persuade her, as the time has come when we each must act in a way we think best, but I did tell her that because of my South African nationality I may have a better chance of surviving than others when we get under the wheels.

After the attack on Thursday, the Lady Auguste hastily packed Aunt Antonia's suitcases, and then taking her own baggage, has fled with Mr. Adolf, Uncle Fritz's milkman, and his family, all in a one-horse waggon. Anna, who knows no other code but that of being loyal and true, stays to live or die with us.

Regarding Helene, after the months we spent together in Piltsch, we have grown very near to each other, therefore I

feel deeply distressed to think that in the dead of night she has
left, taking only a few hastily thrown together necessities to
join the stream of hungry, weary, foot-sore, disillusioned
people struggling along under their packs — may God
mercifully protect them. As for myself, I have definitely
decided to stay in Kyjovice with my children even though
Uncle Fritz and family may decide to leave.

Last night was only disturbed by the snoring of the
maids in their 'Nachtquartier' on my floor. My nerves relaxed
while we all snored and slept soundly. At the crack of dawn,
the firing flared up again with single shots seeming to come
over and explode very near to us, sending a shudder through
the house and rattling the window panes. We seem to be
getting accustomed to the firing because as we leisurely
dressed, Regina came into my room and said that Fritzl must
hurry to serve Mass for a soldier priest who had just arrived
from the front. Happily, Mass was served in the house chapel
again and not in the cellar. It was attended by many fugitives
and peasants. The young priest was accompanied by a choir of
soldiers. They sang the beautiful Schubert People's Mass,
"*Wohin soll ich mich wenden?*" The soldiers' voices swelled and
filled the chapel, deadening the sound of the firing.

*****

Later, the priest had breakfast with us — Fritzl was
delighted when the priest said to him, "For a young man of
seven, you serve mass excellently well." Fritzl beamed and
made all manner of silly capers around the priest. This priest
has been on the Russian front for a long time. He told us of
many tragic happenings, and we know that they are not
exaggerated. Unfortunately, he also told us how — after the
Russians had occupied a certain village — they had put all
men to death whose names happened to be Fritz. They
maintained that this proved that the men were German.
Directly after the priest left us, Fritzl got the enthusiastic idea
to burn all his school books, because his name was on them.
Aunt Toto is very sorry for Fritzl, she says such incidents can
cause a detrimental upset to a child's character. I think it is a
clever idea of his to avoid going to school. However, to soothe

the effect, we have cast around for another name for Fritzl, and as he is my pet, short and sweet, we are calling him "Petty" and Uncle Fritz will be "Papali" to us all like he has always been to his own family, and Aunt Antonia, well — she is just our "Auntie Mother."

Shortly after the episode of the books, Papali called me and said, "Dory, you must pack and be prepared to flee with us, because I would like you to help me with the horses." He added, "We must leave tomorrow morning." With this request coming directly from Papali, I could not do otherwise but comply. Hurriedly, I began to collect my belongings, but I did so with a heavy heart, because I loved Kyjovice dearly, and I was only too willing to be on hand when the Russians came, to see what I could save. Indeed, there are no words to describe our varied feelings, as we all hurried on with the necessary packing. Filled with the thought of our rapidly approaching departure, the word "tomorrow" tugged at my heart and rang like a death-knell. First, we packed our personal belongings: goosedown plumeaux and pillows that are a simple necessity in winter, underwear, and a couple of frocks, skirts and blouses. Now, we were thankful to have our ready-packed rucksacks. Then we saw to the food, scraping together what we could find. In one of the pantries, Anna had a basket of eggs. These I helped her roll carefully in blackout paper and pack in the basket. I was sorry that we did not have suitable boxes to pack our provisions in, but I saw to a number of necessary articles being packed; two large jars of home-made beet-syrup, the rice, sugar and tinned meat that I had bartered for the fowls. I also told Anna we must take suitable pots and pans, a broom and dustpan, and an axe and nails. Anna questioned me about the nails.

"We must have them," I said. Perhaps it is something that I have inherited from the *Voortrekker* days. They would have been stupid to travel by waggon without nails. Then I had three young turkeys killed, so as to have a supply of fresh meat available for quite a while. I ran about searching and found a suitable box in the fowl house to take our six Rhode Island hens with us. Auntie Mother was most sympathetic about taking the hens along.

"But yes," she said when I approached her about them, "and Anna must not forget to pack a box of toilet paper for us."

It was midnight when I finished my packing, and then I went upstairs and found Auntie Mother struggling to choose between her own luggage and the many knick-knacks, prints, books, and valuable pictures that she could not make up her mind to leave behind. I do not think that anyone who has not had this experience can realize what it means to people who have lived in a great old house to have to part with all manner of keepsakes and untold family treasures which we now felt quite incompetent to deal with.

At last, 3 o'clock in the morning, some sense of order prevailed. The firing had ceased. The great house seemed to be quieter than it had ever been before and we went down for a few hours' rest.

Monday, 23 April, 1945

It has dawned sad and dull. Low lying rain clouds fill the skies.

This is TOMORROW, I thought, and we were up betimes. Our departure was fixed for 9 o'clock. The rain clouds did not hamper but rather favoured our trek, as the Russian planes were less active. This morning again, most of the responsibilities rested with Auntie Mother and with the faithful Anna, and in just that same calm, implicit way that they had supervised preparations for the gay banquets of happier days for the beautiful and joyous religious feasts; attending to the Chapel; seen to Laundry Days; doctored the sick; or mothered my own children. They now stood up to this great test, as if they were preparing a pilgrimage to Rome. They divided provisions for the Czech household servants who lived in the village. They tried to decide what was best taken with us. There were parcels to deliver in the village and also some things that they hoped to save by entrusting them to friendly peasants in the village. We know that whatever is left behind in the house will be looted, but we also realize that if we are overtaken on the way, what we carry will inevitably also be lost or looted. So they packed. Then we all made sandwiches until it was time to leave.

The carriage stood waiting by the open door. It was drawn by two horses. There was also the Britzka, a middle-sized heavy waggon with pneumatic tires for our goods and chattels, needing two especially strong horses to pull it up the steep hills that feature this part of Sudetenland. A third waggon was loaded with grain and bales of lucerne for the horses and my box of hens. During the war, petrol has been unobtainable for private use. Papali's big car has long ago been requisitioned, but the small car remained. Papali now hitched it onto the carriage, secretly hoping that if we can get petrol on the way, it will be possible to slip over to the American Army. Our luggage and suitcase deposit before the door swelled enormously. Papali said it was not possible to take everything with us. When Auntie Mother heard this, without our knowledge, she took the cases containing her personal belongings back to her rooms. When ultimately everything was stowed away in the Britzka, we hastily had something to eat and then, being ready to depart, I thought of the silver cutlery upstairs in the small dining room. I found the table set, so I quickly collected all the silver and put it in a basket. There was more silver in a cupboard. Hastily, I also put all I could collect in the basket... it was heavy. When I got to the carriage, Auntie Mother said, "Child, what have you got? No, no, we cannot take it with us, put it back in the dining room." Very reluctantly, I took it back as I felt I could not take the responsibility of safe-guarding it on the trek, as we knew not whither we were going nor what would befall us on the way.

We bade farewell to the few remaining Czech servants who live in the village, and then farewell to the fair white house on the hill... the house within whose hospitable walls the children and I have been so much at home, where we have dreamed idle dreams, where we have gleaned much wisdom during happy hours that were only marred when I saw the grief that the war brought to these lovely people, and my inability to give a helping hand while Europe lay stricken in smoke clouds and blood.

This was a parting of the ways.

With anguish in our hearts, we must say "good-bye." I could have cried out aloud, "Oh, white house, *aufwiedersehn!*" May you stand always alive and enduring, excellent as the cedars, like the great pine trees on the lawn, bearing the spirit bequeathed to you by your gallant owners. The spirit of Kyjovice will live on in our hearts and hover over us always. It is not surprising that as we stepped into the carriage and drove off, Tennyson's "In Memoriam" kept crossing my mind: Help Thy vain worlds to bear Thy Light... A beam in darkness, let it grow... Yes, we were travelling into the darkness... but more of wisdom in us dwell, that mind and soul according well, may make one music as before, but — vaster!

*****

Help Thy vain worlds to bear Thy Light....

*****

Slowly, our trek wound its way down the chestnut avenue — on through the deserted village: Regina sat regal and alone with, I am sure, a heart full of anguish in the motor car, towed behind the carriage, valiantly trying to steer it safely. Like little lost children, we were travelling into the darkness of uncertainty to a future that was more obscure and terrifying than the mist clouds on the hills with the last few earthly possessions packed into the high Britzka waggon.

There were innumerable soldier and refugee vehicles on the road. We therefore travelled slowly to keep pace with our pack waggon. After we had travelled a long way, I was encouraged when, looking over my shoulder, I saw Auntie Mother's calm face. I fancied I could detect a little smile at the upturned corners of her lips. Surely, surely, she too had spoken to the man at the Gate of the Year: Give me light that I may tread safely into the unknown. He replied: Go out into the darkness and put out your hand into the Hand of God. That shall be to you better than light and safer than a known way.

So I did not mind a sprinkling of rain on my one remaining hat.

Several times, planes wheeled overhead. The cannonading continued without intermission. Often a shell seemed to explode very near to us, sending a long, resounding echo down the valleys, causing the highly temperamental grey horse to quiver and toss his head. Papali held the reins, I sat beside him, we were thankful for the steady, docile young mare pulling alongside the grey.

After travelling some miles, we got on to quieter roads. There were fewer soldiers and the echo of the cannonading down the valleys grew fainter and less disturbing. During all this time, the children were thoroughly enjoying this new adventure. With an immense sense of security in our presence, they chirped and sang like two brisk birds. It was when we neared Bilovice, fifteen kilometers from Kyjovice that the sun peeped through the clouds. We travelled down a long, lovely valley, where spring was cautiously shaking awake the snow white flowering cherry trees. Fritzl's gay singing had not disturbed me before, but now he stood up in the carriage and sang; "*Nun Ade Du Mein Lieb Heimat Land, Lieb Heimat Land Ade!*" My heart seemed to turn over with silent tears.

We arrived at Bilovice without incident. Then, travelling up a very steep hill, the heavy Britzka started running backwards, the brakes not functioning properly. The two horses were unable to hold it on the slippery street. As the waggon ran backwards for some yards, it looked terribly dangerous until it struck the opposite high pavement of the street and came to a halt. Anna scrambled out with a very white face and said, "*Du lieber Gott*. I've almost had a fright!" I did have a fright!

Drained and weary, amid tears and raindrops Regina and I ridiculously sang, "*Ach du lieber Schreck, Schreck, Schreck, geht es in den Dreck, Dreck, Dreck.*" (What a shock, shock, schock, we've landed in the muck, muck, muck.)

In Bilovice, we were very kindly received by Count and Countess Sedlnitzky in whose castle we spent three days. Here we rested, revised our lot, and rearranged our belongings in the Britzska because we found it required a major operation to unearth our necessary items among the many heavy packages and cabin trunks where, to our dismay, we discovered the absence of Auntie Mother's suitcases. Dear Auntie Mother, just like the Poverello, the poor ones, journeying into the wide world in only one brown frock with a soft trimming of nutria fur. Fortunately, she is wearing her precious pearls and pearl earrings.

To my dismay also, I cannot find my packet of nails.... They are lost. Countess Sedlnitzky has offered to give me some. I have let the Rhode Island hens out of their box and, like the well-bred birds they are, they do not stray far from the waggon.

Papali cannot obtain petrol and it puts too much strain on the horses to drag the car behind the carriage so it will remain here. The two stablemen who drove the waggons from Kyjovice are married. Therefore, Papali thinks it wrong to take them from their homes — he has sent them back to Kyjovice, and with them Regina has sent two of my beautifully plucked turkeys back to Kyjovice for the servants, as if they haven't got a whole flock of beautiful white turkeys. Or are those reserved for the Russians?

With much difficulty, Papali has succeeded in getting a French P.O.W. and a vagabond Pole to drive the waggons.

Eli, the French P.O.W., promises to be useful. He has already endeared himself to the children, much the same way as Franz, our little butler, has done. The Sedlnitzkys are also preparing to leave home. They have everything packed, in readiness. They debated whether they should join us, but have decided to wait some days longer. After our few days' rest, our nervous tension has slightly eased. We feel more equal to facing the next stage of the fray.

Thursday, 24 April, 1945

Left Bilovice to proceed on our way. We are travelling to Hranice and Potstat, a distance of about fifty kilometers. The rain has momentarily ceased, and by reason of much traffic on the roads, the mud immediately dried and now it is churned to a heavy dust. Very soon, we felt the need of a wash and a good brushup. We looked and felt a sorry sight. In Fullnek, a pretty village, we were glad to make a halt. After vigorously shaking the dust from our clothes, we unpacked our sandwiches made with the last of our rich turkey meat. The Lord is good.

Here, Papali found that two of the horses had to be re-shod. This delayed us considerably: luckily, a smith — an old man — was found. It was while we sat at the roadside waiting that suddenly, among the fugitives and soldiers, Petty saw our Oberstabsarzt riding with his company. We greeted each other like old friends. They were making for Prague, hoping to get across to the American Army, the Mecca that all refugees are aiming at.

Continuing on our journey, we passed many villages, all practically deserted. One homely, peaceful-looking little village called Lindenau inspired Petty's poetic imagination. He chirped; "*In Lindenau wie ist der Himmel Blau, und die Autos machen kein radau*" (in Lindenau, the sky is blue, and the cars make no noise). He kept repeating, "*Der Himmel ist so blau, so blau.*" We had to smile.

After nine hours of steady travelling, we climbed a long road, winding up a wooded hillside: Papali pointed with his whip to a town immediately beneath us and said, "That is Potstat. It belongs to the Des Fours." To me, the town nestling on the shoulder of a stooping hill looked pretty and inviting. Auntie Mother had written to a friend, Count Kuno Des Fours, some time back, asking if they could stop over at his castle should we be forced to leave home. She had not received a reply. It was embarrassing to arrive at the home of a staid and steady bachelor unannounced just before dusk. And to make matters worse for us, we found that the castle had a very complicated entrance if one did not know the approach. The saga of the bewitched castle was realistically brought to mind, travelling round about until we found a grilled iron gate. While the others broached the lions' den, I sat alone in the carriage — for what seemed the best part of an hour — and tried to steady the hungry, spirited horses on a slanting hillside while, flanks heaving, they pawed the ground with impatient hooves and arched their slender, foaming necks, trying to get at the bit between their teeth. My old friend Rosa Bonheur would have delighted in painting them, but I was frightened and it required all my South African knowledge of animals to try to curb and quieten them. It was therefore with relief that I saw two men approaching — Count Des Fours and his coachman. Speaking perfect English, Count Des Fours bade me welcome and apologised for the delay, because his coachman had been called away.

The coachman took charge of the impatient horses while the Count again bade me welcome and took me into the castle to join the others. We entered by the great oaken doorway, the setting sun shone through the tall windows, giving luster to the dark-railed stairs. Somewhere, a great clock chimes the hour. Five o'clock.

Indeed, we soon found that we had come to a place of blessed peace. In this house, like in the Castle of Bilovice, everything is very well appointed. The carpets have a mellow look of age and beauty and the faint smell of mustiness that is always found in these old houses seemed to breathe a pleasant, faded flavor of the past. The Grand Salon is upstairs, also the smoking rooms where Count Des Fours keeps his fowling pieces, antique and modern. Here is also the Chapel where two carved golden angels keep watch, various other salons, and also Count des Fours' great love, his library. I found later that the library contains many precious and interesting volumes ranging from ancient legends and letters to modern romance. I am surprised to find that many of the newer books that Count Des Fours has lent me bear an accompanying note from the author, usually American.

Incidentally, one of the books is the charming 'My African Neighbours', written by that grand old Austrian gentleman, Count Coudenhove, Count Des Fours' uncle, and that our friend Charles Maberly of Duivelskloof said he keeps by his side.

Count Des Fours' private suite of rooms, including kitchen and pantry, are on the first floor. He is well cared for by a capable housekeeper and his Czech serving man. The house is built in the form of a perfect square with an inner courtyard. Count Des Fours has assigned us a suite of cheerful and beautiful furnished rooms opposite his own suite. We have the use of a kitchen and wash kitchen downstairs. This is a house, as in a story, where anything remarkable or lovely might happen: you could meet a knight or a fairy — here, in a dark old wash-kitchen, I met the Russians. Or rather, they met me.

On the first floor it was very quiet, relieved only by Petty and Ilona and the housekeeper's little boy who enjoy nothing so much as to scamper along the long corridors and peep through the large curtained windows into the vine-clad courtyard below, where fugitives and soldiers are continually coming and going.

On the ground floor there are a great many rooms of various sizes and shapes. These rooms are crowded with poor refugees, mostly women and children who are sleeping on the floor, or any sort of makeshift bed, rug or straw. Here, alas,

privation and suffering are horribly acute and notwithstanding
the solemn fact that we have constantly been in contact with
people wearing mourning, it is deeply distressing to visit these
depressed and subdued people. Most of the peasants are poor
people and being forced to leave their homes, their couple of
cows or fowls and geese, has been a great wrench that grows
ever more bitter. Among them all is the question, will we ever
be able to return home again? Home, that is each man's castle,
that he has laboured to build, which has seemed so large, so
big and strong. In this great tragedy it has been swamped and
fallen to the ground. They ask, will we ever find anything of
our hard-won possessions again?

Count Des Fours' waggons are also packed in readiness
to leave. He contemplates travelling with us.

*****

28 April, 1945

We have held a consultation to decide upon the course
we must take. Count Des Fours, Papali and Auntie Mother are
in favour of us trying to cross over to the American lines. I
steadfastly maintained that we remain where we are; Regina
supported me, saying: "If we travel anywhere, it should be
back to Kyjovice." We pointed out that we have already been
surrounded by the Russians, if we proceed we shall certainly
be overtaken, our horses stolen and everything looted.

As this is quite obvious, we stay here.

30 April, 1945

This morning, Auntie Mother came to me. "Dory child,"
she said tragically, "the Americans do not seem to be
advancing and the Russians are closing in. The streets are filled
with fugitives and soldiers who do not know which way to
move. We can't get through any more, so we must be resigned,
if it is God's holy will, to die here."

I determined to maintain an optimistic air. I tried to the
best of my ability to reassure our dear Auntie Mother. Quite
boastfully, I said, "Who is afraid of the Russians? I have a
South African flag and my marriage lines, an antenuptial
contract (with large stamps of King George) that will prove

that I am not German, so surely I can hold the fort for us. Besides, I discredit most of the stories told about the Russians." Nevertheless, I don't think Auntie Mother was taken in by my optimism.

Planes are continually buzzing overhead, flying singly or in grouped formation. Of the *Luft Waffe* there is never a sign. The planes continually strafe the fugitives on the roads. We expect hourly to be bombed, therefore it is difficult to know what to do with all our baggage. Meanwhile it is stored in an outhouse. It is most distressing that we do not know if the town will surrender when the Russians march in. We decidedly do not want to fight, to the last man! In every town and village, the people wish to surrender, but are prevented by the inevitable *Partei*, the S.S. or a few petty officers; so speculation in Potstat is rife as to what will happen to us. The Burgermeister clearly indicated he will surrender, but he has no authority.

With utmost relief, we discovered this morning that the *Partei* and S.S. have all fled. Only a few half-hearted placards are posted up announcing the Fuehrer's heroic death for Volk and Fatherland. No indication of when or how the "hero" died. Nothing more.

No last post. No *Goetterdaemmerung* has been rendered in Potstat for Hitler; his twisted soul has left the morass that he so extensively activated to reach the borderland, to face his Supreme Judge, where we are bound to stand... each one of us, perhaps today, perhaps tomorrow. Meanwhile we each have our pilgrim pack to carry — most people have a heavy cross, therefore there has been no sympathy shown and very little interest in Hitler's heroic passage. Most people believe that the long-suffering people of Berlin have found a dispatch for the Fuehrer; the thought in most minds, however, is:

"When the devil a saint would be,
What a devil of a saint was he!"

Yes, we have our pilgrim packs. It rains incessantly, the slush on the roads is deeply churned up by soldier's waggons and by fugitives. Food is scarce; it gives me an unutterable pang to see small children sitting on rain-soaked waggons; women pushing perambulators; old men unsteadily pulling hand-carts — some are hitched on to waggons while the owner, to keep it in sight, has to run beside the waggon. As horses strain at their harness, all struggle through the slush. The poor animals deserve a very special tribute, especially the shivering, hungry foals that trot alongside their blowing and sweating mothers (this is the foaling season, most of the peasants have a horse or two). They are born to a pitiful plight. I am so moved by these sights that I prefer rather to stay indoors, as I imagine I can see my boys pressing along among the crowds.

We have soon found that our stablemen are eating more than we had bargained for so I spend many hours each day queuing, to get all that is to be had on ration cards.

Sunday, 6 May, 1945

This morning, it seems rather more quiet than usual. The rain has ceased. It is reported that the Russian army is very near to us now. We went to early Mass. Then, being inquisitive, to see if anything untoward is happening in the village. (The *Burgermeister* has decided to surrender without more ado.) I saw that all shops are shut and empty, but at one of the shops, I see people entering at a side door. I entered and found that a small quantity of groceries was being sold without ration cards. As I had some money with me, I was soon spending left and right. I was fortunate in obtaining butter, oats and a large glass jar of jam. When I returned to our rooms, Petty and Ilona whooped for joy at the sight of the sweet jam. Because of the scarcity of sugar, real jam has long been a luxury almost denied to us. After our breakfast, I asked Eli to come with me to the miller, hoping to get some flour. Luckily we found the miller at home and I was able to buy 30 pounds of flour from him with our cards …. the last we had. On the way home I obtained some eggs from a peasant family. For the immediate future, we are provided for.

In the afternoon, Papali was asked to give his horses and waggon to convey supplies from a warehouse on the out-skirts of the village to the shops. Papali complied, although he does not approve of his animals working on a Sunday. In the evening the men returned and said they were required the next day again, when we would receive a payment of sugar. On Sunday evening, we had no bread left. I therefore asked a

baker to reserve two loaves of bread for me, then from some
women I was told that another baker was selling bread
without ration cards. I hastened home and persuaded Regina
and Anna to come with me and try to buy some bread. When
we got to the bakery, we found that a thronging crowd had
stormed the bakery; in desperation, the baker was trying to
reason with the people without avail, and then, as a batch of
bread came out the oven, he cut them in halves and tossed
them far out among the crowd. Regina, tall and eager,
succeeded in catching a couple of half-loaves and so did I,
which Anna valiantly carried home.

Monday, 7 May, 1945

After Mass I spent the morning queuing again and was
able to get some margarine and also the two loaves of bread
the baker had reserved for me. I took my booty home and went
out again obsessed with the idea of obtaining some empty
sacks. During the war, a sack was scarcely obtainable and I am
very fond of an old grain bag. There are so many things one
can do with it. Should we suddenly have to depart, a sack
would be the ideal thing to carry our groceries, bedding, etc. In
I went from shop to shop in a vain quest, until eventually I met
the man who had borrowed the horses and waggons. He told
me that during the night, the German army had ordered the
opening of the warehouse. He said we were at liberty to take
any thing we found there, including sacks.

My heavy wooden shoes sank deeply into the mud as I
sped to the warehouse — I saw a busy throng coming in and
out. Among the waggons standing before the door, I saw our
wagggon, with the two stable-men sitting inactive. Soon they
recognized me and excitedly told me that the sugar and
groceries had already been taken. "And you two just sit here
smoking your pipes!" I said.

With Eli I hurried in to search for my sacks and soon
found some very good ones. Then we opened some large bins
and found that they contained ample stores of grain and
potatoes and while the old vagabond Heinrich just rummaged
around happily, Eli gallantly helped me to fill some of my
newly acquired sacks; four with potatoes, and several with
bran, oats and barley for our horses and hens. It was a hot

morning, and after this little performance, we were both breathless and the perspiration ran freely down our faces. We got the old vagabond to help us load the sacks on to the waggon then we sat for some time to regain our composure and watch the crowd eagerly hurry to the warehouse and coming out with a load, young and old, full of satisfaction, with a heavy load upon their backs or shoulders; one old man and a young girl rolled out a barrel of oil among them quite regardless of the quagmirey state of the road — it was a funny sight!

Some people had the misfortune of having their loads bumped off their backs into the mud. Like drunken men, sacks of grain lay about, or were stored along the road while the owners went home for wheelbarrow or hand-cart, grain and sugar was strewn everywhere, and I wondered where the spirit of "*Kampf der Verderb*" ("Battle of Destruction" — The German policy of leaving nothing behind for the Russians to capture) had flown, that we had been hearing repeated so often.

Some soldiers passed by, loaded with packets of candles. I asked them for some, they kindly threw two packets up to me and also a packet of sugar. As soon as we could get our waggon free through the crowd, we started on our homeward way in good spirits. Our conservative Regina was not as pleased to see us as she might well have been. Actually, she behaved as though I had robbed the Bank of Dresden.

"And what will people say?" she said.

"Blow them," I said. "If they can't collect for themselves, I'll give them some of my potatoes." And I meant what I said.

We have been considering how to keep our belongings from being stolen. The fugitives are complaining of their belongings being stolen from their waggons. I therefore asked Papali if he does not think it wise to have all our goods stored together in a corner of the wash-kitchen, where we can also take refuge instead of the upstairs rooms where there is no water. This morning, with the help of the stablemen, we collected practically everything, with the exception of our Rhode Island Reds, and stowed all in an inconspicuous corner between a big chimney and the wall. We covered everything with Regina's Persian carpet that she had brought along; but as it seemed to illuminate the dark corner, I turned it wrong side up and spread some of my sacks over all.

Sometime later the children rushed in and said, "The butcher is selling meat, he has meat for sale!" I managed to buy some beef; I cut a nice thick slice, salted and hung it up in our kitchen window to dry.... This, I said, for my boys.

###

CHAPTER SEVEN
GOLD WATCHES AND VODKA

Monday night, 7 May, 1945 (V.E. Day)

It has been very quiet. The lull before the storm. The electricity has failed. We sat in our rooms, lit by one spluttering candle, and retired early. The cloud is likely to burst at any moment.

The Germans have surrendered.

Tuesday, 8 May, 1945

Not wishing to be caught in our beds, we got up early. I dressed the children (for many nights, people have been sleeping in all their garments). We intended to go to Mass. Auntie Mother and Anna took the children downstairs while I completed my toilette. Putting on my black tyrolean hat, I hurried after them, when on the stairs Count Des Fours' butler stopped me. Excitedly, he said, "Don't go to church, the Russians are fighting in the streets."

I dashed back to our rooms. My rucksack was ready, it contained my important South African flag and my marriage lines. I slung it over my shoulder, grabbed up our coats; then, in the innocence of my heart, I tried to tidy up the room somewhat and smoothed the blanket over the bed. A bottle of apricot brandy stood on the table, I hastily pushed it into a corner of the room on the floor. A strip of brown paper lay nearby. I picked it up and placed it loosely over the bottle. Our basket of some eggs and groceries were also on the table; hastily, I stuffed them into a small, low built-in cupboard in the wall. I grabbed my swans-down plumeau and blankets and was ready to run down the stairs to our wash-kitchen, where I hoped to find the children, when Regina came running in to fetch her belongings.

"I'm going to stop the children from going out on the street," I called. Regina hastily collected an armful of her things and ran down the stairs with me. (Later, she accused me of not guarding her belongings, as she had asked me to do, that she thought she had left on the lower stairs). I was totally unaware of this request, thinking only of getting to my children. For once, Fritzl — alias Petty — was where I hoped to find him with Ilona. Anna was busy boiling coffee, Auntie Mother was in the act of leaving with the children. I stopped them and only just had my flag and my papers ready out of the rucksack, when the door burst open and two stocky, bearded Russians entered with tommy-guns on their backs. Each was also armed with a "Pistola," and each had a long Bowie knife stuck in his long Russian boots. They came threateningly towards us and made harsh demands, which we did not understand, but made our blood curdle. One of the men had a blurred face and looked tipsy, the other one had little cruel black slit eyes. Unfortunately, Auntie Mother was wearing her gold watch, which they demanded. She took it off and with a kindly smile handed it to them and said "Andenken." They could have it as a keepsake. They failed to notice that she wore, "for safety," her long double string of pearls and the pearl and diamond earrings, worth many thousands more than the watch.

They almost leapt up to me and threateningly demanded my watch. I produced my South African flag and said, "I'm South African." It did not seem to impress them as much as I had hoped and I was afraid they would demand my rings, but they turned away from me, looked round the wash-kitchen and demanded, "Vodka!" but as we plainly did not have any and seeing that the room looked poor and bare, they almost ran out and up the stairs. "Now what characters!" calmly remarked Auntie Mother.

From the curtainless windows, we heard the approach of the Red Army, the thundering grind of the tanks, waggons, trucks, and jeeps, but especially bewildering were the voluble shouts in harsh foreign voices and the tramp of many feet. We did not know which way to turn, what to do, my courage failed; my inside seemed to churn in mad turmoil; I asked myself repeatedly, "What must I do? Where is my intelligence?"

As we had arranged we would all meet in the wash-kitchen, but now where was Regina? And where were Papali and the stablemen? Although my children clung to me, they seemed unafraid. Russian soldiers now continually came banging at the door and demanded, "*Davaj, davaj chasy! Vodka!*" (Give me watches! Vodka!). Seeing only women and children in a half-empty room, they hurried away up the stairs to find better booty. We heard the children of the other fugitives crying. Russians seemed to be in all their rooms. We wondered what was happening to the people.

And what has happened to Papali and Regina? Should I run upstairs and find out? Can I face the staircase alone with all these Russians? Now....? Where is my intelligence? What about my Motto? "Only a little simple, not afraid." But I am hopelessly afraid!

After what seemed an age but in reality not many minutes Regina came in. Over her burnished hair she had tied a red paisley kerchief, thinking to disguise herself like an old woman; she carried a few of her belongings.

"Where is Papali?" we asked in chorus. Still up in our rooms, among the soldiers? What if they take him prisoner? I thought of hard labour prison camps. I gave Regina my flag and said, "Take care of my children, I am going to fetch Papali."

Russian soldiers were everywhere on the stairs and in the corridors. I was trembling, but I thought I must find him. I pushed my way in amongst the soldiers and when I got to our rooms, I saw Papali. He appeared to be guarded by two armed Russian guards. At first I thought they had hit him as he was bending forward, but then I perceived he was picking up some bank-notes on the floor. I helped him pick up the last of them.

"Come on, Papali," I said, "we are waiting for you!" and I took his arm.

"Halt!" said the guards, "That man is our prisoner," and they made as if to march him away. "He is master of this house and he must show us where he keeps his guns!"

"He is not the master and we've got no guns," I repeated, "but I can show you where the guns are."

Feeling very much the traitor and very conscious of my own black hat (the aristocracy traditionally wore black hats), I led the way to Count Des Fours' smoking room and indicated the cupboard. Already a lot of Russians were in the room. They were trying out Count Des Fours' spectacles and binoculars and pulling open drawers. The guards forced open the cupboard that I had indicated. We hurried away as they pulled out the guns, snapped them over their knees and with a great splintering of glass, threw the pieces out of the window. On the stairs, I said to Papali, "Perhaps you should not wear your black hat." I never saw it again, perhaps it also went through one of the windows. Luckily, Papali had a little skull-cap in his pocket and he put it on.

When we got back to the wash-kitchen, Papali told us that the Russians had met him on the stairs. They ordered him up to the room where I found him. Here, they systematically searched him, they took his signet ring, his gold watch, studs and cufflinks, the bag of gold coins from his pocket and his other money. The bank notes they had thrown on the floor as worthless.

As we had had no breakfast, I suggested we have some coffee. I was surprised how my hands trembled, I could scarcely pour the coffee. The hot coffee did us all good. We were all much too perturbed to eat anything, Russians kept coming into the room. Anna remained in the background, almost speechless.

There was no electricity and we had very little firewood left, but as the fire was burning… I suggested, to save fuel, that we boil some potatoes in their jackets for lunch (we had some butter and cream cheese that I had collected the previous day to eat with the potatoes). Auntie Mother tried to assist me to wash the potatoes and put them on to boil…. We wondered if we would have any appetite eat them! What with armed men storming and out and demanding "*Chassis!*" and "*Vodka!*" Anna stood mute, only laying a restraining hand on the children to keep them out of harm's way. Regina, fancying that she had disguised herself by muffling her head in the red paisley kerchief, but with her golden eyes bright with excitement, flushed cheeks and auburn curls peeping out around her face, I can only say she looked terrific! Courageously, she faced the bandits with me. I spoke to them in English; she addressed them in French. They did not understand a word, but with much pointing to my flag and waving of hands and feet, our meaning was clear and, reluctantly, they turned back. We heard many distant explosions. Sometimes the ground shook. We waited, not knowing what the next few moments might bring. However, as nothing shook the ground under our feet with the exception of harsh voices and the tramping of the army, I plucked up courage to look through the small back window that commanded a view of the village square. It was with a shock that sent gooseflesh creeping down my spine that I saw, from the high dominating tower, the Russian flag with hammer and sickle flying. From numerous other buildings on the square, the red flag also fluttered. Henceforth we shall walk under the shadow of the hammer and sickle. In our dire distress, we could only call out like the psalmist, "Out of the depths I cry to you, O Lord, Lord hear the voice of my supplication and let my voice come unto you!"

About 11 o'clock, Count Des Fours came to us. He looked quite desperate and tried to apologize for his appearance. He said, "They pulled my boots from my feet, and they took my loden jacket and my green forester's waist-coat. The house is completely overrun. They are taking whatsoever their fancy pleases… from pantry to cellars there is nothing left; you can see them chewing my apples." Indeed, a truck full of women soldiers was parked in front of the window — I had been surprised to see the red-cheeked apples they were eating, thinking what nice apples they have in Russia!

The fact that we did not hear any further shooting gave me some courage and when quite an ugly and evil looking soldier came in and insisted upon searching my suitcases, without even producing my flag, I said, "Africa! You get out!" I was relieved that he went — and we were furthermore relieved not to see a Mongolian-looking face among the soldiers; we had heard much of the cruelty of the Mongols.

At 12 o'clock, our two stablemen appeared, whom we had concluded had joined the Russians. Eli, with his French beret set far back on his head, looked like a high tension rabbit. He spluttered, "They have taken the horses, the silver-mounted harness… everything!"

Our potatoes were cooked, we invited Count Des Fours to join us. We were a party of ten, and our pot of potatoes soon vanished. Many times, our lunch hour was disturbed by Russian soldiers whom I quickly intercepted with my marriage lines and Regina with the flag. When soldiers saw the stamps of King George — no, not Hitler — they departed. But it was when I decided to make some tea (while my back was turned) that nine soldiers pushed their way in and started turning over and opening our suitcases. I dashed up to them and ordered, "Off!" Seeing that we had four men at our table, they departed, with me accompanying them to the door, but alas, they took my rucksack with them and after about two minutes, a most evil-looking soldier returned. Gesticulating and talking loudly, he pointed to his revolver and I understood him to say, "You, look out!" I answered (with my flag in hand), "*Pistola dobre, dobre,* (Pistol nice, nice), but you get out!" and I took him to the door. Afterwards, I felt distinctly frightened, thinking, "He will surely return tonight."

Count Des Fours, seeing my "courage" asked me to accompany him to his chief forester's house. The forester, quite a young man, with his wife, had come the previous evening to speak to Count Des Fours. They told him that they had decided to shoot themselves with their three young children when the Russians marched in. For two hours Count Des Fours had endeavoured to dissuade them… in vain. They had shot themselves at dawn; it was said the forester was still living.

I was very loath to leave my children, even for a short while, but I found it my duty to see if anything could be done for these poor people. I gave Regina my marriage lines and said I would try not to be long. We walked the little distance down the hill to the forester's house. Before the castle door and everywhere, it swarmed with soldiers, among whom were a great many women soldiers, also armed with tommy guns, some of them comparing the time on their newly "acquired" watches; two of the women were turning many gold rings on their fingers. If our Zdenka had been with us, she would have crossed herself twenty to the dozen! And if it were not for the solemnity of the hour, our walk would have been like a masquerade. Count Des Fours' trousers were stuffed almost up to his knees in a pair of long, broken Russian boots, in his shirt sleeves, minus coat and waistcoat, and with a grim expression. Yet he walked with that unmistakable air of quiet good breeding that gave me courage which I needed as I felt weak. My knees knocked together, I had to say to them, "*Staan stil, jou baas is mos nie bang nie*" (stand still, don't think your master is afraid). We passed many truck loads of soldiers about to

leave for Prague. On one of these, I spied the evil face of the
bandit I had ordered out of the kitchen with his "*Pistola.*" With
a feeling of intense relief, I saw him drive off.

At the forester's house a gruesome sight awaited us.
We entered hesitatingly, Russians were looting in every room.
In the bedroom, the three little children lay in their cots on
blood-stained pillows. Apparently they had first been given a
sleeping draft before receiving the fatal bullet through the ear.
The baby, about a year old, with rounded cheeks and soft little
hands, was dressed in a blue suit. The little head seemed to
rest peacefully on the lurid pillow, sleeping its long last sleep.
The mother lay on her face with her hands pressed to her ears.
A scarlet stream from her pillow reached across the floor to
mingle with the blood of her husband, who lay dead in front of
her bed…. They were all dead. Even the dog was shot. There
was nothing we could do for them except cover the
unfortunate mother with a sheet, all the blankets had been
stolen. There were ten Russians plundering the room over the
bodies of the dead, every drawer was pulled open, doors that
had been locked were broken open, the room was littered with
shoes, papers, medicine bottles… everything imaginable.

As we entered, the Russians showed their fists at the
dead man and I understood them to say: "Men do not kill
children!" (Actually, to my knowledge they never harmed a
child.) It took all my self control not to show the horror I felt. I
was glad to get out of the house, leaving the dead and the
Russians to their plundering, but especially the one the others
called "Kapitain," who was showing off by senselessly banging
on the piano.

We returned via the Priest's house where we hoped he
would be able to arrange for the burial. I was relieved to sit
down for some minutes, but we were startled to hear the news
that the war is over. Germany had unconditionally capitulated.
But plainly with these Russian communists there would be
scant mercy for the vanquished. Without any elation of spirits,
the priest promised Count Des Fours that some Czech people,
who were practically unmolested, would try to arrange for the
burial.

Speeding back to my children, I was relieved to find all
well, but we had scarcely arrived back when a Russian
entered. Here was a spectacle to frighten any self-respecting

person, a huge barbarian, as shaggy as an African gorilla, with brawny arms and lantern jaw. He stepped right into the room. After my recent intimidations, my courage failed me. I sat down too shaken to remonstrate. He placed a sack and a large smutty pot on the table and only when he announced belligerently, "I have come to cook for my officers," I stood up and produced my marriage lines. They had no effect on him. Instead, he ordered me to "Cook the pot!" and to boot, he ordered us to give him half a bucket of potatoes! Which, after some thought, I gave him. Then he ordered: "Now peel them!"

"Oh, no," I said, "I have some work to do," and I sat down to reverse the cuffs on my shirt blouse. By this time Anna had "come to," and she obligingly helped him to peel the potatoes. He made up the fire and then, from his sack, he produced a large loaf of black bread and two chickens which he had roughly plucked. Anna helped him to cook the fowls and our potatoes (we did not know that they were also our fowls… my poor little hens).

Ere long an officer came in. From his pockets he produced seven eggs and gave them to his man to cook. We looked at each other, for we recognized them to be our eggs by the paper they were wrapped in. They had been taken from the basket that I had pushed into the little low cupboard. Two more officers came in. They also produced our eggs. Apparently they foraged together! Soon the man had our two dozen eggs boiling. I told the officers that their servant was using the last of our wood, so they sent him out for more. He returned with a couple of ample armfuls. The officers asked for water to wash their hands and also the inevitable request for vodka (which, of course, we did not have), and seeing the eggs, I wondered if they had also discovered the apricot brandy upstairs. When the fowls were cooked, the servant asked for a white tablecloth, and as he would not take "no" for an answer, we were obliged to give him one of our sheets. He used our crockery without asking for it.

The officers were clean-shaven and their long boots were polished. They did not carry tommy guns; but I cannot say that they ate slowly or with gentle table manners. They smacked their lips and the chicken bones were spread around their plates. After they had eaten, they said kindly to me, "Give the soup that is left to your children."

Then they sat for a short while and became quite affable. They told us from which parts of Russia they came; one from Moscow, one from Leningrad — you won't like it, they said, it is too cold. The third, a likable, handsome dark man, came from Iran — we would have been glad if the last named had stayed in the house, as we felt almost sure we had gained a protector. Indeed, as the afternoon was already drawing to a close, we dreaded what the night would be like, so we almost regretted seeing the dark young officer continuing his journey to Prague.

Before they left, Anna quickly scoured their very smutty pot; it came out a nice blue enamel, and as they were on their way, with much waving, she ran after them, but the man declined the return of the pot, and now it stands us in good stead as a hot water pot. But it was after a while that we saw the man on the stairs and then I understood why he had declined the return of the pot, for in the bag he carried on his shoulder, he had collected a much more ample and precious booty in Count Des Fours salons.

And so with the noise of passing vehicles, harsh shouting of soldiers, the sun set and dusk fell. We sat quietly in our room quivering with apprehension, dreading the dark. I was now quite convinced that every Russian was a thief and likewise everyone was addicted to vodka and as drunk men are not responsible for their actions it was clear why every woman was in mortal fear of being outraged…. This had all along been quite our worst fear of the Russians. It was distressing that our door had no inside lock. We prepared to barricade it and spend the night together, but we had nothing to put against the door until I thought of my axe and nails. So I quickly spiked the nails all along the door frame and bent them over the door. Thus consolingly together, we presented a solid front.

I made beds for the children, to their delight, in two wooden wash-troughs and they soon settled down (after their soup) snugly. Regina prepared the very narrow, high table used for folding the laundry. For herself; Anna spread Papali and Auntie Mother's rugs on the floor near the still-heated stove, as even in May the early spring nights can be very cold in Czechoslovakia. Anna asked me if she could spread her rugs next to mine, so, like two watch-dogs, we settled down side by side near the children. The two stablemen made themselves comfortable in a small adjoining alcove. But there yet remained a cabinett de toilette to be thought of — it was out of the question to think of venturing down the passage, nor up the stairs. In one corner of the room stood a ladder, so to form a little nook, I spread one of the horse blankets over it, with a wash bucket for service. Little did we dream that in this order we would sleep for the next three weeks. Outside, the courtyard was filled with soldiers; in front of our wash-kitchen window, several great camp fires blazed; as we had no curtains, the room was partly illuminated. We were thankful for the strong iron grating in front of the windows. Around the fire the soldiers held high revel, with much shouting and rude laughter (real savages!), women and men. There was continual tramping up and down the stairs, banging of doors, the continual ringing of a bell, and what was puzzling were the discordant trumpet and horn blasts. It was a little reminiscent of those far off historical days of Jericho, when the priests made a "long blast on the trumpets of rams' horns and the people made a great shout." Our spirits were as flat as the walls of Jericho.

During the years of the "*Dritten Reich,*" thinking people in Germany were fully aware of the forces of evil that were gathering, by every means of deceit and propaganda, to destroy man's holy concept of his divine origin; Christians meditated and prayed for deliverance from past and present sins and… they prayed for peace. It was therefore fitting, before we tried to settle down, instead of looking into the dark and gloom with sorrow, that we knelt down on the flagstones and Papali prayed the age-old Sequence of Pentecost: *Veni, Sancti Spiritus…* Come, O Holy Spirit, fill the hearts of Thy faithful, kindle in them the fire of Thy love.…

Several times, there was loud banging at the door and a light shone through the cracks, but evidently the intruder saw no way of entering and made off. Regina murmured low on her high table and eventually got off and spread her rugs under the table. The children slept; tenderly I pushed the hair back from their faces, repeating many times the beautiful traditional Angels' greeting: *Ave Maria, gratia plena, Dominus Tecum.…* A few more *Aves* and then the little prayers of my childhood came to soothe me and while the cacophony continued outside, I fancied I could hear the sweet voice of John McCormack singing: "The Lord is my life and my salvation, whom then shall I fear? whom then shall I fear?" This brought a real measure of comfort and almost a smile as I recalled how my nephew John, aged seven, had commented on this song, "And yes, Auntie, we still have the South African Defence Force!"

Alas, at this hour the S.A. Defence Force was 10,000 miles away! But now it was long past midnight. With a few more harrowing blasts the noise slowly subsided, the fires died down and peace descended upon the Russian *lager*. And from sheer exhaustion and misery we also dozed fitfully. Next morning betimes, all was astir, our toilettes were short. We had not dared to undress. The children gaily crept out of their wash-troughs. We could not think of going to Mass and did not know if the church had remained undisturbed, therefore spent the morning arranging and ordering our belongings as best we could in our limited space and endeavouring to make ourselves as inconspicuous as possible and to attract as little attention as possible to ourselves. We already knew the unfledged truth experienced by every woman in the village, that as soon as it was known there was a woman in the house, the soldiers came immediately and ordered her to accompany them. Many women over seventy years old had to submit to the ruffians; our life has been made a hell, they said. We sat quietly in our corner trying to keep the door shut, which was difficult without a lock. At nights, my nails were invaluable. During the day, we put an iron bar up against the door, which fell down with a thud every time the door was pushed open (this frequently happened) and I was warned in time to run and intercept the intruder with my South African flag and antenuptial contract.

11 May, 1945

This morning there seemed to be a lull in the activities of the Army about the house, and as we were anxious to know if any of our belongings were still to be found upstairs in the rooms, I ventured up with Regina and the children; we had to walk carefully to avoid the filth on the stairs; two armchairs still stood on the landing, but they looked very strange, as if spiders had spun a web over them. Filth and spiderwebs, it was really strange. Even when I walked up to them they appeared to be embalmed in webs. It took some seconds before it dawned on me that it was the under-cover of kapok, all the leather had been stripped from the chairs.

In each room of that carefully appointed house, we stood aghast. A normal person can never picture the disgusting sight. In the rooms we had occupied with the handsome inlaid furniture, the air was thick with what we now recognized as a typical Russian stench: garlic, vodka, and something putrid. The inlaid chests of drawers had been wrenched open and thrown upside down, the brocade was all torn from chairs which lay smashed up about the room. The display case was broken open, all the delicate cups with their soft colouring and egg-shell transparency were gone. There remained only a few Meissen and Viennese saucers in the broken cupboard — the cups have no doubt been taken as drinking vessels. All the pretty, priceless figurines were gone. Mattresses lay on the floors; feathers from the pillows were all about the rooms; the carpets gone; pictures taken from the walls lay about the floors; letters, photos, bottles, and many items that belonged to the castle were discarded in the rooms. A carpet was rolled up in one corner of the room. "We'll take this with us," I said, but when I proposed to unroll it, I shuddered with disgust, it was full of feathers and filth.

Our pillows, coats, and groceries that we had left in the rooms of course, were gone... but in the corner, under the strip of brown paper (I smile to think of it), stood Papali's bottle of 3 Star apricot brandy! So much for the Russians who had slept and "housed" in this room. I think if they knew of its whereabouts, they would speed back from the four corners of Czechoslovakia to demand it. But what must I do with the bottle? The Russians must positively not have it. I stepped to the window, opened it wide, uncorked the bottle, and slowly started to pour the liquor down the stone wall of the castle. The delicate aroma came floating up to me... "Stop! This is a crime!"

In remote times, these old stone walls have possibly had baptisms of sweat and blood and tears, but surely never such excellent stuff. I recorked the bottle, put it under my coat, and took it down to the wash-kitchen. Yes, this is the state of every room in the house; indeed, I can truthfully say, in every

German house throughout the length and breadth of the country occupied by the Russians.

Walking down the main corridor, we noticed that Count Des Fours' oddments of armour, hunting horns and bugles that were a decorative feature on the walls have all disappeared. This then accounts for most of the noises of the night which were so disturbing, puzzling and frightening to us.

Yes, we were puzzled and now I can ponder the deep truth of St. Augustine's words: "Now what is more absurd to say that things are made better by having lost all good? Therefore, if they are deprived of all good, they shall then be nothing...." We stand on the threshhold of a great abyss, with nothing good underfoot; and yet, I had tried to tidy up the room before the Russians marched in.

This morning I took Eli, the Frenchman, and the children for a little outing and to see if we could find anything of our hens. We saw the Britzka standing crippled in the back yard; the two front wheels have been removed, doubtless for the pneumatic tires — I noticed one sack of grain still lies on the waggon. After searching about in the empty sheds I saw that the animals have all been stolen. We found three of our hens, we caught them. The others have doubtless been eaten and quite likely by the officers who sat at our table and stole our eggs, and kindly offered me the soup that remained for my children. These poor, scared, hungry birds seem to have escaped a brawny hand, as two of them are without tail feathers; these birds will be invaluable to us.... but where to keep them? I pondered — in our wash-kitchen! I've prepared a corner for them next to our baggage, with two planks across the corner. I hope they stay behind the low barricade. Regina and Anna are not enthusiastic about my arrangement. To make matters worse, our wash-kitchen is as airless and sultry as if we were living in the tropics, flies buzz in and out of the high window, we have no energy to chase them. I've covered my "biltong" (dried meat) with a serviette. We need a real thunder storm to clear the atmosphere, or a good elixir to restore our energy and spirits.

Potatoes for supper; what a pity those Russians walked off with my rucksack containing the treasured piece of smoked bacon and the two little sausages on which Ilona wished to have only a little nibble. Now my children will blame me always for being miserly and storing up for thieves. Alas, my rucksack is gone. Despicable characters.

Saturday evening, 12 May, 1945

The thunderstorm that we have been wishing for is likely to burst at any moment; the heavens are dark and our men must go out and bring in my bag of grain from the waggon.

They refused point blank to go out, said it is dark and going to rain. Regina said, "Don't order them Dory, you have no authority to do so, because we can't pay them any more."

"And as far as I'm concerned," I said, "they'll get no more food either."

I put on my old loden coat and walked out to rescue the grain. The minute I walked into the corridor, I regretted my impulse. The whole Russian army, rank and file, seemed to be around and about the house. "In for a penny, in for a pound," I thought, as I walked through the soldiers and across the yard towards our waggon. "*Pani!*" the soldiers called out to me, "*Pani!*" but I walked straight on. I intended climbing up on the waggon and throwing the bag of grain down, but the waggon is high and as I hesitated to consider how I should climb up, two Russians came up to me. "*Pani! O, Pani,*" (woman, O woman!") they said, as they playfully each took one of my arms.

"I want to get the bag of grain from the waggon, won't you get it for me?" I asked them. "No, no," they replied, "We have just had our Sunday bath, but you come with us," they ordered, and firmly taking hold of my arms, they urged me along, at the same time petting me and using endearing words. "*Stara Maminko!*" (old mother) I said, but their reply only sounded something like "Old mother be blowed!"

My blood ran cold, the worst was happening, they were leading me to the Russian *lager*. "Where is my intelligence? St. Michael, mighty in battle, help!" For some paces I walked freely with them and then quite suddenly I stopped, and for nothing better to say, I said, "Now *voetsek!* ("hoof it!" usually said only to dogs or beggars) Both of you!" At this, they seemed to be surprised; quietly, they let go my

arms and without another word the brawny fellows
disappeared among the crowds of their colleagues. No one
could ever have been more surprised than I was; they could
not have known the significance of the ugly little Afrikaans
word, but it was a narrow escape.

Trembling, I started back to our kitchen, when a
sudden clap of almost homely Transvaal-like thunder made
me halt; for this sound I had no fear; soon the clean sweet rain
was falling, so I returned to the waggon. I managed to climb
up and by degrees managed to get the grain off and dragged it
into one of the empty cow-sheds. As I walked back to our
kitchen, the lightning was running along the ground, the
Russians had all disappeared. I had often heard that simplicity
is the chief charm of the Russian character. I think these
fellows are mighty simple, and notwithstanding the assertion
of a recent bath, they stink to high heaven! When I got home to
my family, they had been decidedly uneasy about my absence.
I was not furious any more with our cowardly men, nor was I
offended by Regina. I was thinking about "*voetsek*" and I felt
emboldened by the thought that I had ventured out alone, that
I had met the challenge and had been able to pull my wits
together! Yes, I felt "high hat!" I congratulated myself: I can
accept life. (I suppose Carlisle would say to me like he said to
another lady, "Gad, ma'am, you'd better.")

The hens behave well in their corner, except that
yesterday one of the hens in flying over their borderline barrier
made a splash on the floor.

"Look Dory!" said Regina, pointing a disdainful finger.

"It shall be cleaned up at once," I said and I spread
some ash over it and swept it up. "They must have some
exercise," added Regina. "They will lay eggs," I said
stubbornly, "for exercise."

This morning, Papali called out to me (he went to get
something from his cabin trunk) "Dory, come and have a look
here!" Almost timidly I went up to him, fearing the hens had
made a similar spectacle on Regina's carpet, but lo and behold
a nest with six brown eggs laid in a little hollow made by one
of my sacks! We're calling them Faith, Hope and Charity.
Auntie Mother thought it a sacrilege to name them after the
three Cardinal Virtues, until I explained that these are also

commonly used as Christian names. The precious birds have earned for themselves a small word of precious meaning: "Peace!"

So in peace and siege, our first line of defence is, and remains: Faith, Hope, and Charity.

Yes, I had felt "high hat" and I thought I was able to bear the bumps and jars that have become our latent lot but alas! This morning my new-found strength was sadly watered down when I heard a commotion in the corridor before our kitchen door. Hurrying to see what was happening, I saw all the poor fugitive women hurrying out, dragging their children and little remaining bundles. I asked them what was wrong, hurriedly they told me that they had been given half an hour to quit and clear the rooms that a lot of Russians were arriving. These they said were the dreaded Mongols and Tartars that were now upon us. Oh, dear, how dreadful! We had been hearing about the Mongols and Tartars — the dreadful scourge of the Russian army, feared as much as the dreaded Secret Police. The vanguard of the army was known to be mild compared to the cut-throats and robbers who came after in the persons of Mongols, Tartars, and the like — the dear Lord preserve us! Thoroughly dismayed, I hurried back to tell Papali what was on foot, and that doubtless, we would also be ordered to leave. I collected my sacks and we immediately started packing our most necessary items; we had often seen how other fugitives had been obliged to discard their belongings. Almost in a blind frenzy, we sorted and packed, discarded and packed again… thinking only of joining the stream of frightened humanity. Fearing to be seen from the curtainless windows, as already truck-loads of Mongols were arriving, we stooped, crouched, and rushed this way and that, collecting and packing… dreading that every moment they would be upon us. This was most lamentable, as we were only just recovering from our recent jars and shocks and here was my stomach quivering and turning over again. The Mongols! Faster and faster we went through our trunks, stooping and crouching, turning everything upside down. Someone kept asking, "Have you seen the toilet paper?" Our two servant men watched us with astonishment; they did not know what was on the go. Suddenly there was a loud knock on the door that peremptorily brought us all to attention. I rushed to open the door and there stood the very unpleasant-looking officer with the bandaged head whom I had previously encountered on the stairs. He ordered us, "Out!" Fearfully, I took his arm. "*Kamerad*," I said, and I led him to the window, where I showed him our beautiful South African flag and my own marriage lines. These imposing evidences had the desired effect; he motioned with his hand and said, "Stay." *Deo Gratias*, we stayed! But still quivering and thinking that at any moment the Mongols would be upon us, yet hoping that they would be easier to cope with in our own corner. For by now we were regarding the wash-kitchen as a veritable haven, a refuge.

The courtyard and space beyond our window rapidly filled with men, and when I ventured to look out of the window, I did not discern a Mongolian face among them. They sat down in the spring sunshine, and they removed their military overcoats. They dozed and cracked their lice and appeared grim and lean and dejected. Soon, my heart was full of sorrow for them. I called the others to the window; soon we concluded that they were prisoners from German prison camps.

Later, we found that they were prisoners indeed, poor fellows, a portion of the so-called "Vlasov Movement" that got its name from Lt. General Andrey Vlasov, one of the defenders of Moskow, who was taken prisoner by the Germans and who set up the Liberation Army, composed mostly of anti-communist Soviet troops. The tragic account of Vlasov's efforts, his conflicts, hopes, and frustrations, and then his tragic end, when the Americans handed all the "traitors" over to the Soviet Union where they were all executed, are historical facts that point an accusing finger at the fallibility of our statesmen.

The trial of these men in the Castle of Potstat lasted about ten days, and then these sad-faced fellows were ordered to pack up their tins and cans in which they had received their meagre rations of pale-looking soup, cooked and dished out to them in the park in view of our kitchen window. Guarded by M.V.D. with ferocious police dogs, they were put into closed prison vans and all transported off to the Soviet Union. Thus "Our little systems have their day, they have their day and cease to be."

By this time, nothing more filthy can be imagined than the state of the castle and grounds; the two lavatories downstairs were long since choked and had overflowed into the corridors. In the rose garden, of all places, latrines had been dug, and the stench coming from them was appalling!

While the trial of these prisoners was being staged, we were also ordered to appear. Escorted by members of M.V.D. we were led singly into one of the Salons, where some officers decorated with Red Stars sat before Count Des Fours' large desk. Here, our antecedents were written down in what looked to me, in my frightened state, like the Dooms-day Book.

Very soon after the trial of these men had taken place in the castle, we noticed another file of people being escorted into the castle — old men and boys. They were lodged in the rooms downstairs. All morning the M.V.D. brought in more prisoners.

Women and children with tear-stained faces stood outside the gates and along the fence. The proceedings were all conducted very quietly, scarcely a murmur was heard, not even from the women and children. We did not know what was taking place until Dr. Mimi Des Fours (Count Kuno's cousin who lives in her villa in the village) came to us and asked me to accompany her to the "Trial Room," where she said the men and youths are being tried by the usual method and will doubtless be transported to Russia to labour prison camps. "There is not an able-bodied man among them," said Dr. Des Fours. "They have been collected from all the German villages around; most of them have been my patients for years."

In the "Court Room," Countess Des Fours endeavoured to speak to the Russian officers, she valiantly tried to tell them that many of the men were invalids and were her patients of long standing. "Are you a Russian doctor?" she was asked.

"No," said Mimi patiently, "I received my degree in America."

"Then you are not wanted here," said the Russian shortly, and he added, "*Pritch Pani!* Go! — "Both of you!"

We went. Then we spoke to the women and children outside the gates; most of them had walked a long way to bring little packets of potatoes, a piece of bread, or items of clothing. We returned to the castle to get permission for the men to receive their packets. This was grudgingly given. "But only after, when the guards have been changed." The women had a long wait.

The next morning, the unfortunates were all put into closed vans and transported off. We never heard where they were sent.

After the men were taken away off, a bombshell seemed to explode over my head. I was ordered before the Russian police. The unpleasant tall Russian was seated before the desk, a Czech officer sat next to him. I stood there feeling very forlorn while the Russian asked me the usual questions (all had already been answered): Name? Age? Why was I in Czechoslovakia? I could not think what was on the go, when suddenly, looking straight at me, he dropped a thunderbolt: "You can't stay in Czechoslovakia, you must come with me, I am leaving this evening."

I stared back at him. "From Russia," he continued, "there are English battleships in the White Sea, and it will be easy for you to travel back to South Africa."

I tried to answer calmly, "I must first find my children." The Czech police officer was looking not unkindly at me — I turned to him and said, "You will allow me to take further advantage of your kindness and permit me to remain here, until I can fetch my other children?"

He nodded. "Yes," he said. After a little more palaver, the Russian still tried to convince me of the advantage of driving through Russia in a M.V.D. van (while I pictured Auntie Mother's distress if I was forced to leave) and the Russian seemed to have made up his mind. Firmly, he said, "You cannot stay here. You must come."

But the Czech had also made up his mind. "The *Pani* is our guest." And then he spoke some words which I could not understand, and then, "*Kamerad*," and "Vodka." Smiling, he saluted me, and they both walked off together.

I returned to our "kitchen," and I could not control the tears that streamed from my eyes. They were not so much in self-pity, because I seemed to have escaped travelling with a Russian policeman in a closed van across Russia… to the White Sea to find a British battleship. No. In our little "safe" corner, my tears flowed to think of the fate of all those poor invalids, travelling in closed vans to an unknown destination, while their mothers and wives wept outside the castle gates; pity for the unhappy boys; pity for the poor animals; and a great pity welled up in me for a brave people, who had so often showed me a moment of real human warmth, whose blood flowed also in the veins of my children — the Czechoslovak people, who will henceforth walk in the twilight of the great Russian bear.

*****

It was during the trial of the Vlasov army that I became a virago. My little Fritzl was finding the time in our wash-kitchen dull and wearisome. We did try to think up ways and means of entertaining the children. Auntie Mother read them her little homilies, Anna sang her doleful songs, while I tried… not very successfully… to concoct stories about monkeys and lions, pygmies and giants. Ilona is always a sweet, accommodating little girl, but Fritzl? He has found that he can squeeze through the gratings of the small window and like a bird out of a cage, he is out talking to the prisoners, or to the nasty-looking guard who paces up and down before the windows. He has given Petty a present, a little toy violin — no doubt stolen from one of the German homes. As I think the friendship is dangerous — the guard has already intimated that he would like to come in — I have asked Petty to stay away from the window, explaining that he may be kept as a hostage, and so enable the guard to gain an entrance, or make demands. But again, my Petty was out and away. So when he returned, I was ready. I led him to the window for the benefit of Heinrich and the guard, and I said, "Didn't I tell you that when things are more settled, I'll take you for a walk? Didn't I tell you not to slip through the window?" And then I took off my wooden-soled shoe and Petty got a real old-fashioned spanking from me. The Russian called out, "We don't beat children in Russia!" I said, "That is a pity."

I think I have earned some respect, which I am not happy about.

###

CHAPTER EIGHT
A DISMAL RETURN TO KYJOVICE

Saturday, 12 May, 1945

Today has been spent like the preceding days, living in fear of our lives like wild beasts in a lair. We have not dared show ourselves outside. The children have also been very subdued and the Russians have been less voluble, except that this afternoon, we heard some considerable squealing coming from the pig sties. They were killing some more of Count Des Fours' pigs. Later, the smell of roast pork came floating in at the window... surely, if one scent can put an extra edge on a hungry person's appetite, then it is the odour of roasted meat! I tried to persuade Eli to go out and ask the soldiers for some pork, but Eli had no courage. I tried to be extra diplomatic. "Eli," I said, "Your Grand Army carried the Eagles of France to the gates of Moskow, so if you carry the basket to the camp fire and ask the Commandant to give you a piece of pork, we can have a fine Sunday dinner. You are brave, Eli." I am sure Eli did not give much thought to his Grand Napoleon, but he must have thought, like Charles Lamb, I had made my stand on pork. He put on his beret. I tried to encourage him further. "That's right," I said, "show them what manner of man you are!" Eli squared his shoulders and walked off with the basket. Quite soon he returned with a chunk of pork, but alas, he was accompanied by a Russian. Now, what in the world have I done! I was frightened, but Eli's grin was disarming. To my relief, the soldier only came to ask for some salt in return for the pork.

Deo Gratias, the night has passed without event, only an occasional bump on our door.

The shining spring days passed. We remained in our lair. We heard of several people being taken away by the Russians; the local butcher and his wife were found, after a search of several days... murdered in the forest; outrages and robberies continued; we tried, resignedly, to endure the flies and the stench, while fully conscious that in the meadows, spring flowers were blooming, and in the green forest glades, pleasant zephyrs were blowing.

*****

It was a cruel time especially for the poor refugees, I think the worst anybody can experience. For me, there is the constant uncertainty about the fate of my boys. We look grim but we have to endure the rude laughter of the soldiers, the tramping up and down of the guards, together with the pestilent hot air and the blow-flies buzzing in and out of the window. I try to renew my pictures of white, but a word that is uppermost in my thoughts... a word that comes to the fore, many times a day... "Disgusting!" said Count Des Fours and "Disgusting!" said Papali when Heinrich put his smutty finger in our salt pot, but he said, "We must try to preserve our natural sense of tolerance and good will."

"And courage, yes," said Count Des Fours, "while one school advises a grain of salt and another a glass of vodka!"

And now there was quite a conversation about salt. Auntie Mother said something about, "Graciousness seasoned with salt," while my Petty asked Ilona, with big serious eyes, "Does Uncle Poldi (Count Podstatzki) also *smoodle* (mess) with salt on his toast like Uncle Fritz does?"

"No," said Ilona solemnly, shaking her head. "He did not use salt on his toast, they still had butter, when I was with them." Uncle Fritz — Papali — gave an unamused laugh and said: "Really, do I?"

Little did we know that during that time the Podstatzkis were faring far worse than we were.

Now Pentecost was drawing near, and this night as we knelt again on the flagstones, I listened more intently to Papali praying the Sequence: *Veni, Sancti Spiritus* — "Come, O Holy Ghost, fill the hearts of Thy faithful and kindle in them the fire of Thy love; Heal our wounds, Our strength renew.... Guide our steps that go astray.... Give us the Salvation, Lord." My knees grew cold from kneeling on the stones. I looked at Auntie Mother and Papali, at Regina and Anna kneeling with the detachment and serenity of the saints and I felt very guilty about the tumultuous state of my mind during these past weeks. Carry your cross, as old St. Thomas says, and it will carry you — so I prayed a lowly prayer: "Lord, I am a fool, help me not to be a fool." After that I felt better and I slept like a log.

Auntie Mother has confided her pearls and earrings to my keeping. I said I'd do my best to keep them safe. Now the precious, lustrous pearls are around my neck, under my shirt blouse, but I will not presume to wear her earrings. They rest in a little pocket within my pocket; I imagine I can feel the sparkle of the diamonds and pearls!

Papali and Regina are speaking of leaving for Kyjovice. They think we should remain here for the present. Oh dear! It is rumoured that no German people are permitted on trains or busses and that everywhere people are being collected and put into any sort of makeshift barracks and labour camps.

Eli is well behaved and helpful, but I'm feeling decidedly worried about Heinrich, he rummages around; today he came in with a large suitcase. It would not surprise us if he intended taking a store from our belongings. Papali has noticed how he watches us, so he has asked him to return to his people. We must keep our eyes and ears open as last night Heinrich turned my nails around, opened the door and stole out quietly. I promptly turned them all into position again and barricaded the door; he stayed out for the rest of the night.

Anna has helped me to collect some odd scraps from our packs. I've secretly made a rag doll and further, its stuffing is secret and very precious, containing, together with Auntie Mother's pearls, all our treasures. Now I opened the little packet that Gretel Gemmel had given me for Ilona from Auntie Mother: it contained a ring (a broad band of gold with a turquoise stone) that had belonged to Ilona's great grandmother Bertha Princess Croy — we will cherish it. Anna asked if I would include Franz's signet ring and tie-pin that he had entrusted to her. Poor faithful Franz, his ring is safely stitched in the fat tummy of the doll. We call her Majenka. My own precious ring, given to me by my mother-in-law, is similar to Ilona's but with an amethyst. I'll not hide it in Majenka; I look often at my beautiful blue-violet amethyst. It is my birthstone, said to have many virtues; chiefly, the amethyst is said to ward off intoxication, so I'll keep it on my finger.

Majenka's tummy is fat, her face is dirty, with a crooked eye; we keep a vigilant eye on her. I think Majenka is too ugly for anyone to steal; the Russians are kind to children, Petty likes to strum on the little red toy violin the Russian guard gave him.

Papali and Regina are speaking about finding ways and means of travelling back to Kyjovice. Therefore, Regina and I determined to speak to an officer about getting the return of our horses, and when we heard that some likely officers were lodged in one of Count Des Fours' Salons upstairs, we plucked up courage and went up the stairs, hoping to speak to them. We found a big-limbed man, wearing a shiny display of stars; when he had ascertained the nature of our request, he looked around the room and then, reaching up for one of Count Des Fours' ornate lace fans that still happened to hang on the wall, with a friendly gesture he handed it to Regina but further refused to discuss the matter we had come to speak to him about. However, he appeared to be chagrined or rather disappointed that he had failed to make a favorable impression on us. Our disappointment was great. Regina took the fan which she later handed to Count Des Fours while she muttered something about, "Two wrongs not making one right." I said, "It's adding insult to injury, but let us try to find another officer."

All the doors of the castle were wide open, crowds of soldiers were roaming about the rooms, avidly poking into everything. The floors are littered with articles, china, pictures, autograph albums, bottles, etc. The soldiers were not a bit embarrassed by the litter or by our presence, they jovially went on poking about. We were so mortified by the wanton destruction that we gave up all thought of looking for another officer, and instead, we returned humbly to our wash-kitchen.

After this little episode, we ventured out once more, having been emboldened by Eli excitedly coming to tell us that he had seen the silver-mounted harness, but strange horses.... We approached some officers standing before the door. Laughingly, they said, "We have no horses." We hastily retreated when they became too friendly, especially quite a young Russian, who tried to fondle Ilona. Regina was quite distressed, and said that with her winsome little face, we must keep her right out of sight of the soldiers.

Enemy planes are still active overhead, but we are thankful that the army seems to be moving to other parts of the country — it is said, to Germany. The Czechs believe that the Russians will soon remove their armies and influence from Czechoslovakia. Papali and Count Des Fours are not so convinced. Hitherto, the church has not been disturbed, except for the church wine taken. Countess Mimi Des Fours has not been actively molested, but as a last kind gesture from the Russian General, after having been billeted in Countess Mimi's villa. During the night she heard much whispering and shifting about, in the morning it was found that the General had decamped with a large portion of her belongings.

Another tragic event took place at the clinic of the local vet, Dr. Vodizhka (he was quite a friend of ours). Dr. Vodizhka and family left before the Russians came to Potstat and like all the other houses, his house and clinic were over-run. When I took the children for a little run, past his lane, it was a sorry sight to see bottles and medical tubes, large and small, half-squeezed out, lying along the lane and about his premises, but the great tragedy was that a drum of methylated spirits had been imbibed by the soldiers. Not very sensible, because when we went to the cemetery we found, next to the grave of the forester and family, a row of Russian graves. We could not read the memorial inscription, but being translated, it said simply: "Died for Folk and Motherland."

I agree with Count Des Fours, that mankind has many philosophies.

*****

Papali and Regina have packed their rucksacks. Anna washed socks and did stitching repairs for them. They leave at daybreak tomorrow and will hitchhike the sixteen kilometres to the station.

I have spoken to Papali about Heinrich, they will take him with them, so we have also packed some food for him and he has packed his large suitcase, a hold-all and a bag. What do they contain? He came to us emptyhanded. We are relieved to see that he seems almost happy to go. I hope he does not return tomorrow or the next day. Regina and Papali are very brave, may God protect them. There are ghastly stories circulating about the treatment of the German population by the Czech-Communist authorities. We do not know how true they are, or how any of our relatives are faring. I am chiefly concerned about my boys and Helene and her family. I have no peace.

Papali and Regina (with Heinrich, trundling his load) left at dawn. We feel desolate.

*****

The Russians seem to have a peculiarity of appropriating whatsoever comes their way. In other words, I think they are plain greedy. No one can think otherwise when they see the way the soldiers lay hands on things and with the next breath the article is unceremoniously thrown away — usually through the window. The usual aspiration is after watches and clocks and cheap gramophone records. Actually, we've noticed the simplest soldier seems to have some knowledge of carpets. For the rest, valuable furniture, whole libraries of books that could not be bought for love or money… like the library of Peskau… are ruthlessly thrown out and set alight. It is a usual sight, after the Russians leave a house, to see a group of villagers collecting articles beneath the windows. Fortunately, Count Des Fours' books remain in his library. But the two golden angels from the Chapel were thrown through the window. They lie in the courtyard, their pretty faces defaced and their spreading wings broken off. A sinful act.

After Papali and Regina left, we felt very miserable and cooped up in our wash-kitchen until we found that there are truly many wonderful people in the world and in Potstat we learned to know one of them in Mimi Des Fours. She comes across to see how we are faring and brings us the news and because she is not only a good doctor but also a good friend to the Czech people (who still have cows and pigs and fowls), she receives many gifts. I am sure that many of the gifts find their way to other unfortunates, but some of them find their way to our wash-kitchen, and I don't think Mimi has any left over.

*****

June, 1945

The Castle has been taken over by the *Narodne Vibo* (Czech Military Police). Events are moving rapidly; we must vacate our wash-kitchen. We wish to return to Kyjovice, but everything is still too uncertain. Count Des Fours thinks if Papali and Regina are not permitted to stay in Kyjovice, we should remain here a while longer and they can return to us. We searched about for a suitable residence. Count Des Fours suggested his porter's lodge, and got some village people to aid us in cleaning up the Russian mess. The locks have all been broken from the door. Never mind, my nails can be put in place with a steel bar across the door. It is such an unpretentious little house, leaning against the garden wall and sheltered by a huge chestnut tree and rendered more inconspicuous by comparison with the imposing structure of the castle so that troops passing by will not bother to look askance at it.

From the front door, a small passage terminates in a bath and toilet room. A small kitchen leads from the passage; it is complete with a little white stove. Adjoining the kitchen is a breakfast room and a bedroom. Our chief attraction is a tiny stairway leading up to a substantial loft that is light and airy and filled with fragrant hay. Our old porter predecessor evidently owned a pet goat or rabbits.

We relegated the hay to one side, scrubbed the floor and converted the loft into a bedroom. Count Des Fours has lent us some beds; they stand in a close row. We have sufficient room to hide our stores (under the hay) which is important. Eli, of course, has shifted in with us. He sleeps in the kitchen.

Words cannot describe the relief we felt on our first night in our new home away from the deadly stench of the latrines, the noise and nocturnal parading up and down the stairs and all the other disturbing elements in the Castle. We are fully aware of the danger our situation, but in this tiny house, we hope to be free from molestation. Eagerly we all anticipated the pleasure of sleeping in beds again!

I bathed the children, their prayers were short in their eagerness to get into bed, they both declared that a bed is more comfortable than a wash-trough! Then, for a long time, I sat at the open window and deeply breathed in the cool, sweet night air; once more the myriad stars seemed to smile as they looked down. I feel like a prisoner freed from his clanking chains. *Deo Gratias!*

And *Deo Gratias* again, the night was undisturbed.

The post seems to function again, but no word from Regina and Papali. I am sure Auntie Mother is more worried about them than words can say. I have casually said, "Maybe I'll go and look them up quite soon." By the grace of the dear Lord, I have three big items on my programme: a journey to Kyjovice; a journey in search of my boys; a journey in search of Helene and her children.

*****

The local communist leaders, Russians and Czechs, have not been able to locate Count Des Fours' secret safe; therefore, they ordered him to show them where to find it. He came over and asked me if I would accompany him when the safe is opened.

The men came at 3 o'clock in the afternoon — despicable looking characters, especially the sallow-faced Czech, and the Russian general with the militant moustaches. Count Des Fours was ordered to lead the way. When he took them to the room where the Czech officers have been sleeping, they were plainly very much surprised. Count Des Fours produced two different keys and then I was allowed to see no further for the sallow-faced Czech ordered me out.

"*Pritch, Pani!* — Out, Woman!" I was forced to leave.

I walked back to the cottage, and then I thought, "Surely, they will also ransack Count Des Fours' rooms, — his pantry, where I know he still has some silver, a lovely tea pot and other odd pieces — why should I not bring them across to us? But how to do so without attracting attention? As soldiers are continually walking to and fro?" I thought I'd better hurry, as it may not take the bandits very long to empty the safe. Looking around, I spotted our enamel bucket — hoping it will not look suspicious. I put a couple of towels in the bucket with a piece of soap on top, walked across the courtyard and up the stairs. The soldiers who passed me paid no attention; it did not take me long to collect the monogrammed silver and — in case I was questioned — I would lay personal claim to the crest and I could prove that "D. F." are also my initials. Luckily, no one took any notice of the innocent-looking washing with which I returned to our cottage. After quite a while, Count Des Fours came back to us looking very pale and shaken. The large secret safe is located under the wainscotting built into one of the bedroom walls and can only be opened with two different keys. When the safe was opened, the men gloated over the treasures — the solid silver toilette sets with large and small basins and jugs, etc. These the Russians immediately claimed and then they obligingly told the Czechs they could have the large kist with the linen.

They came upon a box with Count Des Fours' medals and keep-sakes which the Russian general grabbed. Count Des Fours asked to be allowed to keep the box, as it contained some of the things that one collects during a long life — there was a medal of distinction that would have to be returned after his death; a silk handkerchief that he had used to wipe the death-dews from his mother's face; there was the jewelled brooch; there was the diamond ring, a demure little ring that he had bought almost half-a-century ago; and a golden thimble. Count Des Fours, hoping that the Soviet hero would relent, showed him the letter he had in his pocket that the Russian prisoners of war had given him before they left, thanking him for having been a good master to them.

The Russian general read the note and said, "*Dobre, dobre!*" (good, good) but refused point blank to hand over the box. They went on with the ransacking until they pulled out a case of liquor. Count Des Fours had selected and saved up this case of liquor — so he said — especially so that towards the end, together with the choice volumes in his library, he would be able to live the old days over again until he fell asleep. The thieves smacked their lips, congratulated each other, and carried the case with the bottles into an adjoining room. The safe was locked up, and each of the two parties took one of the keys. The wily Czechs whispered, "Why did you not tell us you had this here? We would have acted differently...." They called for cups, toasted each other, and Des Fours was dismissed.

The setting sun shone low on the castle door before the heroes came staggering out. Their pockets bulged with bottles and, in addition, the sallow Czech carried a jar of conserved meat under his arm — the last jar that he had stolen from Count Des Fours' pantry. (I regretted not having brought it along with the silver, under my "laundry.") "But what characters," said Auntie Mother, as we watched them from our window. With a grunted "*Sobirayem*" (collecting) to each other, they went their several ways.

And now a little mock-comedy followed on the heels of this drama. The stocky Russian general staggered to his jeep. He climbed in and we hoped he would drive off, but no, he settled himself down, stretched out his legs and soon he was comfortably snoring. Auntie Mother looked anxiously at me — the jeep stood ten yards from our window and our door had no lock. I mumbled something to the effect that he slept like a baby and all is in order.

"Really!" said Auntie Mother innocently, "but if the man is a good Catholic then we may rest assured to-night. Dorothy, child, how do you know that the man is a Catholic? Did he cross himself?" And she solemnly crossed herself.

"Yes, yes," I said, although I was quite surprised, as I had not intimated anything to the effect that the man was Catholic. But Auntie Mother is rather deaf, and so the matter got happily misconstrued.

We had tea and I put the children to bed; and afterwards Anna brought in our "acquired" blue enamel pot with hot water for Auntie Mother to wash.

I barricaded the door as best I could with a few extra nails... and then, with a sinking feeling, I sat at the window and watched the jeep for a long time. The Czech soldiers, sitting in the courtyard of the castle, chatted and sang choruses harmonizing beautifully. Their voices, softly human and rather melancholy, came floating across to our window. I kept repeating *Aves* and I said to myself, "I am not afraid, I am only a little simple." However, I was distinctly relieved when I saw in the grey half-light a number of young Czech soldiers steal up to the jeep. Silently and rapidly, they shoved it along and left it standing in the shrubbery away on the opposite side of the park; whispering and sniggering, they returned to the courtyard to resume their singing, and I stole off to bed.

In the morning early, the "Catholic" general drove off.

How good it is to be like Auntie Mother, always to look for the best and find it in humanity.

*****

The Little White Hen

As our graces are strictly bachelor girls and carefree of family ties, and I think it necessary for us to have some young stock, I thought it a good idea to try to buy a broody hen and set her on a clutch of eggs.

"Where will you set her?" asked Anna, skeptical of my *hoender boerderei* (chicken farm).

"I've thought of that, Anna. The only safe place will be in our bedroom loft."

"*Meine Guete*! (my goodness)" said Anna, and again when I prepared a nest, placing the eggs in readiness with a box to put over the hen (should we be fortunate in obtaining one).

With Eli and the children, I set off to a distant peasant village somewhat off the beaten track where we hoped the poultry had not all been carried off. We took a footpath across the hills and we were delighted to see the unusual verdure of the hillsides. Wild thyme and sage spread inviting little cushions, while tall spiked thistles and *Koenigs Kerze* (king's candles) bloomed profusely in their own designated colours of purple and yellow. We did not venture to linger, as we must be home before dusk, and we walked with trepidation, as this was our first real outdoor venture. When we got to the village, I asked where Mrs. Messing lived, with whom we were acquainted. After being directed, we found her at home, and when I inquired from her if she knew where it was possible to obtain a broody hen, she said, "I have a hen sitting under the wood pile, but no eggs."

"I have eggs ready, but no hen." Mrs. Messing needed the money, and as I was in the act of counting it out to her, three Russians entered the room... an officer with the usual display of stars, and two of his men. The officer stepped up to me and unceremoniously took my purse out of my hand. Without hesitation, he opened it and started counting the coins.

"What are you doing?" I asked him in German, at the same time producing my flag, and then I held out my hand for the purse. He looked at the coins, hesitated a second, and then returned the purse to me. "And now my friend," I said, "what are your men doing here?" I saw that they had opened cupboards and were stacking crockery in two grain bags.

"Oh," he said, "we officers are having a party tonight and we need some crockery, we will return it tomorrow."

"Nonsense!" I said. "Not from my friends. Tell your men to go back to your camp." I assisted them in unpacking their sacks and was much relieved to see them walk out and get into their jeep. Our encounter had been brisk and short. It could have been otherwise. We waited until the jeep was out of sight, I paid Mrs. Messing for the little white hen that was brought out from under the wood pile, put her into our sack, also conveniently brought, and soon we were on our homeward way.

The children are calling the white hen "Dufa," after the white dove in the Icelandic "Nonnie" books. The transfer does not seem to have made any difference to Dufa, she sits quietly on her eggs in the corner.

"*Meine Guete!*" said Anna when eleven chicks were hatched.

After our successful adventure in buying the hen, we tried to buy some butter. On being told that the Russians were collecting large herds of cows in a nearby village prior to transporting them off to the Soviet Union, I decided to try to buy some butter, so our little party set off for the village. It is a criminal outrage that the Russians are collecting every beast from the starving German communities. I have seen animals that have always been stabled and well cared for brutally driven through Potstat; and now, as we walked, we saw suffering animals lying dying or dead along the pathway.

Numbers have foot-and-mouth-disease, while others are too weak and starved to lift their heads. There was nothing we could do to help them.

In the village, we asked someone to direct us to where the Russians milked the cows. "The Russians?" they answered. "You mean where the German girls have to milk them!"

We were directed to a once-wealthy peasant's *Hof* (barnyard). His living room had been converted into a dairy. German girls, looking most subdued, were diligently whizzing separators and churns. A Russian woman with newly frizzed hair, wearing high-heeled white satin shoes and trailing a white evening dress, directed operations. The bodice of the frock was far too low cut and too tight for her; she looked a frightful sight. And I felt out of place, especially when she seemed to stare malevolently at us. Nevertheless, to add a little weight to our request, I said that Eli is a Frenchman and that I came from South Africa. She came across and stood in front of us and seemed to rock on her high heeled shoes; her large bosom heaved (like a coffee percolator on the boil), then she said, pointing to Eli, "You are from France?" Eli was innocently delighted, he eyed her amorously — and I believe he was thinking, in Robert Browning's phrase, "Oh, the superb abundance of her bosom!"

"You can go back to France," she said unceremoniously, "and eat butter." Then pointing straight at me, she said, "You can go and eat butter in Africa. The Russians will eat all this butter!" She waved her hand across the great pats of butter on the table."And the Germans," she said, snapping her fingers at the German girls, "will get nothing at all!!" She turned her back on us, trailing the white evening frock across the dirty floor, to give her directions from the other side of the room. We got no butter, so we soothed our hurt feelings by collecting some wild spinach on our homeward way. When we told Auntie Mother about the woman, I agreed with her, that she is indeed a character.

*****

12 June, 1945
The Birthday Lunch

Tomorrow will be Auntie Mother's birthday. Anna has baked a wholesome-looking honey cake using our last jar of beet syrup. I must try to obtain some victuals and, if possible, meat; I feel reluctant to kill one of our graces, they are laying, each brown egg so eagerly welcomed.

*****

13 June, 1945

Truly, an egg a day keeps the axe away. Fortunately, yesterday I had a good idea. We took a basket and went into the forest for a walk. Count Des Fours accompanied us; he showed us one of his favourite paths through the forest and led us to where wild strawberries grow, then he helped us to collect a small basket full of ripe, aromatic berries; for a while his spirits lifted, he became relaxed and communicative and very kindly. We walked on a bit further and then, not far from where the strawberries grow, Count Kuno pointed to some white objects and he said: "Those look like... champignons?" The children ran to investigate. True! Fresh, meaty champignons!

We arrived home a little breathless, and a little drunk from the fresh air; our treasures, which include a bunch of wild thyme, some blue-bells and dog-roses, are put out of sight, as they are to be a surprise for Auntie Mother.

Early this morning the table was laid for breakfast. Countess Mimi brought us some butter from some of her Czech friends; the table was decorated with a bowl of wild flowers, and graced with a brown egg for each of us. Auntie Mother's place looked festive with a wreath of flowers and leaves around her plate. Dear Auntie Mother is touchingly grateful for our small efforts to make this a happy day. If only we had news from her loved ones! She has thanked us graciously for our good wishes and for the jug of blue-bells and tall grasses on the window sill. But she is sad, much more so than she will ever acknowledge, at not hearing from the absent ones and I am more worried than I can say, because surely, if possible, today they would have sent news! I must set out without delay for Kyjovice. Oh and I must find my boys!

Dear Father in Heaven, bless them and help me to find them safe and secure!

I asked Countess Mimi and Count Des Fours to come for 11 o'clock tea. Auntie Mother and Countess Mimi are two dauntless, strong people and their prayers give me strength.

Afternoon

Our birthday lunch was a success, and no wonder! for many hands made light work. We each took part in the preparations. Eli, wearing his indispensable beret and his crooked French smile, busily chopped a big handful of food ably assisted by Ilona and Petty. And then they peeled potatoes. Anna picked some fresh young dandelion leaves and washed them carefully, while I fried champignons and potatoes. Auntie Mother made the mayonnaise, she sparingly took a spoonful of oil, a gift from Mimi, one egg yolk, and some vinegar and mustard, Petty brought her the big wooden spoon, and drop by drop, they made a mixture in which they tossed and stirred the leaves; we were lavish in admiration! So to add extra flavour, they add extra fervor, tossing and stirring the salad. Anna had the strawberries ready, and as a surprise, some goat milk cream, from a village friend. So all acted what we only remotely felt (except Ilona and Petty): *en jolie compagnie.*

Afterwards, Auntie Mother gave me a little slip of paper with these words: "White Dove of Peace, Great God of Consolation, Brood over the souls that moan in tribulation, and with the whisper of serene tomorrows, soothe all their sorrows." Yes, one day we'll know those Serene Tomorrows, but meanwhile, only God can shelter the souls that moan in tribulation. It was from one of Auntie Mother's teachers that she learned the sense of these lines a long time a-gone.

If I could write a song of triumph about a flower, it would be about a very modest one that few pause to admire, but that some of the great ones... Duerer among them... has exalted in his "Little bit of meadow." It must have been some forgotten scientist who thought that the leaves — long, slender and rugged, reminded him of the teeth of a lion, so he called the plant *"Loewen Zahn," "Dent de Leon,"* "Dandelion...". It was this same dandelion that we enjoyed as salad, and we also got our main source of vitamin, a very real need at present.

As I sat at 'our' little loft window last night, I marvelled again at our "Threads of Loveliness" in God's great web: the moon high up in the starry heavens, a warm little wind that came floating up to me... with all the voices and atmosphere of summer, crickets that chirped under the chestnut tree, my children speaking quietly to each other in their new bedroom. The world seemed to have grown almost sober again. And there and then, I decided, sober or not, I must set out for Kyjovice. It is not yet our "true safety, our serene tomorrows," but Anna must pack the red hold-all.

I am glad to leave the children in Auntie Mother's care; in her quiet influential way, she strives to put first things first. Don't let them have everything they want. The body must remain subject to the will of God; instill it in them, drill it in them; don't give them everything they wish for, she almost implored me.

On another occasion she said: "Remember, you have a duty: they must learn that they have a responsibility towards one another and to our neighbour. It is a poor kind of family which lives only for itself and considers that it owes nothing to its neighbour."

At last, a letter from Regina. Then she is safe, I thought. Half fearfully I stared at the letter. Yes, she is safe, but the address written to me is strange... foreign. Can this be my name? I have never seen it written this way before. *Pani* Dorote Prazmova; is it a detachable name, must I cultivate it and wear it like a cloak? I stared at the envelope wondering why it is necessary for Regina to change my name and why has she not written to Auntie Mother. My thoughts flew to Papali. I ripped open the letter!

"At last I can write to you. By the grace of God, we are safe and in Kyjovice. Papali has been rather ill; he arrived here after ten days. I got here sooner. The house is bare; as we feared, everything is looted. We have no authority. We sleep in the green suite, we have beds but no blankets. In this suite it seems to be safer and somewhat cleaner. For the present, we are tolerated by authorities.

"Peasants and villagers truly wonderful. Write if you receive this, to *Pani* Amelia Hrovatova; Milka is as safe as a rock and quite well, then I'll write to mother.

"I embrace you all dearly. R.S."

A very distressing letter, but they are safe! They have friends in the village, and Milka, Regina's old ladies-maid, has not been influenced by the new rulers.

I must take blankets and food to Kyjovice and then I must act. Yes, I must act. My boys!

Anna and Auntie Mother have packed the red hold-all and a valise with blankets, groceries and candles, and I have packed my rucksack. The old man with a pot-footed horse will take me to Hranice Station, where I hope to catch a train. I do not intend being away longer than necessary. I know how eagerly Auntie Mother will look forward to news of her beloved Kyjovice... perhaps a couple of days. Count Kuno will keep a vigilant eye on the house and Eli will carefully look after the household and children. He seems to be more courageous now that the Russians have left. And so I return to Kyjovice.

With my rosary in my pocket, I am ready. Auntie Mother, Count Kuno and my little ones stood at the gate to see me off. "God speed," they said. The day was warm and homely, but like an explorer on a great adventure, I had not a few misgivings. Will I be allowed to buy a ticket to board the train? Will Kyjovice be full of Russians? There was the red hold-all and my rucksack looking more conspicuous and seeming to grow larger and heavier as they lay at the bottom of the cart.

The ancient pot-footed horse stepped out bravely. We plodded along. It only took us two hours to travel the sixteen kilometers to Hranice. The driver told me to speak English and not German when buying the ticket; I did so, but had to resort to German to be understood. The ticket was issued without comment.

All stations and trains are crammed with Russian soldiers. I fancied everyone was eyeing my red hold-all. At Svinov I took the rucksack on my back and the hold-all on my shoulder and walked across to the Kleinbahn Station. Numbers of factory workers on the train seemed to recognize me and stared with friendly curiosity. The train was crowded, but two of the men kindly made room for me. Arriving at Kyjovice Station, these two helped me to alight and then insisted upon carrying the pack the four kilometres up the hill to the village; it would have been impossible for me to carry it alone, so I accepted their kind offer. One of the young men is a blacksmith from Polom (one of Uncle Fritz's villages). Almost confidentially, he told me, "I am strong! I am not afraid of lifting an ox!" By which, I think he meant to say, he is not afraid of communist opinion. He also said he would be glad if Regina or I would help him to write a letter to America, to the relatives of the American pilot Howard Schmidt, whose grave is in Kyjovice.

The young man set the bags down at the back door. There seemed to be no one about. I was relieved not to see any strangers, but my heart was beating... I was afraid of entering the house, I felt like stranger! I stood at the door. I looked around and then I saw a man coming down the garden path carrying a load of wood. It took some moments for me to recognize... Papali!

He wore a brown Hessian apron and with a neatly grown beard (not grown previously) he looked as if he had stepped out of a picture of St. Joseph. I embraced him... wood and all! How dear he is to me! We carried wood and bags into the house, packed out the groceries and made coffee. Regina came in from the garden, she has been ordered to do manual work with the maids. The garden work is a great strain on her and her poor hands look dreadful, but her auburn hair still has the lovely lights of a brand new penny.

It was late before we got to bed, all three in the Green Suite. There was much to relate, all tragic. The servants, with the exception of the Czechs, have all been put in forced labour camps; Joseph the butler and his only son are dead. Franz is believed to be dead... poor kind little Franz. Otto Stolberg, Papali's cousin, is dead... whipped and starved to death. His wife Countess Herma is in a forced labour camp. It is not known where the children are. The Potstatzkis are said to be in a labour camp. Nothing has been heard of Helene and her babies. Baron Gemmel is dead, they also fled from home and were overtaken on a bridge by the Russians. Everything they had was looted, including Auntie Mother's parcel. And so on and on....

When Papali and Regina tried to return to Kyjovice, they had been ordered off the train and were interrogated by the police. Their rucksacks were taken from them and they were both put into labour camps; then, fortunately, the local shoemaker Mr. Drastik, by some unknown means, got to know of their whereabouts. Together with some of the local peasants, they valiantly applied to the *Vibo* (police) to get them tried in Kyjovice. Regina was sent home after some days, but Papali, who has never been strong, was kept in the camp with about twenty other men. They had to unload coal at the station and were barely kept alive by receiving a slice of dry bread and some watery potato soup twice a day.

After ten days Papali was too weak and ill to continue the labour, and was discharged. Again, the good samaritan, Mr. Drastik was at hand... he slipped some money into Papali's hand, which enabled him to struggle on to Svinov, where, beyond recognition, black with coal dust and with a harsh growth of beard, he was taken in by the priest.

"Here," Papali reiterated, "wearied to death, I enjoyed the best bath of my life."

In the *lager*, among all those men, they had received one basin of water where with to wash themselves. This meant that when it came to the last man's turn to wash, scarcely a few drops of filthy water remained in the basin.

But he added simply: "I want to forget about it all, and further... there is no hope of us remaining under this communist set-up." And I would like to forget the sad state of affairs I found when I had time to look around, the next morning. But a few things hit me so forcibly that I can never forget them. The first is the chapel — it was literally used by the Russians as a lavatory. All the vestments that for generations have been reverently cared for, lie trampled in the filth on the floor... never to be used again. When Auntie Mother heard about the chapel, it brought scalding tears to her eyes... the only time I have ever seen her weep.

The other things are of lesser importance, but they tugged at my heart. All our store of treasures that had been carefully and secretly masoned up in the cellar were discovered by the Russian soldiers. They had entered the cellar by digging a hole through the wall and they took everything they fancied... silver, pictures, knick-knacks and ornaments — with what remained, treasured books, pictures, and Missals, they made a bonfire in the cellar, where the charred heap remains.

Outside, I passed a rubbish heap and there I saw, lying among stacks of broken crockery and glass, the crystal prisms of the beautiful chandeliers. On the lawn, the lovely old spreading, enfolding, old pine tree, the one nearest the house, was struck down by a heavy artillery shell. The massive trunk lies splintered on the lawn. If the shell had not been intercepted, a large portion of the house would lie in ruins; so the big old tree that had harboured the fowls of the air, to whose strong black shade we had fled from the tennis court when Russian planes buzzed overhead, has fallen and saved the house which, but for the broken window panes, stands intact... but very lonely, with only the colourful company of the purple-leaved smoke plant that has survived and holds a truce, like a time-honoured philosopher, puffing his pipes and making the best of this sadly changed world.

I was glad to see Zdenka's house intact, as many of the houses in the village are in ruins. Zdenka looked different from her old self, but like an old friend she greeted me. "*Frau Graefini*, I am so glad to see you! And you truly are alright? And our *Frau Graefini*, how is she? And the children, are they alright?"

"Zdenka, we are truly all alright, except that I do not know where Lekkie and Peter are. Tell me about yourself and your mother and your little boy. Are you all alright? We have always remembered you in all our prayers."

And said pretty Zdenka, who looked so different, "I also have said many Our Fathers for you all and how many Signs of the Cross? Believe me!" And she continued: "*Frau Graefini*, did you manage to save your large cabin trunk that you took with you?" Zdenka was glad to hear that our belongings had not been looted. She said, "If your belongings had been left in Kyjovice, they would also have been placed on Russian trucks that were loaded high from our village. You see what the castle looks like?

"And our house," she continued, "such a cleaning we did have, because it stank like our cowshed when our cow has eaten wet clover. You know we had the German soldiers for months in the village; those that were billeted in our house used to help us with cleaning and fixing things and even on the last day before the Russians entered, they came to look for us in the forest to give us the ration cards. The next day, the Russians marched in and their stink is still everywhere!"

Indeed, the stink is everywhere. Here, like in all villages, the fallen Russians are being exhumed, German women and girls are told to lift the bodies with long iron forks. They are placed in large black boxes and carted off to be buried in a soldiers' graveyard. (For the German fallen, whose comrades had whittled little crosses, they were mostly buried along the forest paths where they had fallen. The crosses are now ruthlessly pulled up and burnt). I would rather wish my body to rest where an old tree may gather sap and strength for its roots.

"But the Russians, *Frau Graefini*," continued Zdenka, "they slapped my bottom and said, '*Krasna*, you sleep with me tonight and I'll sleep with you tomorrow.' I was so bewildered, I had to sleep under my mother's bed." And Zdenka still looks bewildered.

From visiting Zdenka, I went to visit other friends in the village, where I was made welcome. They had much the same story to tell as Zdenka. Fortunately, with few exceptions, horses and cows were not taken from them (apparently, Russians did enough looting from the German communities). It was now my opportunity to enquire if it would be possible to hire a conveyance to bring us back to Kyjovice. Franticzek, to whom I spoke, agreed to come and fetch us himself. He was ready to start off almost at once. I explained that I first intended to go and search for my boys and then we would give him word. I hitchhiked back most of the way to Potstat. Anna wanted to start packing immediately, and Ilona and Petty were very much prepared to catch the chickens and put them in a box.

"Not yet, not yet," I said, "I must first try to find Lekkie and Peter." The family were not in agreement and grew restless and Eli also grows restless.

*****

10 July, 1945

Yes, Eli becomes restless, he wants to return to France not to eat butter, but because he must return to the girl he left behind.

When he told me his intentions, I felt quite a pang.

"Eli," I said, "she must wait a while longer, as I must first find my children... it may not take long, but I may have to travel a long way... it may take me weeks."

Since that vivid dream of meeting Stalin, I do not believe they are in Russia — but I can still see those dreary, desolate landscapes before me, through which I passed in my dream. I said imploringly, "Eli, stay with us please; you can return home when I get back."

Eli seeing my distress readily consented to look after Auntie Mother, Ilona and Petty until I return. He looked kindly at me and said, "*Je comprende tres bien.*"

In my rucksack, I have packed a few small items... the usual things, towel, soap, handkerchiefs, aspirin, toothbrush, a shawl to tie around my head if the nights are cold. Of course, my loden-coat accompanies me. For *padkos*, (road food) I have my skimpy piece of *biltong* and a packet of *harde-beskuit* (hard-tack).

On the 17th of July it will be my Peter's birthday, what can I take for him? I have nothing. I must endeavour to find a gift for both boys.

At the postern gate, where the long flight of stairs leads down to the main road, Auntie Mother and Count Des Fours, both looking pale and distressed, stood with my two little ones to see me off.

My load was heavy as I added the three pounds of sugar the German soldiers gave me. The sugar is all that I have to take for my boys, and I'll carry it through fire and smoke!

*****

11 July, 1945

At Hranice, I managed to board the overcrowded train. I had to stand most of the way to Prague, where I arrived at daybreak. It was too early to get in touch with Leopoldine Princess Lobkowicz, so I had a wash and sat in the waiting room until I could call 47647. Her husband, Rembert, answered and said, "Come up."

Eight o'clock found me at Prague, section 111, where I had another wash and a brush up. Both Rembert and Leopoldine were most solicitous, inviting me to share their frugal breakfast. Afterwards, they directed me to the American Embassy, which is also conveniently situated in Prague 111. They were not optimistic about me obtaining the desired permission to cross over to Germany; however, they said, "Try your luck."

First I went to the British Embassy. Consul Hanow was sympathetic but regretted being unable to assist me, particularly as Regensburg, to where I felt inexplicably drawn, is in the American Zone (A.M. Zone).

At the American Embassy, I waited my turn in a queue of anxious people; when my turn came, one of the gentlemen saw me alone in a large room. The interview lasted about two minutes. I heard only two words: "Sorry, impossible." I was not even given the chance to explain my request, for he had turned on his heel and I was left standing alone. Desperately I cried after him, "I must find my children! I must get over the border!" My voice seemed to echo through the vast hall.

After the long months of waiting and suspense, I was violently shaken by this disappointment.

Once more I was out in the glaring sunlight, my eyes ached, I felt as if I was bleeding from an internal hemorrhage. I longed for a cool place where I could weep and pray. I walked aimlessly. "Angel by my side, walk with me." I walked for a few more steps and found myself in front of the great St. Nicholas church. The interior of the church was cool, deserted and as silent as a tomb. I entered by the wide open doors and sank down.

Some time later, when I lifted my head, I felt tranquil. Only my eyes ached. Again I implored: "Angel by my side, walk with me."

In spite of the heat, there were many people on the street; as I hurried along, a woman stopped me. "I saw you in the church," she said softly in German. "Can I help you?"

"I have been turned away from the British Embassy and from the Americans, where I tried to obtain the necessary permission to cross over to Germany," I said. "My children have been lost since January and I am trying to find them; meanwhile, so much has happened."

"Why do you not try to make it from Pilsen?" she said. "It should not be difficult to slip over once you are on the border!"

"Thank you," I said, "thank you again." And I hurriedly started off on the first stage of my journey to Pilsen.

I hastily called to collect my rucksack at the Lobkowicz Palais. I said farewell to Rembert, who was alone at home. Rembert was plainly distressed at my intention of travelling alone.

He said seriously, "Consider that all the riff-raff of the Continent has been turned loose in this poor country and you are not likely to get the permission to travel to Pilsen, which means that you will be turned back halfway, that will be very unpleasant. No," he shook his head, "these are not normal times, you cannot do it."

"Rembert, yes, these are not normal times, so one does not do normal things… I must be off!"

"Stay a minute," he said, "while I look up a train for you. At 2:00 o'clock, the fast train leaves and arrives at Pilsen at 10:30 tonight. Good luck and God bless you…." he called after me.

I caught a tram to the station by a hair's breadth, and within seconds of my arrival at the station, I was at the counter asking for a ticket to Pilsen. "Have you a permit?" asked the young man as he stamped the ticket. "But I fear the train is leaving," he added, "it is 2:00 o'clock." "Yes, yes, hurry please!" Thank the Lord — he did not insist upon seeing the permission.

On the platform, the fast train was already in motion. Some Czech soldiers hurriedly cleared the way, some others hastily drew me up. And I was on the fast train to Pilsen.

After recovering my breath and straightening my hair, I realized that I had indeed been motivated beyond the limits of my phlegmatic nature, a power vouchsafed to me by the angel by my side and the counsel given to me by the soft-spoken greyhaired woman.

I looked for a seat. Some way down I saw a vacant seat amongst some soldiers. They wore the wide beret and khaki uniforms of the unit newly returned from England. I sat down and felt that I was among friends. I spoke to the young men in English, likewise they spoke some lively words in English, and by the time they opened their baskets of sandwiches and fruit... having spoken together, we knew quite a lot about each other. The soldiers encouraged me to think that if I made a stout effort, I should surely be able to cross the border, so now, for the first time since walking down that long flight of stairs at Potstat, I felt I could relax. I sighed, "So, *ja*," deeply, gratefully.

When the summer afternoon was well advanced, the train started slowing down — and drew up. "Now don't be nervous," said the soldier sitting next to me, "the authorities board the train here to look for unauthorised persons." Two Russian examiners came walking through the compartments; when they reached us, the soldiers laughingly teased them and said, "We have got nothing here to show you, you go next door and look at the pretty girls." Good-humouredly, and without asking for my pass, they went next door.

Now followed two Czech examiners. They took their duty seriously, clipping, examining, and commenting. Meanwhile, the soldiers had invited me to share their refreshments. The examiners, no doubt concluding that I was associated with the soldiers, passed us by with a few casual words. When the train was getting up speed again, I ventured to look out of the window. I realized how fortunate I was when I saw the long queue of people being conducted away from the platform, and I was deeply grateful to my angel and to the soldiers.

Again they invited me to partake of their sandwiches. I also had to assist them to eat their fruit; red and black currants. "But these biscuits," they said, "you must take to your boys." Thinking of Peter's birthday, it did not take much persuasion for me to put the little packet of homemade biscuits in my rucksack. Later, they asked me if I was acquainted with anybody in Pilsen — they suggested that I get in contact with the American Military Police, who patrol all platforms in the A.M. Zone.

When we eventually arrived in Pilsen, the first people I noticed on the platform were the military policemen in their pudding-shaped helmets. The soldiers had to hurry away, but they first introduced me to a policeman as a South African lady, and they added, "You will know how to assist her." Then, with a friendly "*Dobre noc,*" good night, my good samaritans went their way.

The young policeman was plainly worried as to what to do with me, so he fetched a colleague. Together, they decided to take me to the British Consulate. I objected, as it was very late now, 11:00 o'clock.

"Can I not stop at a hotel?"

"We will take you to the consulate and nowhere else," they announced. Their jeep — the first one I had seen except those the Russians arrived in and we had assumed were Russian cars — stood ready at hand. And it took only a few minutes to arrive at the consulate, where they peremptorily knocked at the door and when it was opened, they unceremoniously announced, "Here, we have brought you a woman, a British subject."

The consul gravely thanked them for their trouble and invited me in. I felt most embarrassed and immediately the door was closed on them. I tried to explain my presence. "I am not a British subject." And I went on to tell him about my search for my children.

"Don't worry," said the consul soothingly, "I believe I can help you. In a couple of day's time I shall have to send a car to Germany…. Perhaps I can fix you up," and then he apologized for the absence of his young ladies, saying, "They have gone to the theatre, but I will make you a cup of tea." If a few letters can spell one word to put a person magically at ease, then surely it is the word, "Tea."

With his offer, I accepted my situation. "But may I please make the tea?" His Excellency took me to the kitchen, lit the gas, and showed me where to find things, and then left me to the job, saying he would also appreciate a cup of tea, if I would bring it to his office. Soon, however, he returned with a plate of bananas and oranges.

"You will enjoy these, if you are from South Africa," he said. They were indeed a good sight for tired eyes.

His Excellency showed me a tiny bedroom and bathroom.

On this night in Pilsen, old Father Time's ever-rolling stream hurried along in galloping presto, for no sooner did I seem to float away on a cloud, my head on the soft English pillow, and the angel by my side, then it was time to be up; church bells were ringing some little distance away, I hurried to attend Mass. Afterwards I seemed to be so much nearer to my boys. When I got back to the consulate, the young ladies had prepared breakfast for me. They asked me many questions and I asked myself, "What may this day hold in store for me?" After breakfast, I went to the American Consulate, where I only wasted my time, for I was politely informed, "There are millions of persons misplaced in Germany depending on our authority for food and transport. We cannot, therefore, permit anybody to cross over the border."

"That is ridiculous," I said, "How then can I find my children?"

"You do not expect us to help you also?" said the official in charge.

"Then you are not prepared to assist me? Good bye!"

A woman who was dusting the room accompanied me to the door. Timidly, she said in German, "Why don't you try U.N.R.R.A. (The United Nations Relief and Rehabilitation Administration)?" I thanked her and from the first person I met outside, I inquired my way to U.N.R.R.A. "Straight along the street, pass the bombed out buildings and the beer factory, and a short ways out of town you'll see the barracks." Innumerable Jeeps and trucks were travelling to and fro. Soon, I located the UNRRA barracks, where two white-starred trucks stood ready to depart. People sat crowded on both of them.

"Where are you off to?" I called to one of the drivers.

"To Muenchen!" came the reply.

"Please, take me with you."

"Alright lady, get up."

"No," I said, "I must first obtain permission. Where is your officer?" The officer readily gave me his permission.

"Hurry," he said kindly, "they are leaving soon."

"But I shall first have to return to the British Consulate for my belongings." And what was most important, I wanted to get a note from the British Consulate to enable me to return to Czechoslovakia — I was getting used to red tape.

The officer considered and then called to one of his men, to whom he said, "Take this lady to the British Consulate, and hurry, as she is leaving for Germany."

Am I really? I thought as I got into the Jeep.

Back at the consulate the young ladies greeted my re-appearance with pleasure and while I hastily gathered my ruck-sack, the Consul prepared this cautiously worded note:

> To whom it may concern:
> Mrs. Dorothy Praschma is
> authorised to proceed to Weiden for the
> purpose of visiting her sons and
> returning them to Pilsen.
>   (signature) Acting Consul.
> 12th July, 1945

"Farewell, good luck," they said as I thanked them all. I did not have a chance of thanking the officer at the U.N.R.R.A. barracks, as the trucks were about to leave. I got myself up and sat uncomfortably on the hard floor-boards of the truck among the crowd of misplaced persons and their numerous bundles. They spoke in various languages, but they spoke very little, for refugees are people who have learned to act and not to speak. They had many wishes but seemed to have no definite plans or purpose, and meanwhile, they were all just intent on getting down to Munich. I did not want to go to Munich, I only wanted to get across the border and I still had grave misgivings of getting across without the necessary permit.

There were fleets of trucks on the road, but I did not see one German vehicle. Our two trucks kept together and we travelled for what seemed to me to be a great distance. Surely, we must have crossed the border? Indeed, we had, and without a challenge! I breathed freely, for I was beyond the Iron Curtain. But no, I must attract the driver's attention and ask him to put me down. I did not intend going to Munich, I was inexplicably drawn to Regensburg.

On and on we travelled through Bavaria's magnificently wooded and peacefully domesticated landscape. Eventually, on a bare stretch of road, the trucks drew up and we were invited to stretch our legs... it was necessary!

Refreshments were handed around — a large tin of thin jam and a tin of water biscuits. I asked the driver to put me down at the next cross roads.

"Indeed!" he said, "I have my orders to take you all down to Munich, and to Munich you are going."

"Munich is a lovely old city, but I am searching for my children and I want to start my search from Regensburg."

"No," he said stubbornly, "I am taking you to Munich. Tomorrow I will take you back to Pilsen and you can start travelling out with a lorry to Regensburg."

This was the last thing I wanted to happen, as quite likely, I would not get another chance of slipping over the border so easily again. He interrupted my thoughts and said, "It's devilishly hot — at Munich we can have a glass of beer together." He eyed me and wiped his steaming face with his hand. "Okay!" I said, as I saw that further argument was useless.

Some people on the other lorry came over and spoke to us. I mingled with them and when it was time to start, I climbed on to the other vehicle. Then — asked this driver to put me down at the next cross roads. "Oh, no!" he drawled, "I cannot put a lady down on the road. It's dangerous, you know, there are all kinds of people travelling on the roads."

"Never mind," I said, "I am an old soldier and I am trying to find my children. Please, just put me down."

The first lorry had already started and we hurried after. On and on we travelled. I became desperate, thinking that he had forgotten. But suddenly he drew up and I slipped off. They travelled on, leaving a trail of dust. I looked to left and right and felt very desolate. I did not want to take the wrong road when I could and should take the right road. "Angel by my side, please direct me to the left or to the right."

In the hazy distance, I saw a village. It seemed a good direction. I walked to the village… a very sleepy village in the noon day's heat. I did not see a living soul about, so I knocked at the door of a house next to the Church. It was opened by a young priest. He invited me in. After drinking a few glasses of water and washing my hands, I asked him which would be the best way of getting to Regensburg. He said that from a station about six kilometers distant, a train left that evening at 8:00

o'clock and would arrive at Regensburg at 2:00 o'clock in the morning. Cars and horses from the village had all been requisitioned by the American Army, so — perforce — I was obliged to start walking at once.

It was dusk when I arrived at the little station, no tea room, nothing; I sat down and gnawed at my biltong and had one harde beskuit. In due time, the train arrived. I was disillusioned with the picture I had had in mind of a comfortable seat in the train which consisted only of flat, open trucks used for transporting timber. To make matters worse, a chilly wind was blowing and it looked like rain. I was assured that this was the only train, all others had been bombed out or had been taken into the service of the American Army. I was not alone, there were crowds of refugees with bundles and also some children. We travelled shivering under the stars of heaven in the open trucks. I was thankful that I had thought of bringing my cashmere shawl for my head and my old loden coat.

Duly at 2:00 o'clock we arrived at Regensburg. I had made up my mind to have a wash and sit in the waiting room on my arrival. Again, I was disappointed. This was not the Regensburg station that I knew. We arrived to find everything in total darkness. The station had been bombed out; we groped our way among the debris. With rain drops falling, I sat on a block of cement until it got light. Then, feeling the imperative need for a wash, I looked around for some water, but the taps were all smashed; it was good to get away from that once clean, trim station. I walked down to the Danube. Soon I found a place where I could dip out some water. I washed my hands and face, and though I began to feel desperately ill and thirsty, but I did not dare to drink any water.

The bridge over the Danube into the city had been destroyed by retreating S.S. troops; now a stretch of rickety planks joined two sections which we had to negotiate. The river gurgled and eddied many feet below and I feared I would be precipitated into the water, but I braved it. I wanted to attend early Mass, which I did at the Carmelite Church. After Mass I decided to make immediate inquiries regarding the whereabouts of the nuns from Juliasberg. I came out of the church feeling really ill. After walking a short distance, I saw a nun hurrying along the opposite street. I felt a very imperative need to speak to her. As if my very life depended upon her, I hurried across the intervening space. My rucksack bobbing up and down on my back, I was breathless when I caught up with her.

"*Liebe Schwester* (dear Sister), I must talk to you, I have come a long way, from Prague." She did not beat about the bush. "Come to our convent," she said kindly. "It is just a short way down the road."

She opened the gate and we entered. Meanwhile, by her habit, I had already noticed that she belonged to the *Arme Schul-Swestern Orden* (Order of the Poor Schoolteachers), the same as our Juliasberg nuns. I first asked her for some medicine — I had a splitting headache and felt an attack of dysentery coming on. In a tiny room, the nun bade me lie down while she fetched me a cup of mint tea and some tablets. Afterwards, bringing me more mint tea, she said, "You can drink a gallon of this, it will clean and soothe and rest your nerves," she said. I then took two of my aspirins and went to sleep.

When I awoke, I felt quite better. Some more mint tea and a slice of toast, and I was telling her of my search for my boys and that I was trying to trace the nuns from Juliasberg. She did not know their whereabouts, but assured me that a nun was expected that same evening who belonged to their community and would be sure to know where these nuns had taken refuge. So I had to be patient and wait until evening. I washed my stockings and underwear and sat under a tree in the convent garden. Several nuns came and spoke to me. Everybody was anxious to know how we had fared under the Russians. They told me that although there were many untoward happenings in the American Zone, they had a great fear that the Americans would withdraw and the Russians would take further possession.

The nuns then told me about the bombardment and the surrender of Regensburg, how the inevitable S.S. and the *Partei* were determined that city would not surrender, how — although bombs were falling and shots were fired — the population of Regensburg bravely came out into the streets calling for surrender and peace. This continued until a young priest tried to address the people, hoping to persuade them to go home. He stood up on the sidewalk, lifted his hands and said: "My people...." but he got no further, he was arrested by the Gestapo and immediately strung up by them on one of the church buildings. The shocked and distressed people of Regensburg went to their homes (taking the example of the young priest... hanging in full view of the passers-by on the church wall) to pray for surrender and peace.

Meanwhile the American Army advanced. The S.S. decided that the city would be defended street by street and house by house; they blew up the old stone bridge, seriously damaging many of the fine old buildings and churches. When night came, a mighty battle was fought. The terrified nuns huddled together and prayed in the cellar. They were saying to each other, "Our city is a city of the dead," but the Reverend Mother comforted them and said, "Only if God allows, may He bless and deliver our city this night."

The nuns continued, "Thus she comforted, while we prayed in the musty cellar with the air reverberating with artillery fire. At dawn the cannonading ceased, and then the nuns plucked up courage to view the ruins of the ancient city. All eyes were turned to the steeple of the church, but we rubbed our eyes — for the church was untouched.

"We looked to left and right — there was no evidence of destruction anywhere! Not a stone seemed to have been touched. All the bombardment had been blank shots. Rejoicing, the people came out into the streets. The *Partei* and the S.S. were still determined to fight! Therefore, with fireworks cracking overhead, we endured another night of suspense, we could not know if they were bombs or blanks. Many rumours were circulating, but everyone was asking the same question: 'How long will the Americans have patience?' Nobody slept, we huddled and prayed, people all felt they could not endure much longer.

"With the dawn there was an eerie peace again. Like ghosts, the people crept out of the shelters and cellars to find — the Lord be praised — that the S.S., the *Partei*, and the Gestapo had fled!"

This is what the nuns told me while I waited under the linden tree in the fair city of Regensburg, a city of great and glorious history called the pearl in the bright string of gems that adorn the Danube's banks. Regensburg derives its name from the river Regen; ancient roadways lead down the valleys of three rivers: the Nab on the north, the Danube and the Regen from the south. Where the rivers meet and merge and the roadways cross, arises the city of Regensburg.

Here, history recedes into the mists of ages; stone implements and weapons have been found that were fashioned by men some 2,000 to 3,000 years before the Birth of Christ. It was about the year 14 B.C. that the Romans extended their settlements to the Danube. Away to the eastward ran their great military road via Militaris Augustana, leading to Straubing and further along the Danube. For four centuries the Romans held sway, ably checking wild tribes of fierce ruthless warriors who descended on them from primeval forests and mountains. But other tribes always followed on, until the settlements of the Romans fell before their onslaughts, and very little now remains of the walls and castles built by the Romans. Ultimately among these wild lawless people came venturing the monk Saint Bonifacius with a little band of followers; where the strength of the Romans had failed, the Cross succeeded. And in the year 300 A.D., Regensburg bloomed again.

But with the passing of centuries, other conflicts raged around the walls of the city. An array of barons, knights, dukes, princes, kings, kaisers, emperors, also a few counts and bishops thrown in, warred, outlawed, plotted and had their quarrels. Among them was Charlemagne, greatest of the Franks, with his Paladins. At a later date came another historic figure: Friedrich Barbarossa (the man with the red beard), whose numbers camped outside the walls of Regensburg. One and all of them wore a white cross emblazoned on their shields — The Crusaders!

Suddenly it was dark in the room and I began to be fearful that the nun would not arrive. But then my good little Sister came in with mint tea and something for me to eat and said that the Sister I was waiting for had arrived. After tea, I went down to speak to her and met one of the most beautiful women I have ever seen.

"We have word from our Sisters," she told me. "At present they are at a place called Thyrnau, in a Cistercian Convent, on the Austrian border. It is about eight kilometres from Passau. We have not heard if they have any boys with them. To our knowledge, they had endeavoured to leave, or send the children to their parents."

This was very distressing news for me. Unfortunately, communicating lines between Regensburg, Passau, and Thyrnau had been destroyed. The Sister told me I could travel a short distance by boat then by train. For the rest, I would have to hitchhike.

With the first red streaks in the sky, I was on my way. The low land still smoked and the mist was on the river when I caught the first train and travelled to the terminus. Here I was fortunate to persuade the American police to stop one of their cars and give me a lift. This was kindly done contrary to regulations; civilians not being allowed to travel in army cars. They took my as far as Plattling. Here I stood at the roadside hoping that I would be fortunate again. Meanwhile, fleets of jeeps and trucks sailed by.

I saw that there were barracks nearby, so eventually I decided to see if I could see an officer and ask for a lift. A young soldier on duty went to make my request to his officer. He returned, and said, "He is unfriendly and says you must 'beat the line.'"

"How can a gentleman say such an unkind thing to a lady?" I said. "Please go and tell him that in South Africa we say 'Hit the breeze!' Tell him also that I am most anxious to hit the breeze or beat the line if I can get a little assistance."

I did not expect the young soldier to return to his officer but he did so and after a few minutes come back and handed me this official Credential:

> To whom it my concern:
> 14th July 1945
> The bearer of this note is a British subject and it is requested that all authorities give all assistance possible in aiding this woman.
> Anything that is done will be greatly appreciated.
> For the Military Government
> (Signature Stamp, U.S. Army).

Hastily thanking the young soldier, I said, "You see, he is a good man and I beat the line." Once more on the street, I waved my document to a passing jeep. The driver stopped, friendly soldiers gave me a lift all the way to Passau where I arrived at 4:00 P.M. I had no German ration cards, so I could not buy any food. I was famished, there was only one way for me to obtain food and that was to enquire my way to a Convent and, most essential, perhaps they would know how I could get to Thyrnau.

I was directed to the "English Sisters." These nuns have a very ancient establishment in Passau. I expected the nuns to be able to speak English, since they are called the "*Englische Frauleins*" but they were just kind, shy, little German nuns, who readily gave me some balm tea and bread. They had no connection with Thyrnau, so I hurried on my way — first paying a fleeting visit to the baroque Church of Passau, with a stately organ, the largest in Germany, or so the proud people of Passau maintain.

In the narrow streets of Passau, like in Regensburg, there is much evidence of things of long ago, linked with a sense of the eternal. It was here, in a narrow *Gasse*, I seemed to walk side by side with a leisurely Seventeenth Century courtier in cravatte, doublet, and hose. This gentleman flung his cloak over his shoulder and rattled his rapier in disgust at the way I was hurrying. I feel sure I heard him call after me in no uncertain manner: "You cannot take care of a mouse!" His words echoed in my mind, until I was challenged at an old stone archway by a Roman guard, for the road I walked on, was it not the Via Militaria Augustana?

Soon, I arrived at the Danube, where my reflections were cut short by finding that another stone bridge had been destroyed by retreating *S.S.* troops. The river was also spanned by an improvised plank bridge. Here a soldier stood directing the traffic. I approached him, waving my "credential." The soldier was very understanding. He scanned it and stopped a number of cars for me. Eventually, one of them was passing through Thyrnau and I was given a lift. With my goal so near at hand, my heart pounded with illogical apprehension and I felt a great, dire weariness, whilst in my mind I questioned foolishly, fearfully, "What will the nuns be able to tell me about my boys? Are they safe, will I find them?" How I prayed. Angel at my side, help us to find them at Thyrnau.

It was dusk when I found myself at the Cistercian Convent. Almost bordering the village were forest lands. From out of the shadows of the trees, I saw two nuns appear, carrying baskets. Soon I recognized Sisters Edith and Gunda, and after them came gamboling a little troop of barefoot boys. Their faces were stained with blueberry juice and they carried baskets of fruit. I believe this picture of those barefoot boys, as lean and brown as genuine Gypsies, with blueberry stained hands and faces, will remain as the dearest of my life and like the signs of the zodiac, I could wish it to have international recognition.

In an instant I was recognized and surrounded. Characteristically, Lekkie threw his arms around me, too overcome to speak. We wept together until my Peter, standing erect and almost aloof, said, "I knew you would come, I prayed for it." Just short like that.

Deo Gratias, my boys are safe, they are both well.

A deep peace fills my soul; how often I had seemed to stand in a desert place, a waterless waste — now everything that lies in the past is forgotten.

I am the first parent to appear after seven months. What must these other boys feel? I hope and pray that my unexpected appearance heralds good news for each one of them very soon.

###

CHAPTER NINE
FINDING LOST CHILDREN

17 July, 1945
Peter's Birthday

We stayed up late last night, I sat and marvelled of what the nuns told me of some of their adventures. How they had been roused by a murderous artillery drum fire to learn that the Russians had broken through the German lines and were rolling westward, in a broad offensive, while the German corps, without ammunition, perishing from hunger and cold, fought on in every Dorf and village.

Hurriedly, the nuns got the boys dressed in their warmest clothes; they shouldered their rucksacks — already packed, and in the bitter cold dawn, the little band of nuns and boys marched out to join the vast stream of fugitives on the roads. From their rear came continuous low droning sounds and detonations speeding them on their way.

How they trekked through snow banks before the Russian advance. The boys added many colourful sketches. I marvelled at how the boys had walked, carrying provisions and clothes in their rucksacks; sometimes they could hear the guns roaring and they had to run. How when Peter got ill and his legs were so swollen he could walk no further, they had managed to put him on a waggon for some hours. How they had passed through many deserted villages and how the ingenuity of the boys had enabled them to locate mouldy potatoes in the cellars of the empty houses, to catch some stray fowls, to milk a stray cow (which was a blessing for the sick boys). How, frostbitten after weary weeks of travelling roads and byways, they were picked up by a *Lazarett* train for wounded soldiers. The officer in charge gave strict orders for the nuns to leave behind any sick children, especially boys with contagious diseases, and how the nuns had contrived to

wrap up two of the boys who had measles in their blankets
and stow them away amongst their rucksacks and bedding.

"This was not difficult, said Sister Edith, "among such a
crowd of youngsters."

How on the train, they had travelled to and fro, twice
they had been very near to me in Prague. How when the sirens
sounded at midnight, and the bombs were falling, the train
had managed to steam out of the station. I marvelled, thinking
that this was that night when I found myself on my knees in
front of my bed, cringing and beseeching — "My Lord, and my
God, mercy! Spare, only spare my children!" I marvelled at
how the sick children were comforted on the train with their
heads resting on the nuns' knees whilst they prayed their
Rosaries; and how the boys continued their studies while the
nuns tried to exercise the necessary discipline — thus helping
the boys to retain their strength of character. I marvelled at
how the nuns had struggled to feed the boys, approximately a
hundred meals a day, only two nuns with a few provisions.

But I sat and marveled, mostly at the ingenuity of the
nuns, who never doubted, despaired and who never asked
anything for themselves — poor little School Sisters — who
sacrifice all — and I know they will never cease to pray for
their boys in all ways and always.

The 17th of July and because it is Peter's birthday, the
boys have been given a holiday. The nuns, looking ahead, are
canning their blueberries. We have been busy. I have made
toffee. To lengthen the three pounds of sugar (carefully
transported in my rucksack all the way from Potstat), I grated
a bowl of carrots given to me by the Cistercian nuns next door
with a lump of butter. The toffee filled three plates, enough to
go around among all the boys. I wish I could have given my
Peter a toy for his birthday — something near a boy's heart —
instead, he has handed his toffee around amongst his
colleagues and been rewarded by their unassumed pleasure.

The biscuits the British soldiers gave me are not enough
to go around. We shall have a small private party.

Lekkie and Peter will be very disappointed when they
learn that I have decided to leave them here for the present. I
feel that they are safer with the nuns in the A.M. Zone than we

are in Czechoslovakia. As soon as our position is more defined, I shall either fetch them or join them in Germany.

19 July, 1945

I have promised to fetch them before Christmas if possible. They are satisfied.

My boys are safe! And although Peter is painfully skinny, they are well. The nuns assured me that they get enough to eat, they obtain food from the Cistercian nuns and also from the cook at the A.M. Barracks which the boys fetch daily in a basket.

No pleasant news from Czechoslovakia, only very distressing reports. I must hurry back. After two nights of being peacefully happy and reassured, I am feeling fresh and eager for my return journey.

I am very heartsore to leave my boys, but they are both brave lads.

We must all be brave.

*****

The return journey was almost without incident (I seem to know the ropes) except that at Schandorf, where it rained, I spent an unpleasant night sitting on the muddy cement floor of a shed with many misplaced persons.

Arrived back at Potstat as the sun was setting, just one week after venturing on my search. The first words I said to Count Kuno were: "Look at my shoes, they are in ribbons."

"And you can still smile?" he asked.

"My boys are safe and I am at peace with the world!"

Then I had to tell the family about my journey, my experiences. Count Kuno said: "You have been to Thyrnau on the Austrian border and back?" And I had to recite everything once again.... How I travelled and how I was able to trace my boys. Count Kuno said: "My family fear to visit me from Prague, although they have Czech passports, and you have travelled all that distance on a South African antenuptial contract!"

A day or two later, I sat in the sun with my feet in a bucket of hot water — my toenails were blue (later I lost them) — when a sad-faced woman asked to see me: Mrs. Raeder. She showed me a mysterious crumpled note received from her daughter Ilsa, 18 years old. The note said: Ilsa is in a prison hospital, desperately ill and starving; she cannot possibly survive without speedy help and food. Mrs. Raeder implored me to try to find Ilsa. I tried to put her off and showed her the condition of my feet. In a voice breaking with tears, she said: "You know, no German is allowed to travel by train; there is not a soul to help me, only *Pan* Czeck (a beau of Ilsa) — he will accompany you to Prague. We will provide money, and the man with the pot-footed horse will take you to the station."

Count Kuno Des Fours said, "Rubbish, don't go, you will get your name underlined by Communist authorities. Be careful."

Mrs. Raeder said, "My poor child, she never harmed anyone, she never committed a sin. Four months ago she left here to try to escape the Russians, and now, this shocking note. What can I do?"

What can I do? I thought. We are women together, bound in a bond of motherhood. My heart must not be too small for a woman. I must aid her.

*****

A wild goose chase — but I am assisted by the Czech police.

With two bottles of goats' milk that I had advised Mrs. Raeder to boil down with sugar, a packet of rusks, and two loaves of bread, we are ready to leave for Prague.

At Hranice, the fast train came steaming in. "Come along, *Pan* Czeck," I called. "Can you hear me? Come along!" Russian soldiers stared good-naturedly at me calling to *Pan* Czeck. I squeezed myself inbetween the Russians, trying this way and that, there was not room to set a foot down. Eventually I got into a small compartment that seemed less densely crowded. These Russians stink above the average, I thought. Nevertheless, here I am, taking my stand! Then, as I peered round, in the semi-darkness, I saw a soldier sitting on a seat, a lavatory seat, while the other soldiers were queueing for a turn. I had boldly squeezed myself into the midst of a lavatory full of Russians! I got out of that lavatory quicker than I had gotten in and off the train! Mr. Czeck had not attempted to get on the train at all.

Breathless, two of my coat buttons ripped off but, stll in possession of my rucksack, I was much relieved to stand next to *Pan* Czeck on terra firma. Fortunately, the night was quite warm, so it was agreeable to sit on the open platform and wait for the midnight train to Prague. Although this train was also overcrowded, we both succeeded in boarding it. We stood all the way to Prague, where we arrived in the early hours at the Masaryk station.

By this time, my legs felt like leaden weights and I looked around for a seat. The station was crowded. Soldiers, refugees, riff-raff, men and women occupied all the benches, or reclined on the dirty cement floor. All the people seemed to be wearing badges of distinction, showing that they were not German; medals and flags pinned on to their breasts from every corner of the continent except Germany.

I succeeded, eventually, in squeezing into a very few inches of a bench between two labourers. Mr. Czeck reclined on the dirty floor. One of the men next to me put his oily head on my shoulder and snored. I tried desperately to push him off, but fearing that I would be pushed off the seat, I let his head rest, until after some time, he gave a nauseating garlic-reeking belch on my shoulder. This was too strong! and I promptly cuffed his ear. He sprang up with a startled face and swore some round Slav oaths; his colleagues pressed in with angry faces. Mr. Czeck also sprang up. I shook with fear and did not dare utter a word in German. However, when I motioned the man to sit down, but not to put his head on to my shoulder, they were all mollified.

Quite early, they departed, and we were able to have a wash and find a meagre breakfast on our ration cards at the station. Then we immediately went to the police station to inquire where Ilsa could be found. The police made some inquiries and then gave me the address of a Reverend Dr. Unger, Washingtonova, Room 101. To the Washingtonova we hurried, opposite the Washington Station. Here a queue of people already extended in to the street. We joined them and stood for a long time. I became agitated and tried to think how I could hurry matters when I saw a refined-looking man walk past and enter the building by another door. I darted after him and asked him if he knew if it was possible to see Dr. Unger. "Come up to my office," he said. He went to speak to Dr. Unger next door.

Soon he returned and said, "You may go in." Dr. Unger, quite young and not formidable as I had expected, asked me a number of questions. Then he wrote out the permission for me to see Ilsa and most important, for her to receive the food, but unfortunately not for her to return home until we got the sanction from the authorities at Hranice. When I collected Mr. Czeck from the queue at the door, he was quite surprised as to how I had obtained the permission.

Dr. Unger had also given me the addresses of half a dozen hospitals. They seemed to be spread about the four corners of Prague. We took a tram to the "German Hospital." It was well guarded, but on showing Dr. Unger's permission, we were allowed to speak to the *Chef Arzt* (chief doctor) for a few minutes. He looked up some files. "Ilsa," he said, "was taken to an isolation hospital ten days ago. We were not informed which hospital." I asked him what was wrong with Ilsa. "Not very much, we have many such cases here," he said. "Ilsa is one of the unfortunate victims kept prisoner at the Stadium (in Prague) whom the Russians have brutally ill-used."

(We knew that the Russians literally used the Stadium as a place for ghoulish sporting events. We were told of torture and even crucifixions taking place.)

The doctor gave me the address of a likely hospital in Prague 111. We had to walk quite a distance, took a tram, and then had to walk again until eventually we found the number we were looking for — an old monastery in a side street, a somber building with large iron doors and small grated windows. I rang the bell and eventually the door was opened by a young man wearing the red communist band round his arm. I said, "I have come from Hranice to look for Ilsa Raeder and I have been given this address."

"You have come to the wrong place," he said, "she is certainly not here," and he closed the door.

Mr. Czeck and I then decided to go to a hospital somewhere in Prague XII. Here also we had no luck. We tried two other places.

"Not here."

"Now, *Pan* Czeck, we are going to the police," I said. Again, they were helpful by directing us to a place for displaced persons which had the facilities for tracing people. Here I was glad to find a gentleman who spoke English. After we explained our trouble, he sat down at the telephone and I think he rang up just about every hospital authority in Prague. Eventually he said, "Go back to the monastery, tell them that Ilsa was delivered to them ten days ago and you demand to know what has happened to her — dead or alive."

Not long afterwards, I knocked again at the heavy monastery door. By now it was long past noon. We were famished and I was impatient. But at the same time, I had to be diplomatic as I had no passport and could claim no protection, British or otherwise.

The door was opened by the same man with the red band. We stepped in. He tried to intimidate us. "You have no right to enter an isolation hospital," he said harshly. "Ilsa Raeder is not here."

"I have come to speak to someone in authority. I have Dr. Unger's permission, and I am in touch with the British Embassy." I trembled lest he ring them up!

Now he took us to a small waiting room. "Ilsa Raeder is not here," he repeated.

"Ilsa Raeder was delivered to this place ten days ago and I want to know what has happened to her. If you can't tell me, there is certainly someone here who can!"

He threw back his long, black, greasy hair and combing it with his fingers he started shouting, "Get out! Get out!" Mr. Czeck pulled at my sleeve. "Let us go," he whispered.

Saint Michael and Saint George help, I prayed. These two saints, mighty in battle, did not beat around the bush; they rushed in to help. I stepped up to the red-banded man, snapped open my bag, took out paper and pen. "Your name?" I said. "First your name, and then you call someone in authority.

Or I shall go straight to Dr. Unger and the British Embassy."
Still running his fingers through his hair, he went out.

Mr. Czeck said feebly, "We are getting into b-e-e-g trouble!"

Our friend soon returned with an elderly official. "Tell her! You tell her!" he almost shouted, but the other was not telling us anything. Instead, he stepped in front of the red-banded man and enquired politely, "What can I do for you?" I explained. Eventually, he said, "You see, this is an isolation hospital and we must do our duty."

"Is it this man's duty to lie to us and send us off on a wild goose chase? When I have Dr. Unger's authority to see Ilsa Raeder? And now be kind enough to allow me to see her."

He motioned to the communist to take me to see her; ungraciously he led the way: up a short flight of stairs and through a door directly leading into an enormous room, containing rows of beds. Ilsa was lying on a straw mattress on one of the beds. (I was thankful to see there were only a few inmates). She was very small and weak, her knees were badly bent up by rheumatism, contracted through rain and the experiences of the Stadium. She begged to be taken home. I had five minutes to explain that first I must return to Hranice for permission for her return. "Meanwhile try to get better, I'll fetch you next week."

Mr. Czeck was waiting at the street corner for me; we were glad to get away from the morbid atmosphere of the monastery. The streets were very quiet and as we walked, we complimented and congratulated each other. *Pan* Czeck dared to raise his voice in admiration of the aristocracy in general. "Countess Mimi Des Fours is the best doctor in Moravia, and if humanly possible, she will set Ilsa on her feet again. Count Kuno Des Fours," he said, "courageously worked for the welfare of the people during the war, as was voluntarily testified by the Russian prisoners of war." He looked kindly at me and said, "Come and get some bread at my bakery when we get back to Potstat."

"I'll tell you what, *Pan* Czeck," I said, "I still have fifteen kilos of meal that I brought from the miller the day before the Russians came. War meal. Perhaps you can mix it up in your bins and give me some fresh meal?" *Pan* Czeck was willing, so I clinched a bargain.

This talking of bread made us realize how hungry we were, and as we were near Princess Lobkowicz's residence, I called in and told her what had happened and that we were famished. After refreshments, she gave me a tin of conserved meat for Ilsa. Then I took a tram to the International Red Cross Society. Mr. Czeck begged to be excused from travelling further (his head was queer from the sleepless night on the train and the vibration of the trams). So while he rested in one of Princess Lobkowicz's servant's rooms, I went further.

The chief of the International Red Cross, a handsome gentleman, had only just returned from Switzerland. He said: "There is little we can do; the Red Cross is only tolerated by the communists. We are trying to find ways and means of helping the hospitals and also the unfortunate German children in Czechoslovakia." Then he gave me some ointment and powder and some tinned food. And then, like the two good guardian saints, I did not beat about the bush, but returned to the hospital with the medicines and tinned foods, which I was able to give to Ilsa without fuss.

*****

Permission for Ilsa's return to Potstat was granted when I went for our ration cards. Mr. Czeck says he cannot face another journey, therefore on Monday, Ilsa's father will accompany me to Prague — that is, if he is able to conceal the mark of distinction all Germans have to wear on the backs of their coats... a big letter "N." for *Nemec* meaning "German" in Czech. (Same as the Jews were ordered to wear the Star of David in Germany).

Mr. Raeder was skillful in hiding his "brand." He turned his jacket inside outand no questions were asked. The journey was not as difficult as we expected.

We immediately proceeded to the Washingtonova and obtained Dr. Unger's permission for Ilsa to leave the hospital. Presenting ourselves at the monastery, the red-banded man tried to wave us off, but being unsuccessful, he tried to raise every objection he possibly could to prevent Ilsa from leaving:

"She has an infectious disease, and the germs will spread... she is too ill and too far gone to travel... you will first have to produce a doctor's certificate...." and so on. I saw that there was no point in arguing with him, so I said, "The police are helping me to get her to the station. We are calling for her shortly, please get the patient ready."

I went to the nearest police station and asked the sergeant if it was in any way possible for them to help me convey a patient from the isolation hospital to the station. The sergeant thought a moment and then, to my pleasant surprise, he said, "We can call a taxi for you." He rang the taxi stand. "Sit and wait here," he said, "as it will take some little time." I sat down to contemplate The Cares of the Day on tenterhooks that we would miss the train to Hranice. Meanwhile, Ilsa's father was also on pins and needles waiting at the street corner. The taxi arrived and I said the little straight-laced words, "Thank you," to the sergeant. It should have been a fine big expression but there was no time for fireworks.

At the monastery — with a very courteous driver at hand — I said, "I have a taxi from the police, is the patient ready?" The patient was ready and being brought down — but I would still have to travel to the other end of Prague to get her signed off by the officials who delivered her in here. (If we intended catching our train, there was little time to lose).

"Can't you arrange for her to be signed off here?"

"Impossible," said the communist.

The taxi rattled over the cobblestones of Prague at an alarming pace. Ilsa, a little white skeleton, was lying in her father's arms. At the hospital, I said hastily to the Czech official in charge, "I have come from the isolation hospital to get Ilsa Raedner signed off. We must catch the train to Hranice."

"Have you got Dr. Unger's permission?" I wanted to show it to him. "Not necessary," he said.

"Is there anything I must sign?" I asked. "Then we must hurry. Thank you and good-bye."

So this was the second wild goose chase I was sent on from the monastery.

At the station I paid the taxi-man handsomely. He went to see if he could obtain a coupe for us. Astonishingly, he did obtain one and helped to carry Ilsa in. We were only just seated when the train moved off. The ticket collector came round, and when he saw that we were not the important "police passengers" the taxi-man had led him to believe, he had a very glum face and he returned repeatedly to make inquiries. I feared for Mr. Raeder's "N" inside his coat! Ilsa became terrified. When he came again, I said, "Look, take this hundred kronen and if there is anyone more important than we are, or anyone more ill than my cousin is, then give them this coupe." We did not see him again.

Ilsa moaned in pain. Throughout the night we gave her sips of milk and water and some Togal (pain medicine). We took it in turns to hold her. She was a featherweight. In the coupe, we were shocked to see the big open bedsores on her back and arms. It was 11:00 o'clock before we arrived home. We had spent many hours holding her gently in our arms.

Ilsa's mother put her in her own bed, with Dr. Des Fours in attendance. "I am surprised," said Dr. Mimi, "to see anyone suffering from such malnutrition and nervous debility can still be alive." It took months for the bedsores to heal and longer for Ilsa's legs to straighten, but with Countess Des Fours' attentions, which helped considerably to put her on her feet, Ilsa made a good recovery. When she tried to tell me about the brutalities she had suffered, I said, "Try to forget everything, you are safe in your mother's featherbed. Drink your goat's milk and soon your pretty dimples will return."

*****

After our return from Prague, I felt I could not face up to anything more, I was *kaput*. I felt like a sick bird — like *Pan Czeck* must have felt. After not lifting my head all morning, I thought perhaps a walk in the forest would be beneficial and I went out in search of Count Kuno, to whom I said, "What we need is a long walk in the forest." The grim expression hardly left his face, but he agreed. So with the children, we set out. We were rather distressed to encounter some Russians riding up the hill — it was strange to see them on horseback, they were usually in Jeeps. Anyway, I thought, we are hardly likely to see them in the forest on horseback.

We walked along ways that Count des Fours directed. The velvety forest glades were peace personified, the only audible waves of sound were the mighty hymn the wind played in the high tree tops and the call of strange birds that seem to beckon to even deeper solitudes. Here we could take deep breaths of clean oxygen-laden air together with the scent of "*Waldmeister*" (woodruff) that grew like lilies under the trees. The children romped around. We stood together beneath the spacious sky, two needy human souls.

Count Kuno said, "Fortune is an unpredictable guest in human life — no one knows when he comes, no one when he goes; but why has fate struck us such a wretched blow?"

"Perhaps it is because, as you say, 'Fortune is an unpredictable guest,' and therefore we must strive never to lose sight of our three God-given qualities: faith, confidence, and goodwill to all mankind; they carry us far and away above the highest tree-tops of your forest."

"You really mean goodwill to all mankind?" he asked very seriously.

"Y-e-s." I said, and tried to be lighthearted, "we must take a good shot at it! Times will not always be what they are today."

Count Kuno also tried to be light-hearted, he took my hand and said, "You know, I often say thank God I'm not mixed up with that bad lot but I'll try to remember your formula." He kissed my fingertips and said, "It could have all been so different. You are the best friend I have ever had."

As we went on our homeward waywith a big bunch of *Waldmeister* for Auntie Mother, we felt better for fresh air and oxygen and good friendship.

The war is over — but the general upheaval and the heartbreak of the people continues unabated. This morning, the German people were all ordered to assemble in the church square. There they were all separated into groups according to age and ability, then they were alloted various jobs: the children have to sweep the streets, dig up weeds and so forth; the older women have been put to cleaning their houses for the new occupants. While the more able-bodied and younger women are sent to the fields and factories or as farm-hands, they have to dig and plant their own gardens and milk their own cows for the new landlords.

Some days past the order was given that all strangers had to return to their own villages or starve as they would not get ration cards. This order caused great consternation, as many villages are completely destroyed and there is nowhere for the people to return to. Others again have come from distant parts of the country, some from as far as Breslau and Berlin, and there is absolutely no transport — all horses and conveyances have been taken from them, like our own. Most of the women are old or they have young children. They have no food or money — nothing to take them on long journeys. Nearly all have endured sad experiences of suffering. One young woman with her three young children told me, before she left Potstat wheeling a pram and the others clinging to her skirts, "We must try to keep body and soul together — but how?" I often wonder what happened to this poor woman. Where possible, the people try to travel in groups, feeling safer from being molested by soldiers and riff-raff. It was a very dejected and poor-looking group (after being plundered by different Russian soldiers) that left Potstat. During the ensuing days, numbers of other groups passed through from villages far and near. These poor people stopped as long as they had permission to rest and beg for food.

Another distressing sight are the herds of cows driven through Potstat on the way to the railway station, from where they get transported to Russia — it is said that not many of these beautiful red and white *Sieben Taler* cows survive the cruel journey. These animals have been born and bred in cow-houses. They are not used to hard ground and so have developed long hooves. They struggle pitifully along. German women and boys are mostly ordered along as drivers but sometimes I saw the animals brutally beaten by Russian soldiers.

Our village, being on the road to Hranice Station, has seen some strange cavalcades passing through. I have seen a string of sick and wounded horses, and once a line of donkeys and camels. We never knew from whence or whither they were going. Here also their new landlords, the party comrades, came marching in. They mostly came empty-handed. One that I personally saw carried his goods and chattels in a bag over

his shoulder; one came with a grey rabbit, another with a
sickle, and so they took possession of the peasants' homes and
the fields to the great mortification of the owners who are
deprived of even the basic necessities of life until they get
transported off, in batches, to Germany. During this time, most
of the three million German people in Czechoslovakia are put
into any sort of make-shift barracks, their homes placed at the
disposal of the good comrades or left to stand empty, like in
the village of Potstat.

We had to queue up for our ration cards; already the
German women, with good perception, say that the official
from whom we receive the cards sits with his beady black eyes
like a spider in his web, ever ready to pounce; he is therefore
named The Spider.

To The Spider I also went for our ration cards. He sat in
his web, and then said: "You want ration cards for yourself and
your children?"

"Yes, and for my aunt Countess Stolberg and for Anna."

"Why does not Anna come herself?"

"Because," I said, "she has a bad leg."

"A what?" he asked.

"She has a very bad leg," I repeated, which was true,
but feeling at the same time that my own legs were not too
good. The Spider handed me the cards, but Anna received the
German cards, half rations and no meat. I was thankful to get
cards, as they were denied the other refugees. Anna
complained bitterly at "no meat." I consoled her by saying, "We
sink and swim together, and in any case we hardly have
enough money to buy meat." Anna cheered up and found that
it was a consolation that the Czechs had not been deprived of
their cattle.

*****

Our return to Kyjovice has been hastened by a letter
from Papali. He is alone. Regina has been taken to a labour
camp in Bilovice. There is no news from Helene. We sit, as it
were, in the dark. It is no use for us to question the why and
the wherefore. We return to Kyjovice tomorrow. Ferdi will
fetch us.

But first there was the Britzka that stands crippled in the yard (from the Russians removing the pneumatic tires) and it was a foregone conclusion that we would never get horses to carry us back to Kyjovice. I made a quick suggestion to Auntie Mother: "What about approaching the Spider to buy the Britzka?"

"Do you think he will be interested? Because if he wants it, he will take it."

"Well, I'll forestall him and ask him if you agree."

So it was decided to see if I could sell the Britzka. Actually, I had no right to do so, as it would now appear that it belonged to the Czech State. However, when I went to fetch our ration cards, I spoke to Mr. Spider. I even suggested that perhaps, one day, he might decide to visit South Africa. The Spider himself bought the Britzka! Later on, in Kyjovice, I was questioned about it, so I said, "You must please ask the Russians and the leaders in Potstat." I heard nothing more about it, and the kronen Auntie Mother received helped considerably in tiding us over. Actually, Auntie Mother thought I had no means at all and I think she was relieved to hear that during the last months, I had placed every available deutschmark possible in the savings bank in Czechoslovakia for each child and myself in separate accounts. The Spider did not know of our impending departure, — otherwise, he may have said, "Just leave the Britzka here."

We have packed up all our belongings in readiness to leave. Pettie and Ilona caught our ten chickens and put them in a box with their mother; our three graces, Faith, Hope and Charity are in another box.

I hardly dare face Count Kuno to say *au revoir*, he is so cast down in spirits. In Afrikaans, we say: "Before you really know each other, you must eat a bag of salt together." We have eaten our bag of salt. We have learned to know and to appreciate, not so much the clanging chords but the more sensitive timbre of a real true worth... the parting cannot be a casual call of "Ship ahoy!"

###

CHAPTER TEN
OUR COMMUNIST LORDS

On our return to Kyjovice, I think Auntie Mother
expected to find the worst, but to find the great house filled
with strangers and to be restricted to the "Green Suite" —
empty, except for a couple of beds — caused her real mental
anguish. The only consolation is the Chapel, a few doors away
from the Green Suite. It has been cleaned and disinfected and
although all the vestments are gone, a visiting priest usually
brings all his requirements with him. Away down the corridor
the Communists have the use of the large kitchen. We are
grateful to have the use of the small kitchen (some doors
further along the corridor). I have our same large old room
that we have always occupied, next to the Green Suite. Yes, we
have returned to Kyjovice. It is autumn, the leaves turn yellow,
Kyjovice has lost its bud and bloom.

Our first thought has been for Regina. Papali told us
that on the evening before Regina was taken away, a man
came to the castle and with many Marxist slogans and made
himself conspicuous. Papali, in his wise way, gave no replies,
but he saw Regina's golden eyes snapping. It was when the
man started speaking of the wonderful things the leaders in
the "New Czechoslovakia" were doing for the people that the
breaking point arrived. Regina very coolly said, "Hitler also
repeatedly spoke about the wonders he was doing for the
German people." That same evening, Regina was ordered to
report to the camp in Bilovice.

"Don't worry," I said to Auntie Mother. "Tomorrow, I'll
go to Bilovice and see what can be done." I was always saying
to people, "Don't worry," but this time, it was really something
serious. From personal experience, I knew I first had to get
permission from the local police for Regina's return. They were
sympathetic, but said that Regina should not have said that the
Czech leaders are like Hitler. I explained that this is not what

she meant, she merely said that Hitler spoke about the
wonders he was doing for the German people. The permission
with licence was granted.

I walked to the station and bought a ticket to Bilovice.
The clouds had gathered and it started raining. When I
approached the authorities for permission for Regina's return
to Kyjovice, the official said, "I am afraid you will first have to
get permission from the police in Kyjovice. When I handed
them the licence, they readily gave their consent, but said it
also had to be authorized by the *Okresni Vibo* (district police).
Fortunately in Bilovice, without much palaver, the sergeant in
charge said, "Orders are orders, and it is all in order."

Rain was falling as I walked along the street looking for
the *lager* when I saw a group of blackened-looking people.
They were pushing hand-carts and wheelbarrows laden with
wood between them — along with Regina. They had been
ordered to get timber from some burnt-out buildings, so
together with the rain and the blackened wood, they looked a
sorry sight indeed. I went with Regina to the *lager* to get her
rucksack; she could not believe that I had come for her. The
internees of the *lager* offered her some soup before leaving,
which was being cooked by some of the older women. They
also had some slices of potato strewn with salt sizzling on the
combustion stove, on which they were cooking their watery
soup. I thought it was perhaps made from potato peels, but
they told me that sometimes they were obligingly given half an
ox head.

Regina hurriedly washed her face and we started off as
quickly as possible — for fear the licence would be revoked,
which had happened before people could proceed on their
way. We were soon away from the main streets and were able
to call for a short while on Count and Countess Sedlnitzsky,
where we had some tea and I unpacked my sandwiches. As
the castle is bombed and without a roof, they are living in a
small cottage. They had the same sad story to relate as
elsewhere, and in spite of being Austrian, they have no wish to
remain in Czechoslovakia under present Communist
conditions. When we were on our way again, Regina tried to
persuade me to travel home by train. "I can quite comfortably
walk home the fifteen kilometres alone, I know the foot-paths

through the forest," she said. "It will be dark by the time we reach home."

"Yes," I said, "we must just keep on our way." I think she was quite relieved to have me stay with her. Except for a few labourers and the falling rain drops, there was nothing untoward to disturb our way home.

Despite the long twilight, it was dark when we opened the great door and entered the castle. I went at once to the Green Suite. Auntie Mother looked imploringly at me. "All is well," I said, "Now come and greet your child; you have not seen her for a long time."

*****

Apart from the purge of the German people, our position here remains unhappily confused. We get no newspapers, we have no radio; but it appears that the Czech communists, urged on by the Soviet Union, succeeded in placing their men in dominant positions, which enables them to subjugate all authority and principles (I say this is just like Regina said of Hitler). All newscasts and, what is most distressing, the Czech Peoples Party to which Papali also belongs and which is mostly Catholic, have ceased to function.

The majority of the people of Kyjovice and neighbouring villages are working hard to help Papali to retain his position here — they have signed and sent several petitions to President Benes and to Jan Masaryk (president and foreign minister of Czechoslovakia) to this effect. To me it seems that Papali, like Kuno Des Fours and others, would rather leave the country than live under Communist rule; but as Papali says, if this comes to pass, it will be bitterly humiliating to have to live from the hand of charity.

*****

All along the lower corridor, the rooms have double doors, this includes the Green Suite. These Czech farmers and peasants, knowing that all our money is in a frozen account, bring gifts when they come to early Mass, sometimes a little slab of butter, bread, sausage, milk or vegetables, and quietly place the gifts between the double doors, so that undesirables do not see them; and then, like quiet little mice, we swoop down upon anything we may find, It is truly wonderful of these good people. One of the women told me that in former days there was always a helping hand when needed and a car ready to take any one to the doctor or hospital; therefore they are now only too ready to extend a helping hand.

*****

Autumn, 1945

Before I go in search of Helene and the little boys, it will be wise for me to get a visa because if she is in Piltsch — now acceded to Poland — the authorities there may hesitate to acknowledge my antenuptial contract. As I am not able to get a visa from the British Embassy in Prague, I applied to the local *Vibo*. To my surprise, they were quite ready to furnish me with one, but I will have to get the *Okresni Vibo* in Svinova to authorize it.

As soon as the visa was ready, I set off for Svinova. Inquiring my way to the police headquarters, I was asked to take my place in an office where I was interviewed by an officer for whom I had to answer a great number of questions. He then looked at me critically and said, "You shall have to answer to someone else." As soon as he left the room to fetch this other party, I mumbled something to those present about returning soon and to myself I said, "These officials are very discerning. If you want your Identity Card, then run away and run quickly… run back to Bilovice before you land in trouble here and your pack of cards falls together for trying to get a South African visa when your husband was *Reichs Deutsche*."

It was when I sat in the train to Bilovice that I rubbed my hands together, thinking that my hurried departure from Svinova was funny.

Without demur, the *Okresni Vibo* in Bilovice stamped and signed my brand new visa.

The good village people rejoice at Regina's return. What the others think, we do not know, but she has been sent off to work in the garden. Our ration cards were handed out to me this morning (without comment) by the authorities. I've prepared the ex-bantam house in the kitchen garden for my little chickens. I say "little," but the large hens and cocks will just have to try to make themselves comfortable on the small bantam perches! Even the ten chicks have grown like young turkeys, especially the five cockerels. We shall have one for Christmas. The kitchen park is situated near the house. I shall not have to walk far through the snow to feed them.

We do not know from one day to another what the communists' next move will be. This is indeed a heart-breaking time for Papali and Auntie Mother; they take events quietly. Meanwhile the so-called "Caritas" (Catholic Relief organisation) has taken over the house for children from a Czech orphanage. There is much activity on the stairs and in all the upper rooms and alterations are being made to the house.

Papali and the boys collect wood and store it up for winter heating. Auntie Mother takes the children for short walks and reads them little homilies. This morning, when they complained about making up their beds every morning, Auntie Mother patiently explained that it is seldom that we arrive at the heights without effort; we must first learn the value of everyday trivial things, we must keep our eyes open and recognize their beauty. But Auntie Mother, there is no beauty in shaking out the blankets — there is only dust! "No, children," she said, "let us finish the job."

When the beds were made up neatly she said: "Now stand with me and look, there is beauty in the neat folds, and value lies in work well done. We must not forget the trivial things — one of such has gone around the world and is a beautiful sacrament, that simple thing that Jesus did when he sat down and washed the disciples' feet. Our Lord God showed man how to be humble."

I am deeply thankful to have the children in Auntie Mother's care.

From the villagers we hear vague rumours of storms of high policy — We have no radio, receive no letters, and cannot read the Czech newspapers; there seems to be division among the victorious powers. Papali says we can only judge by the distressing political system that now prevails through force and fraud. This is a time of great suspense and sorrow for everyone, — especially for Papali and Auntie Mother, to see their home and their old heritage snatched away while they stand powerless, naked before the evil forces. The village people have again sent petitions to President Benes. No reply. Papali thinks that these petitions only serve to provoke the Communist lords and will serve no purpose.

Papali and Auntie Mother were somewhat distressed when I said I was going in search of Helene, I said, "Don't worry, I won't go further than Piltsch, but if anything untoward happens, it may take me several days. I may have to find ways and means of getting out of Poland!"

I had much difficulty in crossing the border into Poland, and with much difficulty again I was allowed to enter the village that had been our home; I found that Helene's villa was razed to the ground as was practically every house in the village.

The building where I had lived was also in ruins except for a tumble-down stairway and a couple of rooms and my kitchen — still with the picture of St. Joseph on a high shelf. I had installed him as house-father. It was there that Helene suddenly appeared with Christian in her arms. Christian was being comforted by Helene because he had a swollen foot. The other three children were in bed with a type of typhoid fever that followed in the wake of the Russian army in Europe, and was brought on by hunger.

Helene was hardly recognisable, the garden overall that she had worn in happier days did nothing to conceal her dreadful, haggard appearance. Embracing me with tears, she said, "I knew that you were the only one that would come and I've watched the bridge for a sign of you. Oh, how I've watched the bridge!"

"Never mind now," I said. "Don't worry, I'm here!" Helene did not know that her husband Fritz was in a P.O.W. camp in England. She had tried by various means to obtain an exit permit — in vain. No German, on pain of death, was allowed to leave "Poland."

After the children had greedily eaten the bread and apples I had brought in my rucksack, we sat down to consider ways and means of getting across the border. Helene suggested that I cross over to Czechoslovakia again with the children and she would swim across the Opava River by night.

"Not possible, I must get the permission for you to leave," I said, "because in any case, the children can't walk... it is too dangerous. I must try and get a conveyance from the Czechs."

"But Dory, you will never get the permission for us to leave. Many thousands of people have tried in vain."

I thought, I'll have to move quickly, before the children get worse. Helene also had a high fever and sore throat. "We must try to get away before suspicions of our intentions are aroused. Firstly, I'll walk to the Czech village of Wehovice (by another road than I entered Piltsch) to see if I can get the permission for you to stay in Czechoslovakia and I'll also try to get a conveyance."

After sitting in a rickety old chair and falling asleep for a short while, I started on the three kilometer walk to Wehovice. Before crossing over, I managed to obtain permission from a Polish general stationed near the bridge for us to travel across. In Wehovice, I went to the *Burgermeister* to ask for the necessary permission and also the possibility of getting a conveyance. He wrote out the permission and said I could get a conveyance from him when we are ready, which he much doubted. I returned to Helene with the good news. The next morning at day-break I started off on my journey to the town of Leobschuetz, a distance of some fifteen kilometers, where I hoped to obtain the exit pass.

Along the roads of Upper Silesia I had always travelled with pleasure. The main roads were macadamised; there were long stretches of leafy fruit trees, cherries and plums, apples and pears linking one village to another; there were wide open fields, meadows and mellow hills; but quite the most distinctive feature along the roadways were the gentle, undulating wheat fields. Upper Silesia was known as the "Wheat Chamber" of Germany, and when you listen to the low muffled music of the wheat, you understand why someone has said, "A field of wheat is one of the three most beautiful things; the others are a fruit tree in bloom and a pregnant woman."

Now I hurried along the road with fear. — I had a terrifying sight of the land, whole villages had become battlefields, houses were demolished; but more terrifying still than the destruction was the plight of the German women and children. I was repeatedly told that the Russians were slave-drivers, but the Polish *Militz* was cruel in the extreme, and there was no law to defend or protect any German. In the fields (that the women had planted last season) the Russians were stacking the wheat in mountain-high ricks. German women and children toiled from early dawn to late evening (the men who had returned from the war had all been placed in forced labour camps) at the threshing machines guarded by Russian soldiers or the much more feared *Militz*.

The tarred surfaces of the roads were torn and broken up by vehicles and machines of war; Russian trucks, supplied by America, passed to and fro in hundreds, carrying the wheat to their various military depots. I had to pass through many villages. Each one offered the same derelict sights: rubble-strewn streets, charred roofs with chimneys standing stark among the ruins added to the desolation. I saw signs stating, "Typhoid fever!" put up. I was very thirsty, but feared to pause and ask for a drink, and also, I was too cowardly to face the desperately needy people, being unable to render them even the smallest service.

At the village of Nassiedel I was stopped by the *Militz*. My visa and also the pass given to me by the Polish general at Wehovice, stamped and signed by the same, did not satisfy them. I had to answer for myself to the Commissar. Fortunately, my papers were in order. Now I took the opportunity of asking the Commissar if perhaps there was a conveyance travelling to Leobschuetz? My luck was in, the post cart was about to leave; however, the two young men took me up with a bad grace and said I could not return with them as they had another passenger. I was glad for the respite for my aching feet, but soon I felt ashamed and mean for adding to the load of the lean, overworked horse. She was put at the trot and kept at it up-hill and down-hill, and I saw that in her weak and half-starved state, she was striking one hind foot against the other with iron-shod hooves; the blood was oozing from her legs. I had never seen this before. I asked the callous fellows not to whip her down-hill, they answered that friends were waiting for them in Leobschuetz and the whip

never left the horses flanks. I asked them if they knew the
horses' prayer:

> Up a hill hurry me not,
> Down a hill spur me not,
> On the level ground spare me not,
> In the stable forget me not.

They had no use for prayers. Instead, they entertained
me with the information that they had been in German camps
for the inevitable five years and partisans for the last two
years. I had long since lost all sympathy for this type of
criminal sufferer. At the next village we passed through, I
persuaded the men to stop the cart and from some women
threshing near the roadside, I got some strips of old sailcloth
with which I securely bandaged the bleeding legs of the gallant
little horse. Meanwhile, the men sat back in the cart and
assured me that my bandages would soon fall off. Fortunately,
they lasted all the way to Leobschuetz, where we arrived at 4
P.M.

Like all other towns, Leobschuetz was mostly in ruins. I
made my way to where the government offices stood. And
now, what I had come to know as the usual procedure took
place. I was sent from one office to another. In each one, I was
asked more or less the same questions:

"Nationality?"

"Age?"

"Where do you come from?"

"Why do you want to help a German?"

And then, "Sorry, we cannot help you!" As I came away
from the fourth disappointment, I was in despair when I saw a
tall, rather well-dressed man walking down the corridor.

I ran after him and I said in English: "Will you be kind
and direct me to the responsible authority where I can get an
exit permit?" When he said, also in English: "Come with me," I
felt hopeful, but when he also asked me the same pertinent
questions and then said, "Impossible to give a German
permission to cross over to Czechoslovakia," my hopes were
shattered. He added, however, that he would help me by
seeing that Helene was put on a train to Germany. It was a
waste of time to tell him that there were no trains travelling
because, surely, he was better acquainted with the state of the

bombed bridges and railways than I was. Therefore, I was inspired to concoct a story of Helene's mother being French, that we had French friends in Prague who would care for her, and also that the Polish Consul (I did not know which Consul to name) was in favor of her travelling with me. I believe the man saw that I was persistent, for, *Deo Gratias*, he took up his pen and wrote out the permission! I thanked him sincerely and left the office — indeed, I fled, being terrified the order would be revoked. This would regularly happen to people.

I hurried a long way down the road before considering the direction I was taking, then from two decrepit-looking old people I enquired the way to Opava — which was in the opposite direction. However, they showed me a shortcut. I had already lost about half an hour of precious daylight. Then I passed some sad-looking women digging moldy potatoes from a cellar in a bombed-out house. When I told them which way I was going, they tried to dissuade me, solemnly assuring me that no one was allowed to travel after sunset, people were hunted down with dogs and shot.

"Stop over with us in our hovel and continue your journey tomorrow," they offered. I thanked them and hurried on.

The main road was less dusty and seemed cooler. Helene had said that the cruel winter was nearly upon them. This was only too evident when I saw how the swallows congregated on the telephone wires. I hurried on and encouraged myself by saying, "*Kom nou my ou goie gras perdjie*" (Come now, my good little grass-fed horse), but mostly I was encouraged by the slip of paper I carried in my pocket.

When it grew darker and then pitch dark, I heard a waggon travelling up behind me. I felt distinctly frightened until a friendly voice said in German, "*Wo hin?*" (Where to?) The driver offered me a lift. He was on his homeward way from carting wheat to the Russian depot; he regretted that his special pass only permitted him to travel to the corn depot and back to his village. I travelled with him for about five kilometers. He was astonished to hear of the permission I had obtained, but said I would most certainly not be permitted to leave; he had many sad stories to relate and tried to persuade me to spend the night with his family.

"Don't you understand that people are continually trying to escape," he said, "and the *Militz* are making game by shooting without question and mercy?" I took the opportunity to ask the man if he knew anything about the Nuns of Katscher, a village some little distance away, where a relative, Monica, Countess Ballestrem, is a white Franciscan sister. He replied, "You know, we have only bad news, but if you write a letter to the Reverend Mother, I'll deliver it at my first opportunity."

I felt rested after the lift and a long drink from the driver's water bottle. The night seemed less dark, but I was not happy about my loudly resounding footsteps on the beaten road, but now I was on familiar terrain. Presently I heard a motorcycle. The *Militz* after me for my permit? I scudded out of the road and lay flat in a stubbly corn field. When the motorcycle was far away, I hurried on again, but not too far, when I heard the baying of a dog. A police dog on my tracks? The wolf-hounds that I had seen with the secret police, the dreaded M.V.K. — when the Russians had carried off those hundreds of unhappy prisoners in closed vans, to an unknown destination — flashed through my mind while the dog baying came nearer. By this time I had scrambled out of the road and was running in a clover field. I ran as I have never run before with the blood pounding in my ears. The dog behind me, I called to the angel at my side — the first dog that I have ever been frantically afraid of, and I hope the very last! With low fierce growls he came after me. I strained every muscle, I felt that death was imminent, then like a flash, the dog leapt upon my back. The shock of the sudden, sharp impact sent me sprawling in the field. Simultaneously, a shot was fired, while the great shaggy animal stood over me. Was it a dream, or did I feel the animal lick my face? My senses refused to register any further.

For how long I lay in the field, I do not know, but when I became conscious I had a weird feeling of floating in the air, and I know that death had touched my shoulder. I am convinced that when the dog leapt upon my back and sent me flying in the field, I was saved from the *Militz*'s bullet. Then the dog became my friend and went back to his master and it was too dark for the *Militz* to see me lying in the field. When, eventually, I had the courage to look around, I realized that I was quite unharmed and quite alone — with my precious paper safe in my vest pocket.

Meanwhile, a great pale harvest moon was shining down. I was so grateful for the light that even when I came within sight of "our village," the ghostly aspect of the rows of chimneys standing stark among the ruins inspired no dread. It was long past midnight when I walked up the dark broken stairway of the house.

Helene wept as she embraced me. "Dory," she said, "I am thankful that you are back, I have been so anxious about you, I think I have grown years older today." Only then, when I realized what this night's vigil must have cost her, I was glad that I had hurried back.

"Helene," I said, as I showed her the paper, "God willing, we shall take the wings of the morning and fly with the swallows." Helene now modestly produced a little dish of cold potatoes boiled in their jackets, and there and then, in that derelict room, lit only by the moon-beams, I enjoyed the best meal of all my life. Which goes to prove that hunger is the best sauce! After the meal, we immediately lay down to rest and the cool night air penetrated through the broken windows and the gentle calm of nature entered our souls for the remaining hours of the night.

The *Burgermeister* of Vavrovice was enjoying his early coffee and eating a thick slice of rye bread and goose fat when I arrived in his yard to ask him for the waggon, I gratefully accepted his invitation to partake of his breakfast. He was, like the others, astonished to hear that I had obtained the permit and he got the waggon ready for me. The horse was lean and old, the good man knew that in dealing with his neighbours across the river, discretion was the better part of valour.

He sent me off with a young Czech driver. We had no trouble with the guards on the bridge. Helene and the children were pleased to see me back so soon. While Helene helped the children into the waggon with a couple of unattractive-looking bundles, I wrote a quick note to Mother Superior of Katscher Convent and asked good *Frau* Christian to give it to the driver.

In the room upstairs, there were still a few articles of my furniture and pictures, there was a Louis XIV table with hand-cut ornamental fittings. The legs had disappeared but the top was valuable and very, very heavy. I made up my mind to take this along with me, so with old *Frau* Christian's help, I was struggling down the stairs, when in walked the Chief of *Militz*. He ordered me to leave everything.

"They are my personal belongings," I said. "I am not a German and I'm not a Pole, I am taking my table." He hurried us down the stairs and amid his protests, we landed the table-top safely on the waggon. "There," I said, "and now we are off!" By way of speeding my departure, he gave me a blow on the South African flag I wore pinned on my breast. The children started crying and I feared we would be detained, — "The Polish Consul will hear of this! (Again, I did not know which Polish Consul). My friends know where I am!" The young Czech driver was only too eager to be off.

Soon we were out on the road experiencing the freedom of travelling the path of the swallows. "*Tot siens, tot siens!*" (farewell, farewell!) I said in Afrikaans, and I did not find it out of place to laugh, to exult, and childishly I cried out, by way of cheering up the children, "*Fonteintje, ek sal noit weer van jou water drink nie!*" (Little fountain, I shall never drink of your water again!)

The children were hushed, but I was shocked by my own drunk feeling when I thought of the tens of thousands remaining in Upper Silesia condemned and doomed to misery and hard labour and I heard their cries as surely as Homer heard the cries in the Underworld; "Names of lamentation loud, Heard on the rueful stream."

We regretted not being able to say goodbye to the dear Reverend Father, whose patience with our children and courtesy were inexhaustible. He had been warned a couple of weeks later to fly, so by night, practically on his knees, he stumbled through the stubbly corn fields and managed to cross the river to safety in Opava. Poor *Frau* Christian, who had done nothing but good all her life, was dragged to an unknown destination. Helene's grandmother, Countess Kerssenbrock, a stately old lady of over 80 years, who did not believe badly of anyone, was rescued stealthily from her once-stately home, Schurgast Castle in Upper Silesia by one of her daughters and an English escort. By night they swam the old lady across the river Neisse in a bathtub, which could not have been very nice. Bishop Nathan, whom I had met in Kyjovice, the founder of the great Medical and Welfare Hospital of Branitz, had sent food to the women and children in a *lager* at Leobschuetz Station. The very next day, he was notified that if the offence was repeated, the church and hospital would be blown up.

We continued our journey to the river; our papers were in order and we were allowed to pass over the bridge…. At the *Burgermeister*'s house, Czech women brought us bread and milk for the children, which they hungrily consumed. We did not let them eat too much. Helene's throat was greatly swollen. With difficulty she swallowed some milk; she was shaking with fever.

When I looked out of the window, I was distressed to see that some men had outspanned "our" horse, but soon I was pleasantly surprised to see that they had inspanned two shiny-coated sorrel horses to the waggon. Ere long, we were on the road again with the waggon swaying to the rapid trot of the sorrels. We would arrive at the home of Baroness Rhemen unannounced, which was somewhat tragic…. A whole family and under such dire circumstances! But as it was more feasible and only twenty kilometres from Troppau, we took the inevitable.

Luckily the road was surprisingly quiet and we travelled without incident, only stopping at the Castle of Wagstein, as we were anxious to know how the Rozumovskys fared. The family was at home and was pleased to get our news. The Countess, a Russian princess, told us she was much terrorised by her compatriots who had unfortunately become acquainted with her nationality, and argued and insisted that she return to Russia. We were pleased to note that the family were still accorded most of their personal possessions. We had tea in what seemed the most peaceful home I had so far visited. The children were becoming very sick and tired; therefore we tried speedily to accomplish the last stage of our journey.

We were thankful when we ultimately passed through the ancient archway leading to Baroness Marika Rhemen's domain. I need not have felt timid about presenting our sick family. Marika accorded us a warm welcome. Gratefully we leaned upon a strong and able guide. Soon, she had rooms prepared upstairs, and from a secret store she brought us soap, as well as scissors and a fine-tooth comb. We snipped off the children's pretty curls, or rather, what had remained of them. We combed our hair and cracked all our lice and then we all enjoyed the luxury of hot baths.

The cook sent up broth, bread, and tea. Soon the children were comfortably settled. There were beds to sleep on! On the day after our arrival, all three children were seriously ill. Baroness Rhemen was able to get the attention of a good doctor from Opava for them. With good food, they speedily recovered.

At Kyjovice they anxiously waited my return. After some months I went back to Opava to bid Helene and family godspeed; together with Marika Rhemen they were all transported off to Germany, where Helene met her Fritz who had returned from a P.O.W. camp in England. Christian's last words to me were, with a dramatic sweep of his hand, "*Aufwiedersehen*, Auntie Dory. Don't let the Poles hit you again!"

******

October, 1945

The mail seems to function again. One of the first letters to arrive is from Auguste, Regina's one time lady's maid. Poor old Auguste! We had hoped that she was well behind the A.M. lines. Instead, she writes from Krnov on the river Oder, from one of the Liechtensteins' estates, where she is stranded with the family Adolf with whom she left Kyjovice. Auguste was never like Anna, in sympathy with the Czech people of Kyjovice. When the letter arrived, I had remained silent. Regina got in touch with Helene and asked if there would be any objection to Auguste joining them in Jaskowice? As soon as Regina got their assurance that Auguste would be welcome to come and assist in their menage, Regina came to my room with her ski slacks.

"Dory," she said, "if you will assist Auguste, these will be warm for the journey."

"You know," I said, and I echoed Papali's words, "Auguste is lucky she is not in a *lager*. She took herself off with the family Adolf in their one horse cart, now she will surely be able to take care for herself."

When I saw the unhappy look of Regina's face, I thought: Auguste gave me a helping hand when I needed one with my sewing. My heart must not be too small for a woman. So I said: "Well, okay, I'll have to see which will be the best way to travel to Jaegendorf."

Before I left for Jaegendorf, Papali said, "Dory, you must see if any of the Liechtensteins are in residence, they will surely be glad to receive you if you want a night's lodging."

In spite of the journey not being too long and the comfort of Regina's ski slacks, it was bitterly cold. I was glad when I located Auguste with the Adolfs — then off to the *Vibo* to get permission for Auguste to travel with me. I had to produce my visa and then had no further difficulty as the Liechtensteins had not involved themselves with the Nazis. Mr. Adolf was employed as one of the dairy hands on the estate.

Between shoals of autumn leaves on the pathways of the park, I walked to the palace, There was no evidence of human life, all seemed deserted and as quiet as any tomb. When I returned to the family where they lived in their one room, Mrs. Adolf was busy preparing our evening meal. They seem to fare very well. Our meal was topped off with delicious strawberries and rich cream.

As it was not yet dark, we sat and related some of our mutual experiences. The Adolfs had been able to stow all their suitcases behind a large wall cupboard, where they were not discovered by the Russians when they had repeatedly ransacked every building. Now, it was time to retire. Someone offered up their bed for me and, instead of sleeping in a princely suite, I had the experience of sleeping with Mr. and Mrs. Adolf, their three children, Auguste and a dog — all in one small room! Thus would my enemies have occasion to say, "How the mighty have fallen!" But I don't think I have any enemies. Still — one never knows!

The next day, as we sat in the waiting room of Jaegendorf station, a tall, fine-looking young man entered the room. He stood for a while looking at the people, then walked up to us. He said softly in German, "You are speaking German, will you do me a kind favor?"

"If possible," I said, "but how do you know we are not Czech?"

"I saw by the movement of your lips, and I think it is very important for me to get to Opava to see my wife and baby, who are most seriously ill." Upon showing my visa, his ticket was also granted without comment.

*****

November, 1945

Since our return from Potstat, we have had no news from Herma Stolberg. We know that Otto is dead and Paskau is occupied by the communists, therefore it was almost a relief to receive one of those mysterious crumpled notes:

"I am very ill and starving in a labour camp in Frydek. Dory, help me, I implore you on my bended knees. H.S."

"I'll have to go to Frydek," I said. The family cautioned, "It may be a trap. Don't go. Consider carefully." To consider carefully would get me just — nowhere.

The next morning, wearing my best tweed suit and my now battered Tyrolean hat, I presented myself at the *lager* in Frydek — an old factory building. "No," I was told by the man wearing a red band round his arm, "you cannot see *Pani* Stolberg without the *Vibo*'s permission."

I made my way to the police station. The officer in charge said not unkindly, "Sit down." I tried to explain delicately who I was and what I wanted, so he said, "Before I can give you the permission for *Pani Hrabenka* Stolbergava (Countess Stolberg) to leave the camp, we must have a written statement from the police in Paskau that she is not wanted by them."

The officer's expression was grave but not unfriendly, so there and then I got a shrewd inspiration and ventured to ask, "Is there any place where the Countess can stay until I take her to Bavaria?"

"I'll stretch the point for you," he said, "and allow her to spend one week here in the hospital." Before speaking to the police officer, I did not have a thought of taking Herma to

Bavaria! And when he suggested the hospital, my relief was great, as I could not possibly have taken Herma to Kyjovice without further jeopardizing our already precarious position.

I took a train to Paskau and sought out the police. The officer was dubious about giving the permission; but when I told him that the police in Frydek were in favour of *Pani* Stolbergova being taken to hospital, he became responsive. With the necessary document in hand, I returned to Frydek.

The late afternoon sun was sending low, slanting rays athwart the blue roof of the twin towered "Church of Grace" (built by the Praschmas), when thanks to the kind cooperation of the police officer, I entered the hospital with *Pani* Stolbergova leaning heavily on my arm.

One week in hospital! It did not give me much time — if at all possible — for getting the necessary permission for Herma to travel to Prague by train. And then suddenly I got very excited because this would enable me to also get across the border to fetch my boys! As I had promised them before Christmas.

I paid another visit to Frydek, this time the sergeant was very friendly — in fact he greeted me like an old friend. He said, "I think I can get the necessary documents for the *Pani* to travel to Prague. From there you will have to find ways of getting across the border." Then he asked me, "Do you belong to the family Prazma that once owned Frydek?"

"Yes, my husband's grandfather was the last of the owners. He sold the estate when the family moved to the more profitable one in Upper Silesia."

"If," asked the sergeant, "one could foresee the turn of the wheels of fate, the family would now still be in possession?"

To which I agreed, but still not knowing if there is more advantage in Czechoslovakia than Poland for German investment. Certainly, the people would be free to travel, while in Poland they are bondaged slaves.

"Have you been to see the Castle Prazma?" he then asked. "Also a street called after your family. Unfortunately, at present, the castle is closed."

Everything was ready for our departure. We sat on the platform at Svinov Station when some officials approached and demanded that Herma accompany them. Poor Herma, terrified, clung to me. "Don't worry," I said. "Our papers are in order, are they not?" I asked the men, while I tried to pacify Herma — our train to Prague was just about due!

A man with a red band round his arm stepped up to me and insolently pointing to Herma, he said: "This woman does not wear the *Nemec* (German) stamped on her clothes!"

"It is very stupid of me," I said, and from my bag I produced pen and paper and hastily wrote two labels, each with a big *Nemec* and pinned one on Herma's chest and back. The train came steaming in. We left the men standing on the platform. Once in the train, I removed the "labels."

The next morning, from the Masaryk Station, we took a taxi to the Dvorak street where Princess Leopoldine Lobkowicz had reserved a room for us. In this quiet street, poor Herma must feel like a prisoner set free. She wanted to eat, she was very hungry, and she wanted to talk. I had to keep reminding her not to talk German, we could get into serious trouble. I did not blame her, knowing what she had been through, but I was thankful when we were able to close the door behind us and put out the light. Then, among many rather mixed up thoughts, I wondered if perhaps the spirit of old Dvorak did capers in the *Gasse* (street). I do not know; it was sufficient for me that I had been able to experience some of his great legato movements.

Now began a strenuous time of trying to find ways and means of getting across to Bavaria. Leopoldine was doing her utmost in trying to pull strings among her many connections. I asked the angel by my side to find a loophole and I hammered the Red X. After a week, when we seemed to lose ground and weight, we were elated to get sudden good news. As a Prior and members of his monastery were leaving Czechoslovakia, the American authorities had arranged for a train to be placed at his disposal. He was leaving that same night, and we could travel with this train across the border. To make the arrangements, we had to see an A.M. official, and he brought something we had not seen for years, a pocket full of small slabs of chocolate! Herma, being starved for something sweet, polished off one slab after another, while I wished to put them all in my bag for my boys. We were at the station in good time for the outward-bound train (after midnight). Herma travelled on to Munich to friends, while, with my angel by my side and a number of small slabs of chocolate, I made a bee-line for Thyrnau.

The boys said they had looked out every day for my coming — they knew I would come, they prayed for it.

*****

3 December, 1945
We are packed up and ready to leave, but I still have a couple of urgent letters to write — one to Rosario, Helene's sister in Munich, to tell her of our welfare and that should Fritz arrive from England, he must on no account try to get to Piltsch as he will immediately land in a prison camp; Helene and the boys are safe in Jaskowice.

And I must write another letter, a very sad and distressing letter, to acquaint the Family Ballestrem that I had received very sad news — a reply to that letter I had written in Piltsch to Reverend Mother in Katscher when I fetched Helene. Reverend Mother wrote that they had suffered dreadful experiences:

> "My dear *Frau Graefin*,
> "Thanks very much for your letter. We are so longing to hear something about the families of our Sisters, but your letter is the only notice we received until now. None of us knows anything from home. I am glad you found your boys, how are they?
> "We had a very bad time and I am sorry to give you such sad news. Our dear Mother Monica Gabrielis Ballestrem died on Easter morning at 2:00 o'clock.
> "On Good Friday, 1945, our little town was ravaged by a mighty attack. Our house was relatively undamaged. That night the Russian forces overwhelmed us. Holy Saturday the house was full of drunken soldiers, looting and plundering.

"It was such a dreadful night! We were all together all night in the dining room. Three drunken Russian soldiers came in, you understand what they wanted. We were clinging all together, but finally one of the men got a young sister outside the group. We held each other tightly but they managed to drag off one of the young sisters.

"Immediately the dear, good, brave Mother M. Gabrielis took the soldier by the arm and pulled him away from the threatened young nun. The man became furious and smashed his fist into poor Mother Gabrielis' face. Probably she was already unconscious, at any rate dazed, because without a sound she sank to her knees. Then the man pulled out his revolver and shot her through the head. Our dear Easter Lamb fell to the floor bleeding profusely and the three heroes hastily left our house. Prayerfully we surrounded our dying sister. Our resident priest gave her the last rites and we prayed the rosary. Perhaps she lived another half hour without regaining consciousness. It was about 2:00 o'clock on the morning of Easter Sunday. She is a true martyr who gave her young life for purity and brotherly love. During the same night we had numerous other visits but we took cover behind Mother M. Gabrielis' body and our attackers retreated immediately, no matter how drunk they were. That night we buried her at the back of our garden under the crackling and smoke of three burning farmyards.

"She is a candid little martyr for Purity and Charity! We miss her very much, but we pray to her, and she helps us faithfully. Certainly she will help also you, dear *Frau Graefin*, and your children, especially Engelbert and Peter, whom she liked so much and called her Sunday Boys. Mother M. Gabrielis was such a dear loving faithful soul, always ready to help. Our house stays and we are glad to be at home, but life is very hard just now. Our Lord went the Way of the Cross and we have to follow Him. During this time, we suffer great privation.

"That night we were forced to leave our house, wheeling a crippled sister in her chair. We endured very hard times and this sister died in Krawarn. After six weeks we were able to return home but four other sisters died as a result of our hardships. We have had to leave our convent, we live in any kind of make-shift hovel or fowl house, but I oft remember a little rhyme of my boarding-school days long ago:

'Ask not how, but trust His will,
Ask not when, but trust Him still.'
Good-bye! When you hear something from family Ballestrem, then write to me please.

— Reverend Mother Maria Antonia,
F.M.M.
Katscher. 13, 9, 1945."

I want my children to keep this record tucked away in their hearts because it is a little chapter taken from our family annals. Sister Monica Gabrielis Ballestrem was the daughter of Papali's sister Agnes. Monica joined the Franciscan Order of Missionaries Maria. These nuns live and work in many parts of the world where the pulse-beat of Il Povarello (the little poor one) is ever present among them. The Franciscans, in their many facets, are the largest in the Catholic Church; very humble, close to the humanity of our Lord, who was born in a stable, endured all the afflictions that flesh is heir to, that we can ever know... walking lonely through the grey, dying naked on the cross. The nuns of Katscher are no exception to the rule, nursing the sick, caring for the poor, giving, always giving... the charity of our Lord.

"Ask not how,
but trust His will,
Ask not when,
but trust Him still."

While the war raged on all fronts, Lekkie and Peter were at school in Katscher for some months. On Sunday afternoons, they would visit the convent; Sister Monica called them her "Sunday Boys." This white-veiled, beautiful blue-eyed nun always prepared a little special treat for them, before joining them in the convent garden. One Sunday when the boys were capering round, a big shaggy wolf dog appeared as if from nowhere and joined them. They all loved animals and were delighted to see the dog, and more so when suddenly a squadron of bomber planes appeared in the sky above them. The big dog, with much wagging of its tail, ran up to Sr. Monica and pressed itself close up against her; the boys said: we did likewise and we felt ourselves a little close, safe company; we had no fear because we knew that Sr. Monica and the big dog would ward off every kind of evil and danger.

###

CHAPTER ELEVEN
READING OLD LETTERS

Mid-December, 1945

It was 2:00 o'clock in the morning. Cold, winter, snow,
but snugly warm at heart with my boys. We were once more
safely back at Kyjovice. I shall have to try and keep them as
subdued as possible, as this is a time of great uncertainty and
suspense. What will the next step be? What will the next hour
bring? I have written many letters and hope to hear from South
Africa soon. Papali has endeavoured to get in touch with
friends of influence, but even Dr. Benes and Jan Masaryk seem
to get shifted out of the picture. There is no redress.

Mrs. Staffin from the Guest House has sent us a pot of
goose fat. The St. Martins geese were fat, and this is good! The
land is grey and sodden and cheerless. The peasants are
struggling to lift the last of their potatoes and fodder and sugar
beets before the ground freezes, and what a mess their
waggons have made of the country roads. The trees are bare,
the heavens are toneless and obscured by low-trailing clouds.
Everyone says it will snow.

Soon the wind comes whistling through the leafless
trees carrying the first light flakes of snow on its stinging blast.
The children call out delightedly, *"Es faengt an zu schneien! es
schneit!"* (it is starting to snow! it snows!). In tiny dribs and
drabs the first snow-flakes scurry and fall. Soon billions of
flakes, like white wafting feathers, fill the air, and while the
countryside is enveloped in a milk-white sheet, we resignedly
say: "The old woman in the sky is plucking her geese."
Through the curtailed, darkening day the snow intermittently
falls; through the silent night, dimly seen, the snow falls softly
on the woodland hills and meadows, on the black slate roofs of
the village and on the hedgerows, glancing airily off the
steeple of the church, waveringly alighting on the churchyard
wall, covering with an ermine cloak all the lowly laid. In the
park the scene has changed to deep rift valleys and pallid

mountains of the moon. It freezes colder, harder, night and day.

Mrs. Staffin's pot of goose fat is very welcome.

*****

24 December, 1945

It is Christmas Eve. Oh the beautiful Christmas that takes us away from all "absurdity," as Anna would say, so that in this troubled world of ours, the angels' song becomes very real and we get that general uplift, a universal uplift that carries us far beyond the Pale... even to the Christmas Star. It is this "uplift" that our household feels today. We are all tremendously busy and I can say happy.... All the villagers are busy and happy. Christmas is an infection that makes one feel good. We have no presents, but Regina has contrived to make some pictures from holy cards found in an old Bible — very pretty. The children made cards for all of us. We are not supposed to see them until tonight, but Ilona and Petty's cards are real treasures.

And I? Yes, I tried to make a big batch of cookies. I started beating up some sugar and eggs and some sour cream from Milka.

While I got the pans ready, Peter and Ilona offered to do the mixing, but when I looked into the bowl. I know whose faces were very red and who hung their heads.... The mixture had tasted too good! And now my cookies will lack the essentials.

Papali went out with the boys into the snowy forest. They returned with red cheeks and noses — and a young fir tree, which they have set up on a bed of green moss. The tree is most comforting in a bare room.

And now, while I am writing this Christmas story, I must count our many gifts. They are mostly blessings that money cannot buy, on which we put a high value and we rest in them in comfort:

1st. — God's own gift, that was made manifest to us on the Holy night: the Babe that was born in a stable and laid in a manger.

2nd.— The invitation from the choir of angels to join in the Gloria.

3rd.— Good health, kind hearts, and "bairns" full of glee.

4th.— Papali's fluffy fir tree.

5th.— Regina's pictures.

6th.— The children's cards.

7th.— Auntie Mother's gracious words to all.

8th.— The beautiful Christmas roses growing on the snow-bank in the park.

9th.— A basket full of red apples.

10th.— A basket full of walnuts.

11th.— A small basket full of eggs.

12th.— A large basket full of Kolaches, lovely filled buns, from the village people.

13th.— A pat of butter and a bottle of milk from the forester's wife.

14th.— My plate of cookies.

Tonight we have a cup of soup and bread; tomorrow, Christmas day, we have:

15th.— Lamb's lettuce salad (from Papali's garden) growing under the snow.

16th.— I suppose I can safely count my chicken pie — a big pie! — in which I put hard boiled eggs and forcemeat-balls. Decorated with pastry leaves, it looks festive... like my mother used to make.

17th.— And now. Last but not least, My Big Blessing: My children happily together; they add a little touch here and there to welcome the Christ Child... on this Silent Night, Holy Night.

As we wish each other a Happy Christmas, our recollections may be very near to tears, yet like the Wise Men, we feel the "Uplift" of His Star... Our Star. And with shining faces greet the New Born King.

*****

A week or two ago I asked Uncle Fritz if perhaps there are any documents in Kyjovice that are likely to be of value to

me later regarding the Praschma estate. "Yes, possibly," he
answered. "Look in the little room, at the back of my office,
where the files are kept. You will find a file that has been sent
to me. It contains copies of the Testament of your father-in-law
and of his father. There is also the *Vertrag* (agreement) and the
Beschluss (conclusion, resolution) which I think you must
safeguard. There are also numerous letters and papers which
may interest you. Ask Milka to try to get the key of the office."

Milka obtained the key and while the communist party
was at supper and the house was quiet, I stole up by the back
stairs, feeling not a little nervous. I opened the library door and
the thought flashed through my mind of how I had felt on my
first visit to Kyjovice; a stranger, with no programme notes to
guide me. I had fancied I was fighting a little Waterloo. I
peered around… and there a big rat, with a rustling noise,
jumped off the dusty table — only a rat! But I was greatly
relieved after he had scurried past me through the open door.
Holding the candle aloft and feeling pretty unnerved, I looked
around the room and was again much relieved to see that the
family portraits all appeared to be stacked up on the floor.
Many books were still on the shelves or lay strewn about. I
wished I could spend a day or two in the library, sorting out
some of the precious volumes and securing the family
portraits. In the little back room, nobody seems to have
troubled about the files of papers, they remain as orderly as
when Uncle Fritz worked in his office.

I soon found the Praschma file and hurried back to my
room. It seems to contain the documents that I need and also a
lot of other papers and letters. I shall look through them when
time permits. I have a feeling of guilty pleasure in dipping into
old letters and dictionaries — it is like reading someone's
dreamy private diary.

*****

Alas! I marvel to read these old letters, I am astonished!
They are not at all like reading a dreamy private diary — I feel
hot because they are much my concern, they are letters mildly
reminiscent of love intrigues at royal courts. It is when you

come face to face with that ugly little word "intrigue" that you marvel to what lengths underhanded people resort! How much more kindly to follow old Mrs. Wilkenson's prescript. Like she says, in her broad Yorkshire accent, "Rather give an ounce of help than a ton of sympathy." Yes, *Deo Gratias* for the good simple folk, but living in the same district are the Mrs. J. Dickes and Mrs. Erika Hartmanns who, unmolested, live their lives in the good old South African Low Country, and they write:

> Your Hon. the Count of Falkenberg, (says Mrs. Dicke, who at one time regularly spent Saturday evenings at our home, with a much disgruntled face if she lost at a game of bridge), overlook the liberty I take in writing. My husband has had a letter from Madam Countess Praschma evidently in full agreement of your son's marriage, which is wrong. She would not be if she knew the people and circumstances, on the contrary, she would be severely against it. The girl, in her way, is quite nice, not good-looking — only capable as a farmer's wife that is all! Her father has no lands, relations of both families are numerous and most of them very poor. Your son will be mixed up in a circle of poor people. The families have been intermarried for generations and are not what we call a robust family. One uncle of the girl had two children, now fortunately both dead, who behaved like little monkeys, made funny sounds, looked queer, more like animals than human beings. It is to be hoped that such creatures will not be born again in the family but who can tell?
>
> We hardly ever see them. The girl has expressed her view of the marriage, that if she marries a Count, it will be a gain for her family. Heaven knows what the young people are going to live from — it is sheer obstinacy that your son will not listen to you. Your son proposed to my daughter, who is of aristocratic birth, and has had a university education, and will be well provided for, but both Mr. Dicke and myself went against it

because we thought it wrong to go against your Hon. wishes. Tomorrow I am going over to Dr. Hartmann.

These are facts that I have stated, that any father would like to hear. I hope sincerely that something will happen to prevent the marriage for the sake of your family.

I remain your Hon. very sincerely, J.Dicke.

This letter was written some weeks before our marriage. My father-in-law, the Hon. Count, must have drawn his own conclusions. There is no copy of a reply to Mrs. Dicke. Included was my own letter to Engelbert's parents thanking them for their good wishes and blessings; I said:

With good wishes and blessings and with a good angel to cheer the way, we shall surely be a happy couple. We are fortunate, because among our telegrams is also one from Holy Father Pius XI which gave me great happiness. This is also a good opportunity of thanking you for the faith and trust you have shown in me. We know that these virtues are the bases of the good life. Now there is something I feel I should like to tell you, I am sure it does not affect anybody but ourselves. The fact is, at present I do not think a title is of any use to us in South Africa where standards are different to what they are in Europe — where things are taken naturally; here you are subject to a certain amount of curiosity and criticism and are even expected to be extravagant! Surely it is better for a man to be accepted at his own true worth and to find his feet.

A simple letter, but unconsciously it must have been of good effect, but what must my father-in-law have thought of the children behaving like animals? It is to be hoped — prayed for — that people are not born suffering from epilepsy. As for the other lies, well, I wonder who will ultimately suffer because of them!

Another letter, one from Mrs. Erika Hartmann. — she could not possibly make a mistake. As I read her letter, I can freely forgive my father-in-law for what I thought he was — a hard and bitter old man — and especially for the letter he wrote that puzzled and grieved me so much which I received when my baby, Rea, died. I had opened that letter thinking it was a message of condolence, but he only said:

> I am sorry the baby is dead. Your husband has never told you the truth, so now I find it my duty to tell you and also I send a copy of this letter to your sister, that should you decide to come to Germany with your husband — you will never be accepted here, instead you will be sent home a penniless stranger. You must know that there are seven (7) millions of people out of work here and times are hard. My wife and family have been forced to leave Falkenberg; at present, they live in a forester's house on our other Estate of Tillowitz. We do not know how long we will remain here.
>
> In giving you this warning, I do so in your own interests. I advise you to get work and to remain with your own people.
>
> From your father-in-law, Johann Nepomuk Praschma.

The letter had brought scalding tears to my eyes, but before Engelbert returned, I had had time to take a square look at myself and to reflect: How we had shared our sorrow — how together we had made the wreath of white roses — how together we had carried the little white coffin of our beautiful child to rest in that little grave 202.

When Engelbert returned he exclaimed impulsively: "My father! How could he write this? Something is not in order! How could he write this! He will answer for it!"

I tried to be diplomatic, I took his hand and said: "No, my dearest, if anything, it draws us nearer together. I shall not let you down, I will not disappoint you. I will not disgrace the people from whom I am descended, whose history my grandparents often related to us — of my ancestor, the

Commodore, who was so good and mild, and yet he did not fear to brave the ocean storms in his sailing vessel. Of those simple but elegant people, the founders of Franschhoek. I'll go anywhere with you. I'll go to Germany."

Mrs. Erika Hartmann's letter lies before me, it gives a clear picture of that troubled scene — from a woman whose face I have never seen, whose strokes of the pen are as bold as brass. She writes a long letter — in German, commenting on the inflation in Germany — that cuts me to the heart — that Falkenberg is assisted through "*Ost-hilfe*" under government management until recovery, that because of the income from the forest alone she trusts that my father-in-law and his family have every prospect of retaining their possessions.

Then:

Regarding the idea of Engelbert returning home with his family, this is now the question for you to consider in advance. How can you defend yourself against accepting the family? May I in this respect give you some advice? Of course it is quite out of the question that Engelbert has explained the true situation to his wife. He will naturally have told her that she will be welcomed at home; letters through his hands will have been accordingly edited. You will be advised to write to her and also to send a copy of your letter to a neutral person, i.e. her sister perhaps, informing her loud and clear, that under no circumstances can you assist her and her child. Therefore in her own interests, she will be advised to remain in South Africa with her relatives. Honoured dear Count Praschma, you can feel well assured that her family will give her every assistance — this bespeaks the hospitality and the unity of these Boer people. For you, under present circumstances, to receive the family, will not only be a financial burden, but you must consider that his wife's origin is from a simple peasant circle. Finally, does not every good old family — be they aristocrats or bourgeois — hang on to their traditions? There will also be other complications — but when his wife fully comprehends that no

recognition awaits her in Germany, she will have
the good sense to remain in South Africa. This
appears to be dreadfully hard, but she will have
been warned; for God's sake stick to your guns —
don't allow yourself to be overruled.

Here we are well off, although things
have been more than difficult, but with a lovely
climate; heavenly free life; no finance officer or
prescribed order. With hard work and diligence
— we are well off!

Erika Hartmann.

*****

Mrs. Hartmann, if it was not that to me your letter is a
serious matter, it would be amusing. You do not have to state
that every good family has its traditions; it is in respect of the
Diary that my great-aunt wrote that can be found in our
Afrikaner Museum Library, that I started my Diary, and, "if
half the world does not know how the other half lives," then it
is just as well that "half the world does not know what the
other half knows!"

Did Mrs. Dicke know that her marriage depended
upon the offer I rejected of being taken to the Police Ball in
Pietersburg, an offer that also included a "dream evening
frock"? I had joined my father as we customarily sat at sunset
on the old blue-gum log, listening to the golden orioles call
and watching for the flock's return. "Daddy," I said, "Mr. Dicke
is coming to ask you if he can take me to the Police Ball. Please
say 'No' — put your foot down, Daddy."

Did Mrs. Dicke know that later, when Engelbert came, I
again sat with my father on the blue-gum log. I said:
"Engelbert Praschma is coming to ask you if he can marry me.
You can say 'yes,' Daddy." Some neighbours jokingly came
and sang a song for me: "I'll rather marry a young man, with
an apple in his hand — Get away old man, get away!"

It is late, my eyes are clouded. I see only a wreath of
beautiful white roses, a picture I want to keep with me always.

*****

14 April, 1946

There was no early bird song, but we have been up early. A dull morning — the rain sprinkled on our faces and mingled with our tears. Auntie Mother, Papali, Regina and Anna sat in an open lorry. They were being transported off, far away from Kyjovice, first to a *lager* in Bilovice and then to an unknown destination. The communist authorities have denied them every request — a last few precious threads from their old home to weave into some sort of a pattern in a new environment; the beautiful table linen; the silver that has been the pride of generations; portraits; books; treasured glass and oddments... nothing that we strove to save from the Russians — nothing is theirs. With only a few odd bundles that each one was able to carry beside them in the lorry, bound for the unknown, they were ready to leave in the rain.

"*Au revoir*," they said and then, to cheer me up, my dear good Papali said, "Be brave like you have always been, and thank you for everything." The lorry drove off before I could tell them how deeply indebted I was to them for everything.

They had disappeared down the chestnut avenue. I am alone. I am desolate! And yet I am sustained by the knowledge ... of how easily our worldly possessions dissolve and crumble into dust but that our essential home is indeed indestructible; *Deo Gratias* for such a background — for the practice of detachment that has now made it quietly possible for them to leave their beloved home and to travel through darkness to the Light Victorious. May God bless them, bless them always.

We hope and trust they will be sent to the British or A.M. Zone.

*****

It is well known to the authorities that Papali and his family were not Nazis. It is also known that I am not German. However, for reasons of their own, they may also decide to place us in a transport; the order may come today or tomorrow. To a certain extent, as long as I am with them, the children would enjoy the novelty of being put in a transport, but I? No! I think of the *veld* and the *kopjes* and the wide open spaces of the Transvaal. No! I would hate to lose my freedom! I must be on the alert and get everything in readiness, especially the things I must try to smuggle to addresses given to me in Prague.

But first, I must take some food to the *lager* in Bilovice. Even the friendly village people do not know how long the transport will stop there.

I went out and killed a rooster, a large bird, there was no one else to do it. I'll pot-roast it and take it to the *lager* with bread.

Princess Bluecher has just called with son Thomas. She was shocked to hear that the family have been transported off. "But why? This is impossible," she kept saying. Then she asked timidly if I thought it would be wise for her to try to see them at the camp. I said I am going in any case, I am pot-roasting a chicken and I am taking bread.

"It smells nice," said Luise Bluecher. "The Russians have eaten all our stock; they caroused in our large salon and shot holes in our family portraits. I want to get back to Guernsey!"

I left very early in the morning for Bilovice, carrying the little load of provisions in a bag that I could also sling over my shoulder; the few peasants that I met on the way greeted me with a friendly, "*Dobry den*." There are about fifty German people in the camp — all waiting to be sent to the British Zone. It is said that some of the transports are sent to the Russian Zone where the poor German people are all virtually kept prisoners. Anxiety and distress are written on every face and I did not dare show my food bag in the presence of all those half-starved people, especially the children. While I was there, they were lined up to receive their midday meal; water, with a few pieces of bread and potato floating in it.

Without exception, every person is systematically searched before leaving the *lager* and every little keepsake and last bit of jewelry is taken from them. Auntie Mother therefore confided her wedding ring to me. Such a demure little ring, it gave me quite a stab when she placed it on my little finger.

Later, as I walked back, filled with gloomy thoughts in the gathering twilight, as I twirled the little ring on my finger, I got a real pang, and I asked myself: is it necessary for people to destroy all the old established order of things? Why don't they

find it saner to try to lighten the darkness than to decry it?
There was no answer... only a small thing that is most
important: I must safeguard the ring, so that it is returned to its
rightful owner, my very dear Auntie Mother.

*****

Kyjovice. April, 1946

Here is a poor woman from England. She can't say,
"*Dobry den*," she can't milk the goat, she can't walk through the
snow to feed the fowls, she can't accommodate herself to a
peasant-woman's life in Czechoslovakia. Why did she marry a
Czech peasant? If a woman wants to walk by the side of her
man, in any walk of life, she must be prepared to say, like
Ruth, I wonder if I am sorry for this woman?

Princess Bluecher has called again. She intends
hurrying back to Guernsey as quickly as possible. Tommy will
stay at Radun, but Lulu says he will never be able to bring a
young wife here — he better marry an old lady if a young one
can't walk beside him. Are there no more Ruths in the world, I
wonder? Tommy is so kind, so genuine, with earnest brown
eyes and admiration for Lord Wilberforce and for all who right
the wrong... and all who lighten the darkness.

Among numerous pieces of broken furniture, crockery
and all manner of household odds and ends are also numbers
of cabin trunks, old fashioned portmanteaus, suitcases, etc. All
have been broken into or smashed in some way or other by the
Russian soldiers. I took one of the big suitcases to the village
carpenter and he has kindly repaired the lid for me. I have
packed the pastel pictures; some miniatures; the beautiful
painting of Kyjovice; a picture of Grandmother Bertha Princess
Croy done in oils, wearing a bonnet with ribbons, sitting in a
high chair, with a little goat beside her; the Stolberg diary — it
looks very impressive, with ribbons and seals. Our Majenka,
the jewellery stuffed doll, will go to dear Leopoldine.

*****

A hurried journey to Prague, Princess Schwarzernberg
not too friendly, Leopoldine her gracious self. Luckily, one of

the Liechtensteins was in Prague... Leopoldine was quite surprised to see what Majenka contained, but it was the demure little wedding ring that brought a catch to her voice.

One of the next procedures will be to get some of the pretty Dresden china and Regina's Persian carpet to Prague. And then some family portraits to another address. Perhaps I'm enjoying myself!

*****

On occasion, when I have done little things for my children, people have said, "You do spoil your children!" Well, if I don't spoil them, who will? They have no father, no one except that fair, beautiful nun in the white habit, Monica Ballestrem, who called them her Sunday Boys. But even if I spoil them, I pray never to involve the principles of life. Our minds must ever be obedient to God. Children must know that they are much loved, but they also must have clear-cut ideas and, to help them out sometimes, a few sound smacks work wonders. So I wonder if I really spoil my children.

I miss our dear Auntie Mother sadly, she had so much good influence on the children... her Wild Flowers, as she called them. On occasion, she said to me: "You must always make them feel that you expect the best and they respond; only don't expect too much."

*****

In the sweet simplicity of their hearts, my four have great faith in me; they don't give a thought about the morrow, about the future, they don't worry about anything — not when the bread tin is empty, or where the next meal comes from. If they have such carefree faith and confidence in me, then how great must my faith and trust be in our heavenly Father's care. Who marks the sparrow's fall? Actually, my faith is the same as the children's. I am convinced that we shall never really hunger, never starve. One must think about these things but I am persuaded (almost) that people will be prepared to steal for us! I have not quite made up my mind about the rights and wrongs of stealing to still the pangs of hunger. If I should have to walk round the village and try to steal a crust of bread for my children, surely no one will blame or punish me? I could never have punished Kittie, our cat, when she stole for her kittens.

I slept well last night, and when, early this morning, I walked among our rows of beans and berries and flowers, I thought about how stupid and confused my thoughts have been about the "rights and wrongs" of stealing. How can a grown woman try to give children clear-cut ideas when she is without them herself? Surely, as our Regina would say, "Right is right and wrong is wrong!" If I steal, I shall have to pay back in coin that I shall be very sorry to give, so at all costs I must be resourceful, and even our bread tin is empty. I must keep my faith — like my children — because God is able to do abundantly more than our every concept, which is quite clear when I look at my beans and berries and flowers and what's wrong with considering myself an amateur economic expert? Or a beggar?

*****

Kyjovice. May, 1946

I have been to Opava again, to speak to the bank manager — he said, "Sorry, (I am losing my sympathy for the word 'sorry') your money is in a frozen account and we cannot pay out one heller." The peasants and friends are all in the same predicament — except people who work for the factories are well paid, to step up the supply for Russian demands.

And then I visited our Zdenka. Her mother gave me some turnips and milk, she said I must cook the turnips in the milk and add a little butter, which she also supplied. "It is a good supper for children," she said, "with a slice of brown bread."

As *Pani* Homula said, boiled in this way, the garden fresh turnips were delectable.

*****

Mrs. Kupka, the lady who I think has my Voigtlander camera, has asked me to give her children English lessons. In payment, she will give me milk and butter. Gladly, gladly I assented. The children are eager to learn and are much better scholars than my children are.

The butter and milk are rich and good.

*****

When in every way we must try to be as unobtrusive as possible, my children seem to become more wayward. I try to be like the other Irishmen. I try to change my tactics. Sometimes I say sternly: "You dare and you know what I think!" When a special crisis arises I speak in English, my voice drops down to zero, it usually works. — They prepare for the worst; it usually comes! A few sound smacks work wonders. I have noticed that whenever anything is particularly forbidden, they delight in trying to circumvent me. Then I say, "Carry on, bump your heads, you'll learn." I never try to punish them together, it is better and more dignified to take them out singly, especially when it so happens that my wooden shoe must have full play! I have never had occasion to spank Ilona — not soundly; Petty is a nervous child, the war has left its mark on him. I usually undress him (because he is tired) put on his pyjamas and put him to bed.

Yesterday at lunch time they were out for devilment. I used my low-toned English — no good — then when Lekkie got up and chased Peter round the table to the clapping of hands, I was so exasperated, I took up my plate and bowed myself out of the room, I sat down in my bedroom and wept. After about ten minutes, there was a knock at the door.

Peter came in, "But Mammie, what's the matter with you?" he said. "Can't we have a joke?"

"If a gentleman thinks it's a joke to behave badly, then you can just go back and think it over. Shut the door after you."

Soon Ilona came in. "What's the matter with you? You have not had your dinner o-oh!"

"Go back to your brothers and have your jokes, I have no appetite."

Again a knock on the door. Lekkie this time, "Do you want us to sit at command like poodle dogs?" he asked. "I would rather have little dogs than pigs. Please go out and shut the door."

Quite soon the door was unceremoniously opened. There they all four stood, Lekkie carrying the tea tray with cups, Peter the tea pot, Ilona the milk jug, and my Petty the sugar bowl; they set down the tray and their faces were very solemn. They all knelt down with hands on their breasts — Peter had difficulty keeping his face straight. Lekkie looked at him sternly. "Your little dogs," they said. I looked down from one to the other, my heart melted, but I said: "If people have no self-control, then they turn into beasts."

*****

I have a few hundred kronen, and not from the bank! (I shall never go and see that surly bank-manager in Opava again.) After making inquiries for a buyer for my watch — it is a good little gold watch — several women came to see me. I sold it to the highest bidder, then I sold the little round table in my bedroom. I had no right to the table, it belongs to Auntie Mother, but it will be snatched up by someone else. Auntie Mother said I must take anything I want that remains. This money is for our homeward trip. I am rich again! What with Mrs. Kupka's milk and weekly pat of butter (a very good arrangement) and with our vegetables, I am able to make an appetizing and hearty casserole — sometimes it's called an "Eintopf," *(one pot") — and sometimes it's called a stew; also, I can never get over the beauty of having our own hens and eggs the young hens are laying. I keep up my reputation of being an amateur economic expert.

*****

Oh, oh — the school master has been to see me. What he actually came for I do not know. Anyway, he reported that the village boys say that my boys are not South African, they are German because they stand shoulder to shoulder and they are much stronger than the Czech boys. I have noticed that they come walking home, up the chestnut avenue, almost shoulder to shoulder. I am very proud of it. I could only say that they must stand together and they must show their school friends love and respect. I hope that this is what he will tell his scholars, but the poor man is plainly worried. He is also distressed because he does not know Russian and now he must teach it in school.

*****

We are not allowed to pick any of the lovely strawberries, apples or other fruit in Papali's garden, but by lucky chance our garden plot is bordered by low spreading red currant and gooseberry bushes and it is flanked by a number of walnut trees on the outer garden wall. The trees are obligingly laden with clusters of nuts as I am sure are seldom seen on walnut trees. Perhaps they are so laden because I told the boys that it is said that "A dog, a woman, and a walnut tree must be whipped." Forthwith, they armed themselves with sticks and I said, "Gently, gently." The trees have responded with a royal harvest. We shall gather the fruit when the first frost tinges the leaves. We'll leave some for the birds — like Papali used to do.

In the vegetable garden we have plenty of rhubarb but alas, no sugar. We don't like it, who does? We have plenty of horseradish but .... no meat. We have plenty of sour, sour gooseberries but what a pity, no sugar. But as to our herbs, well, with plenty of manure waterings, they have come into their own. We have parsley, thyme, anise, dill, sweet basil and mint. Stews, spaghetti, and mince seem very tasteless without sweet basil, when once you acquire the taste. Peas and young potatoes I vary by tossing in finely chopped mint or parsley — I don't let a curl of parsley go to waste. Here where the growing season is short, with plenty of manure water, rain and sunshine, vegetables soon mature crisp and tender. Never have I seen such crisp lettuce — almost fat! I am sure that our broad beans rival those of Thomas Pringle, which he mentions in his 1820 diary.... that the zebras galloped through. My trustworthy gardener Peter said proudly: "Mammie, we can slay a man with them!" Their pods average seven inches in length.

However much I strive to get things in marching order for us to leave, I only seem to run round in circles, like the spotted cow that closed her eye and opened it and closed it once again! I get no further, I feel defeated and dejected. I know I must be logical, otherwise the clearer view that I pray for will never be made manifest to me.

The *Vibo* require triple lists of our personal possessions — every single item — that we are taking out of the country. I got the lists ready — they have been checked and signed by our several *Vibo*s (what a business!) in three different towns where, with a sheaf of papers in my hand, I had to explain to police and custom officials what and why we need our own goods. I suppose it is because of these journeys and other happenings that I feel so glum and exhausted. I perceive that the longer we remain here the more wayward the children are growing. It is not to be wondered at, because there are so many disturbing influences. The boys are not under proper control.

This morning I saw our pretty blue Dresden china tea pot boiling tea on the communist stove in the big kitchen. Some of the cups were lying in the sink. I had to wait until the busy-body of a cook went shopping, then I hurried into the kitchen with a basket, collected the teapot and cups, and also a Rosenthaler vase from the shelf — they need a good scrubbing — and then I'll put them in my trunk. One of the children at school told my boys that her mother has my Voigtlander camera. These and similar incidents are very disturbing and a setback to character; beyond these upsets I also have to deal with the personal temperamental trait of each child. I am actually beginning to think that somewhere in the branches of our genealogical tree there must have been an Irish ancestor, otherwise I cannot account for their monkey tricks.

As I have already written, I especially notice that whenever I am worried or tired, the fat literally falls into the fire. Very likely it is my fault, and what distresses me is that my dearest Peter, my blue-eyed boy, as the others say he is, is often the ringleader. At a solemn moment he will start giggling at something and then of course they all become hilarious. Or like it happened on the day when I was travelling fruitlessly between Opava and Bilovice trying to get an interview with the bank manager: Peter, with Petty in tow, was playing truant. They carried one of the wash tubs to the old stone quarry, and there unconcernedly paddled their "boat" and picnicked on the sandwiches that I had prepared for school. This continued for days, until I noticed their soggy boots, then, my oh my! How the sparks flew!

Again, when Mr. Kupka and all the garden hands chased them through the French garden and over the garden wall, my Peter was in the lead! I am reminded of some Irish characteristics given to me by an old Irish Sister. She said, "We are temperamental, illogical, touchy, capricious, over-talkative, procrastinating, conceited, maddening!" That fits my picture! "But," added the old sister, "amongst ourselves we are not illogical, because we understand each other." "How do you come to understand each other?" I asked her. "Oh, by just being as lighthearted and as clever as the other Irishman!" I realize that I am no match for my children, but a mother must be versatile. — Perhaps I must begin by trying to keep them better occupied after school hours and so give the devil less work for idle hands; it will become more difficult as the long winter evenings advance.

I have started by making a programme for an evening effort. We begin…

Every evening, all see that there is enough wood for the stove.

Monday: Supper. I wash up while homework is being done. If time permits: Reading.

Tuesday: Supper, etc. We all darn socks or mending. Boots get polished.

Wednesday: Supper, etc. Lekkie gives a singing lesson — boots polished.

Thursday: Supper, etc. Songs or reading.

Friday: Supper, etc. Concert, all sing. Lekkie conducts (German or the lovely old Czech hymns).

Saturday: Supper, etc. Socks are inspected and boots polished. Card games or reading.

Sunday: We relax while each one does as his fancy pleases; usually reading.

If any one does not join our "effort," he must be off to bed early on two consecutive nights.

My "evening effort" seems to be a good idea — as the children also realize that socks do not get darned nor do dishes get washed without personal effort, and when our effort is concerted nobody feels a martyr.

The boys are good at darning, and even Petty can stitch on a button; and when he is in the mood and restful, he can sing and harmonize any tune better than the others, except perhaps Lekkie, who is very gifted. When he sings and at the same time conducts — a quaint, erect little figure, standing on the sofa, like he sometimes does — his own idea of "standing above to conduct" — he looks like a teddy bear, very endearing in his suit, but I wonder how long the others will tolerate this "standing above" of his. Anyhow, the entertainment provided heightens our "effort," and when they sing the Czech hymns to Our Lady: "Maria, Maria, flower of the field and Lily of the Valley," the sweet pathos of Lekkie's soprano voice seems to carry the lovely tune and the ringing words — "Mar--ria, Li--llia," — far away from our small kitchen room to fairer pasture lands and still waters; then I am sure Our Lady must — like I do — forgive them their "Irish characteristics."

Growing by the old turkey runs are great, gorgeous, low spreading elderberry trees with a cloud of creamy white flowers. I am glad that the communists and villagers have no use for the purply black berries; they are left to the birds and to me and we shall make the most of them. We know some of their medicinal virtues. I have already collected a few baskets full of flowers and have dried them for our morning cup of tea. I shall make bottles and jars of what I call "elderberry wine." The berries boiled and strained with apples will be a treat for the children — a glass of hot wine after our "Evening Effort" sounds good; elderberry flowers are said to make a good spicy wine, but we have no facilities or inclination to make wine. In an old book I read that the flowers and berries; in fact, the whole tree — lock, stock and barrel, or should I say: root, bark, and berry — have so many medicinal virtues (while the good hard wood can be turned into fishing rods) that Boerhaave, a famous Dutch physician, is said to have taken off his hat to all elderberry trees. My children will take hats off to me for hot drinks into which every grain of sugar that I can muster will have gone. I have also dried vegetables for winter: spinach, green beans, peas, and of course mushrooms that we have collected in the forests — and herbs, lots of herbs. Milka thinks my herbs are a waste of time, as she will give me sauerkraut and the peasants will give me potatoes. "Herbs," she said, "is just grass and some of it tastes horrible. Garlic? Yes, that is for good sense!"

I always tell people, "Don't worry," but I have been miserably worried at not hearing from our absent ones until today and now what a beautiful day it has been! A halcyon day... a day of summer sunshine and lightheartedness... a marvellous day! Two letters! One from my sister Clem in South Africa — all are well. They are also putting the wheels in motion for our visa to come through. A dear letter. And the other, a letter from Papali, I wept, yes, I wept when I read his letter — partly from joy to hear that they had landed safely in Baden, Germany, in the British Zone, but also I wept to read of the hardships they were made to endure... these sensitive, dear people.

He wrote of the first ten days in the camp in Wagstad... all the indignities they were subjected to, then like animals they were forced into a cattle truck. There was hardly room to stand, as one half of the truck was taken up by baggage. There were old sick people in wheelchairs, mothers with babies in arms. This state of affairs they had to endure for thirteen days (without sanitary arrangements). Happily, the unfortunate people travelling in the truck were helpful and friendly. After this ordeal, dirty and exhausted, they arrived at a larger camp in Germany, which although also filthy, they were at lest free to roam about.

Here an old friend of the family, a Count Emanuel Westerholt, heard of their dilemma and came to their rescue. He offered them a respite in an old castle called Gamburg in Baden. Emanuel owns another establishment where he lives in Westfalia. This is a solution to their immediate difficulties. Papali says that Auntie Mother had to be taken, in a state of exhaustion, to a hospital, and he adds, "Now in Gamburg, we are also recovering. From my high window, in the old stronghold, I have a marvellous view of mountain and river. We have no servants, so like always, much work and responsibility rests with our good Anna. Greetings to the children, from us all much love. I kiss your hand. Your true Uncle Fritz."

Yes, I weep when I think of the cruel indignity inflicted on these grand old people by the new, contemptible overlords who are well acquainted with the Stolberg history — that of mercy and charity, but as Papali has often said, more than one person has experienced the bitter taste of man's ingratitude; we must carry the cross and not expect it to carry us..... What words of gratitude are there for those who would carry it for us? What we need is courage, as my Auntie Mother would say, to be worthy of our high calling; but I say the world is still full of heroism.

To prove that I am right, Mimi Des Fours came to see me. I have said before, that Mimi is one of those calm, dauntless people who inspire me with courage. I felt the same regard for her again yesterday, taking the long journey under much difficulty, when others are fearful of travelling a yard or two! Mimi traveled sixty kilometres on a charitable mission. Sad to say, she had many distressing facts to relate about Potstat and its vicinity, where people now have occasion to say that taken all in all, Hitler was not such a bad chap.... by comparison.

In coming to see me, Mimi's mission was to give me two packets, one that I must deliver to her nephew Carl in Prague, and one, which she said, "will help to tide you over to England."

"Mimi," I said, "I can't take it. I shall never be able to pay you back." "You must take the money, it is a present from me to help, to take you and your children out of this poor country, before the Iron Curtain clamps down.... Just send me word now and then to say where you are and how you are faring!" This gave me a pang as if I could feel how "the wind bloweth where it listeth, tossing us about, hurly-burly, like fallen leaves — we know not where we land." I could not do otherwise but accept her offer.

"But this," said Mimi, "this is rather precious." She held up a brooch with the jewels of Carl Des Fours, "It is a golden hyacinth." I saw that it was indeed precious, pearls with two pendant pearls and I "wondered, how can one part with something so precious?" I wanted to ask Mimi about the brooch, but as I perceived that it was indeed painful for her to part with it, I remained silent. Then Mimi spoke about the heartbreak of the German people. She had known many of them from her childhood and of others she had attended to since she had returned from America with her Medical Doctor's degree — all were now deprived of any means of livelihood. But she spoke mostly about animals... animals suffering... people suffering.... But it was when she said, "I could go to Austria, but I must go back to Potstat — to take up my stand," that I realized the heroism of Mimi, Countess Des Fours.

Knowing that informers and thieves are watchful, I feared that Mimi's visit could herald other unpleasant visits, so I tried to think of a safe place for hiding her packet. I sewed a little bag with two compartments, one for Charles' packet and one for myself. I attached a piece of tape to the bag, to hang round my neck; but where to hide the brooch, I was puzzled, so I hit upon the idea of sewing another small bag and putting the gleaming golden brooch with the diamonds into it and stitching the little bag into my shabby old bust-bodice. When done I rolled the bodice up neatly and placed it in the back of my drawer, then I felt very satisfied with myself.

*****

5 September, 1946

The peacocks no more strut and sun themselves on the stone steps of the place. ---The ancient proud assurance of the house is gone, no loving hands tend the flowers and shrubs in the park;... all are rioting wild. It is quite an experience to see the tulip trees; they have turned a vivid gold, looking as if the sun is shining out of them. There are brilliant splashes of colour among the late greens of the hedges; to stand here and look across the park is breathtakingly beautiful and sad — I must not stand long in retrospect, just long enough to see the black crows settling in the trees. They chatter and I fancy they say: Nature is heralding winter's snow, with a flurry of golden leaves.

*****

In the cellar I have a bag of carrots stored in sand, holding the fort against the siege of winter. Also standing in sand is a military-looking row of cabbage heads. Milka will give us sauerkraut — they have a large barrel full. With onions and garlic and a sprinkling of pepper, we should be alright until further orders.

Sometimes I think of that old courtier I encountered (maybe I imagined it) in the narrow Gasse in Passau, who called after me: "You can't take care of a mouse!" Because I believed him, it has worried me considerably; but perhaps he was a bit stupid, because I think I am still the best person to look after my own children.

*****

An Autumn Idyll.

Surely it is time for us to fly home. The last rose of summer is dead, all the colours are fading. Nature itself is grey and drab and sad. We are still in Kyjovice and I cannot be patient anymore. This last rose reminded me poignantly of my first days in Germany, how I had felt strange and unaccustomed and alien — and then, for the first time I had seen a real opera, it was Martha, the sensitive young artist was singing — singing "*Letze* Rose" — Engelbert was with me, how gay we felt, and I thought — nay, I believed that never again could a last rose of summer touch a vibrant chord in me — Oh, no, never again — but now I had not the heart to watch the petals as they fell. Even the swallows have left, for days past they congregated in groups and suddenly, on swift wings, they are gone — all are departed — I have struggled so desperately to get away before the winter.

I must get busy on something. I shall make our living room bright and neat.

After I scrubbed the pine table, it gleamed like white silk. The chairs are polished, the lamp shines. A clean cover is over the divan. After washing the window panes and rubbing them with soft paper, they shine in their settings of lead. I washed the flat grey stones of the windowsill — surely not many window sills are so handsome and broad — it measures four feet! When all was ready, I thought I could rest, but then I decided to put a pot with autumn leaves and starry scarlet flowers on the window sill. It looked a very livable room, and when I called the children in to admire our Autumn Idyll they were enthusiastic.

The afternoon sky is so bright and so clear and as cold as if it has been washed with ice water. I think that by tomorrow the frost will have tarnished the leaves and flowers that remain in the park, so we'll slip on our loden coats and all make a run across the park and have a last look at the display of colour before it lies buried under the snow.

We have had a good walk through the park. I pretended not to notice the unswept walks, with shoals of fallen leaves and the hedges growing wild — but rather drew the children's attention to the evening sky: it looked so high and so cold.

It was quite dark when we returned to our living room. Meanwhile old Illik had visited us. He made up a very cozy fire and by bountifully adding to our idyll, he has turned it into a still-life picture. On the broad window sill, he put a plate of fresh walnuts, a round yellow pumpkin, and a too-beautiful Czech sausage filled and fat with meat and the strong odor of "rank and guilty" garlic pearls. I am sure that Charles Lamb would have hesitated to call this aromatic sausage "a sacrifice to the exterior tegument." Good, good Illik — garlic or no garlic — I praise the Lord for a Christian man — he has brought me quiet comfort and a little bag of grain for my chickens and my duck and now, the echo of those falling petals has receded deep down in my heart.

*****

After Illik's heartening visit the sunshine was still bright and clear. Now, alas, from one day to another the weather has changed and overnight we have stepped into winter. Weeks ago I had endeavoured to buy a few bags of coal — in vain. Mr. Balhar, the forester, had thought it possible to arrange for some wood for us, but nothing has happened, except that now the vast corridors are like ice vaults. And from our bedroom window, we scraped away the ice flowers to watch the snow flakes lightly falling and powdering the park. In no time now the landscape will be changed into strange pallid mountains and deep valleys of snow; the children do not mind the snow, they were excited about getting the sleds and skis out. Yes, I said to them, the snow has come to stay, the peasants will not be working the fields, they will readily help us now with a waggon to bring in some wood, we must go into the forest and collect as many stems as we possibly can. (And to myself I thought, I'll take an axe and the law into my own hands). While the children put on boots and coats, I went to borrow a saw and axe from our friend Joseph the tub-maker. But before starting out, we must first say a prayer to St. Wenceslaus. I said, "Here is a woman, a widow, going into the cold dark forest with her children to try to get firewood for the winter. St. Wentzel, I have seen you in your great Cathedral on the hill in Prague, distributing charity in the form of firewood to a poor woman. You know all about us, St. Wentzel. Help." The children said, "Amen."

We walked a long way in the forest. There were no mushrooms now to gather for supper. There were no dead trees either. The Communist authorities had given us permission to collect only dead trees — destroyed where fierce battles had been fought — many trees had been destroyed. Some had their high crowns mowed off like grass, others stood in various stem-lengths, while many trees had been bodily rooted up; but now we found that the dead trees had already all been collected by the peasants. It was very cold and very quiet in the forest and I was all but tempted to do some private sawing, when the boys said: "Let us go to the bunkers that the German soldiers built. We'll try to pull up some of the wood." Now we saw some men approaching: the forester and police on the lookout for wood thieves. I was thankful that St. Wentzel had stopped me from doing anything rash! When they came up to us I felt forlorn, and I said to them, "We have not found any dead trees, the peasants have taken them all." The men held a little *indaba* (meeting of the minds). Then they directed us, saying that in the vicinity of the bunkers we would find trees where the soldiers had tied up their horses; the poor starving animals had chewed rings of bark — as far as they could reach — from the trees. Subsequently, the trees had all died off and were now quite dry. We could take a limited number, and be sure you saw them off near the ground, they added. We thanked them and we thanked St. Wentzel. We told him that as warmth contributed so much to well-being and happiness, and now that Christmas was coming, we would sing his famous carol. We soon found the bunkers and also the dead trees. The children sorrowfully exclaimed, "Oh, the poor horses! The poor soldiers! Did any of them reach their homes again?" I did not say anything to the children, but I do not think that hardly any one of them escaped that last fiery ordeal. Their life's blood, like the dead pine trees we were sawing, had ebbed away in the dark, silent forest.

As the boys sawed, showers of snow hurtled down from the trees on our heads and backs. We were enjoying ourselves and, soon we were heated from the vigorous work. Lekkie and Peter were better skilled workmen that I had expected. They sawed, drove a wedge into the tree stem, sawed on, and soon the tree cracked and snapped and crashed to the ground! and then another and another! I lopped off the branches while Ilona and Petty busied themselves by collecting stick bundles and fir cones.

Some women, muffled in shawls, passed us carrying their own bundles. "Dobry vecer," they said pleasantly; doubtless it was quite agreeable for them to see that the castle folk could turn a hand to rough work. We answered a friendly "Dobry vecer."

A waggon passed by laden with wood. Then, except for our sawing, it grew very silent in the forest. We worked on, till suddenly the light was gone. Only a few pale stars twinkled over the dark tree tops. We decided our work was accomplished. Tomorrow we would get a waggon to bring in our "booty." We had felled about five times the amount of trees we were entitled to take. Our Uncle Fritz's — Papali's trees, who cared? The winter is long and how gladly he would have given them to us!

With aching backs and blistered hands, but with light hearts, we all five plunged into the gathering gloom, so full of the fragrance of fallen leaves and crunching snow. Then crossing the frosty meadow (known as Folen Weide, where the foals used to gambol), it was a happy family who sat down to enjoy a pot of hot coffee and black bread, for surely, we had earned our supper and the blessing of Father Wenceslaus.

*****

December 1946

Some days after the first fall of snow, the sky grew dark again and a swirling snow-storm began, we knew it meant real business. The snow fell solidly; all the black slate roofs of the village wore a blanket of white... it was a pretty sight — like gigantic iced cakes. Snow blew against the windows and sifted through them in white streaks. I have difficulty in feeding the hens — they are practically snow-bound. To get to their little house, I have to stumble through snow drifts of up to four feet. As soon as the snowstorm ceased, the frost was hard again — we would almost rather have the snow than the ice.

Sunday afternoon, we all sat in the kitchen with as much wood in the stove as it could accommodate. The steam from the kettle was sending out a white stream and I was getting ready to make some coffee, when Lekkie, looking out of the window, suddenly exclaimed: "There goes our lost rabbit!" In the distance, we saw a grey rabbit with long erect ears making its way over the snow hills. The boys immediately prepared to give chase. Putting on jerseys and gloves they let out wild whoops to the other boys in the vicinity to join them. Ilona and I settled down to our coffee, until our attention was arrested by the shouts of the returning hunters.

We watched them as they came tumbling over the snow drifts, Lekkie and Peter holding the legs of the rabbit, assisted by Rudi, while Petty and the other small boys, who had joined in the chase, had their work cut out to keep up with the big boys as they all came sailing over the snow drifts. They burst into the kitchen, snow and rabbit fur flying everywhere. "*Himmel!*" said Lekkie, "He has kicked me in the ribs! and look at my jersey!" It was in a sorry state. Seeing the long ears — the spoons — of the terrified animal, I said, "Indeed, it is not a rabbit, it is a full grown hare." And so it was I tried to persuade them to put it back in the park. "Not on your life," said Lekkie. "After the job, we had cornering and capturing it! If we can capture it, a dog or fox can easily do the same." But I still tried to persuade them to let it escape. "You boys cannot kill the poor beautiful thing, and not here in the kitchen." Lekkie was determined. Indignantly, he said, "You would not expect the old Praschma, who won his spurs by catching a stag with his bare hands for the Emperor, to have been persuaded to let it escape." And off they all rushed, Ilona in tow, to *Pan* Drastik who killed and skinned the hare for them. Among the village boys, this came to be a big event. "Yes," they said, "the Praschmas must be South African." The hare was quite a large animal and in good condition.

I decided to give a Huntsman's Dinner for the children. The boys who had joined in the chase were invited for the next Sunday. Peter assisted me in making a beautiful menu card. A coloured picture of a hare leaping over some sprawling mushrooms. The items read:

+++

Mushroom cream soup.
Roasted spiced venison.
Elderberry "wine"
Red cabbage and apples.
Carrots and parsley.
Roast potatoes, green lamb's lettuce salad.
Caramel Custard a l' Africaine.
Stewed Prunes.

+++

It was a simple dinner, but with the addition of the menu card and glasses of elderberry wine, it was much appreciated by the budding hunters… in fact they said, "It went off like a bomb!"

Quite soon the visitors' reticence and cautious manner dissolved and there was more noise and good-humoured laughter that Sunday afternoon than we had heard for many a day.

*****

We must be sparing with the wood. It looked like a great pile that *Pan* Joseph and the boys split up and stored, but our "kitchen" must be kept warm and we must continue with our Evening Effort. It is bread and wood that are my chief concerns and oh, for a few bags of coal! And I almost think I would give my money (in the frozen account) for a little bag of precious South African *mealie meal* (corn-meal)! Why are we so slow to realize that mealie meal porridge can just about keep body and soul together?

*****

When I was quite young, I had two ambitions — I still have them — and one was to make a patchwork quilt. On and off I have collected patches, in Hamburg again started a collection — all gone with the wind, except for a card of silk brocade samples that lies in my treasure chest. My other ambition has smoked and smouldered, but it seems to be getting on apace. It is my diary. Once upon a time I asked my sister Clem, "What must I say about you in my diary?" She considered, then said, "Oh, just say that old *'bruin oog'* (Clem is the only one in the family with brown eyes) is tall and lanky and quite cranky." That is all that remains of that diary. Our family are all sentimentalists; that is the nearest I can get to being "quite cranky."

These long winter evenings could be spent profitably when the children are in bed — I could revel in a basket of patches — but now I am coming to it. What I want to say is that here, in these Eastern parts, many winter evenings are spent by many peasant families, sitting round the kitchen fire "brightened by its ruddy glow" — each one with a bundle of *mohn* — poppy seed pods — a container, and a knife.

When Milka asked if I wanted to do some work, I was surprised. She added, "The Homulas have invited us to a *mohn* gathering." I did not accept with good grace — it was too cold. Indeed it was cold and dark outside, but very agreeable to come into a warm kitchen. We sat on a sofa near the fire. I think it was the Babushka's bed (old grandmothers customarily sleep in the kitchen; in Russia, I am told, Granny's bed is made up on top of the great porcelain stove). We were each given a knife and a container. Soon we were all busy cutting open the big poppy seed pods and pouring the seed into the containers. It proved to be a merry evening — much talking and laughter — to be wound up by a steaming cup of coffee and a *kolace*, a lovely bun filled with poppy-seed or cream cheese.

Poppyseed fields are very beautiful when in early summer the large white flowers with purple centres pop open in bloom as they wave in the light warm breeze — they are the ladies of the fields.

What I am trying to say is (like an Auntie Mother): If you can't do the things you want to do, there is much virtue in doing something you don't want to do — even without coffee and *kolace* — you will still enjoy it.

I still intend collecting for a patchwork quilt.

*****

Whenever I travel to Prague, the strain and the stress grows worse. On every occasion I make a beeline for Prague 111, Thunovska 14, The British Embassy. A Consul Heynau speaks to me — very official. I get no satisfaction — very sad. I think the poor man is tired of me. I am sick of him. Surely they can do something about arranging a visa for me? I stress that I am a British-born subject and so are my eldest-born children! No good.

*****

Oh! Christmas wishes from home. Good cheer. All well.

Christmas wishes from Papali — a card that he made for us: Papali on the Gamburg and then on the opposite side, the crib, with four children standing beside it: Lekkie, Peter, Ilona, and Petty. The children bear the good wishes from the Christ Child and the family to us all. And now we prepare for Christmas.

*****

Christmas Eve in Czechoslovakia
24 December, 1946
The Good Czech People

Our fire is burning brightly and my heart is so full of gratitude that it can burst. But only last night I was ridiculously disconsolate; for was I not alone in Kyjovice with my children — without our relatives and friends — all have been transported far from this land. They had always made Christmas the best remembered feast of all, and as I sat at the window, were my hands not benumbed with cold as I looked at the snow drifting in sheets over the desolate park — and worst of all, was our bread tin not empty again and no word from the British Embassy!

But overnight all has changed, thanks to the charity of men and women of great good will.

It was dark outside when Milka called to me. Crescenzia stood without, with two of her friends, each with a little sled. "We have come," they said, "to make your Christmas warm for you and the children; but we must hurry," they added mysteriously — "there are people in the village who need not know about these coals." On each of three sleds was loaded a sack of coal. "What can I say? How can I thank you?" I said to them. "Never mind, we want you to know that the Czech people are not all hard and bad." They off-loaded the coal and then muffling their heads in their shawls, they silently stole away into the white silence of the night.

Quite early this morning Silka, the forester's wife, came to greet us with a jug of warm milk from her cows, and also a packet of dried mushrooms. From then on various womenfolk from the village have visited us. They shake the snow from their thick boots and come in with a kindly greeting, — "*Dobry den. We have brought you some kolace* from the Christ Child." Papali maintains that only Czech women know how to make *kolace* — light lovely buns, filled with either plum jam, ground poppyseed or cream cheese, topped with butter and cinnamon — and I can add that only Czech women know how to generously express a greeting, especially when it comes from the Christ Child. We counted our buns — one hundred and twenty!

Lekkie, Peter and little Fritz, assisted by the forester, went into the forest to find a suitable fir tree. They set it up in the middle of the room then I let them decorate it festively, with strips of tinsel that we had assiduously gathered in the forest months ago, where it had fallen from American aeroplanes (part of their radar intercepting equipment). The tinsel was carefully avoided by the peasants, believing that it contained poison — it did seem peculiar to collect tinsel in the forest! The children then cleverly made a decoration with soft green moss and spruce twigs. They added a tall candle for the carved crib — for Mary, Joseph and the Christ Child. Ilona and Peter added some Christmas roses that bloom in the snowbank by the kitchen window. If my Visa had arrived, I would have put it high on the Christmas tree, but instead, I dusted and put a high polish on the furniture and with the settee and chairs put into position round the tree. We were all but ready to greet each other as a welcome to the Christ Child when the two crowning events occurred to make our Christmas Eve a Holy Night, a Silent Night, lit by a Star in the East. First Milka arrived to say that a young priest arrived from Ostrava to celebrate Midnight Mass in the chapel. Two doors away from our bedroom, the chapel had seemed so cold and neglected although we had decorated it with greens and some candles that we had begged from the village church.

Shortly afterwards, there was another tap at the door and Neuwert, Papali's coachman, stood without. The first time I had seen Neuwert had been quite an experience. He had met us at the train station with red hair streaming out under his tall bear-skin cap, wearing his great coat and a scruff-haired fox-skin cape over his broad shoulders. He had tucked us comfortably into the fur bags of the sledge and then, with a steady hand on the reins and his whip hand ready, to the accompaniment of sleigh bells, Neuwert had directed the fiery black stallions on the slippery ice from the station to the castle. I had pictured him then as the image of a Norse god — "I am the god Thor — I am the war god — I am the thunderer — Here in my Northland, fastness and fortress, reign I forever!"

But now Neuwert entered very meekly. He doffed his bear-skin cap; it was jewelled with little snowflakes. Then he greeted us: "And *Frau Graefin*, I've come to see if you are wanting anything, and here is bread and here are apples." From his basket he took out a rounded loaf of rye bread, freshly baked and almost as large as one of his own cart wheels. My children crowded round. We thanked him profusely and we asked him to sit down and admire our Christmas tree. This he was far too modest to do, but I think it was a good, if only a small way of expressing our thanks. While Neuwert was having a glass of our hot, spicy elderberry "wine," I said to him, "We must have your gifts here on the green moss by the crib, where we have the pleasure of seeing them." The large precious brown loaf and the fragrant apples that have the rich autumn tints glowing under their skins were laid next to Mary and Joseph and the Christ Child.

I wonder, if in bringing us these gifts, did this old image of a Norse god divine something of my despair, and did he come, as Scripture itself says, "To comfort me with apples." And now, because peace on earth has been so abundantly vouchsafed to us by these eager Czech people in their far away snowbound village, I feel very humble and so full of gratitude to Him who lit the star in the East, that my heart is ready to burst.

###

CHAPTER TWELVE
DEEP SNOW AND CHARITY

25 January, 1947

Since Sunday it has been snow, snow, thickly flurrying snow; the first real snow storm since the beginning of the year. The falling snow is a relief instead of the penetrating frost and wind. We were virtually "prisoners of winter," fearing to put a foot down on the slippery ice. The peasants say it is one of the worst winters they have experienced. I am thankful that the temperature has risen — but still many degrees below zero.

The boys left almost joyfully for school this morning, there will be much snow-balling. Ilona has a temperature and pains in her legs; I have kept her in bed and am trying to keep the room warm. St. Wenceslaus knows that our wood and our spirits are getting low. I have to remind myself to be brave, and I braved the whirling snowstorm to give our hens some warm mash and grain. Their little house is like an igloo, nearly buried in snow. Charity and Dufa, the little pets, have each astonishingly come up with an egg again which I rescued just in time. If eggs are left out in the freezing cold, they expand, burst and split open. The children will have an omelette for lunch.

Tomorrow Milka will try and get us a soup bone. Snow whirled all night and Mr. Ribka's dog howled in front of our window. We had to let the poor fellow in; I told the boys not to encourage him — we have no soup bone to give him.

Yes, no soup bone, but Milka got us two nice leg slices of mutton. From where did Mr. Ribka get that sheep? I'll make a macaroni casserole. It will be marvellous to get a taste of lamb!

After frying the meat lightly with onions, dried green peppers, a can of peas, mint and boiled macaroni, it looked like a meal for a hungry family! In this cold weather, the children have enormous appetites. True enough, they come in declaring: "We are as hungry as bears! Is there something nice to eat?" Judging by the way the macaroni casserole disappeared, it was quite in the order of things.

Custom, yes, custom. Well, the old Czech peasants are accustomed to their own brand of food: kraut and potatoes, cheese and meat. They have no use for tinned foods that are distributed now through UNRRA from America. A good sausage? Yes. But sweet corn? Peas? Beans? We give it to our pigs — and sometimes a tin to *Pani Hrabenka* Prazma. We of course find this very acceptable! And also the shoes, little high heeled, pointed shoes — so ugly! Give them to the *Pani Hrabenka* Prazma. Our *Pan* Drastik in the village makes beautiful solid shoes. *Pan* Drastik also made a pair of boots that are a boon to me.

*****

16 February, 1947

Today is my birthday. Oh, news from home. Oh, and a cousin, Joe Steele, sent an address in England. He has never been to England, he is not Catholic, but somewhere he found the address of The Priory of Our Lady of Good Counsel in Haywards Heath, Sussex — beautiful names. I'll write and explain our circumstances. If I can get accommodation and employment in England, visas will be granted to us, and in London there is South Africa House! I seem to be on the way!

With a visitation of angels, my good angels; they have come crowding in. At first I thought they were birds — at least some of them. A good start, I woke up early to the sound of twittering birds. Birds? No, it is midwinter. The room was dimly lit with one shaded lamp. The twittering continued, the sounds coming from my children, who, as bright and brisk as birds, at this early hour, astonished me by speaking softly in Czech. This made me very inquisitive. I slightly opened one eye to a busy scene.

Lekkie was attending to the high porcelain stove; Ilona and Petty were busily making up beds; Peter was busily sweeping. Apparently Lekkie did not notice when my eye closed with a snap, when he looked my way. He only said a warning, "*Ticho!*" — Silence! — to the others, and for a few moments an uncanny silence prevailed. Then came the question, "*Cerna kava?*" — black coffee? — then I remembered it was my birthday. My dear children had not forgotten and they were preparing a surprise for me, speaking the while in Czech to prevent me from understanding what they were doing — it was a surprise!

When everything was in readiness, including my robe and slippers laid out, they stood round my bed and in joyful spirits sang: "*Viel Glueck und viel Segen auf all Deinen Wegen*" — Much luck and many blessings on all life's ways. And now came another surprise: I must look at the table, laid with a special white cloth. On it stood one tall candle and I must look at the cake — a yellow and white iced cake set about with spruce greenery, lit up by the blessed candle; and the coffee-cups and plates were ready. Without further preamble, I embraced each one in turn. All faces were red and eyes were bright while I showed my delight. Now they explained that the cake was made by our friend Slecna Crescenzia to whom they had expressed their special wish and she had managed to scrape together the ingredients; *Fraulein* Katke, another friend, had applied a thin boiled icing, but they were not satisfied. Then they found a novel way of decoration with strips of my pumpkin compote from the pantry shelf, which proves that necessity is often the means of creating a novel invention. With the addition of some rye bread and a little sausage, we have never had a better early breakfast.

A few friends came in to wish me well. Of course they included Milka and Crescenzia and little Hilda, with this little poem:

> Not a star shines to greet you tonight
> only the flurry of falling flakes,
>   Jack Frost's performance is persistent and chill
> with patterns of fern and flowers of ice
> pressed on your white window sill,
> I find no flowers to send you....
> No roses white and red in the bud
> No forget-me-not blue, in a nosegay for you.
> But *ei!* Who then are these?
> 'Tis Lekkie and Peter, Ilona and little Petty, to say:
> *Viel Glueck* and a happy Birthday to you!....

Full well do we know, it shall finally be
when you reach the gates of pearl and pure gold
to face St. Peter firm and old,
The angel by his side will fling the gates wide!
and wave you all herein! Inside!
Yes, with Lekkie and Peter, Ilona and your little
Petty close by your side,
because even now in heaven they let some of their
sunshine come through.
Ei! there will be bud and blossom and flowers for you!
        Amen. From your Hildegard.

We all thanked Hilda for her beautiful bouquet and poem and invited her to sit down to some of our cake.

And now what do I say? Shall I try to understand more of the human heart? Or shall I just believe that it is a storehouse wherein we must keep good virtues and never allow the *Daemmerung* and snow, that I thought would never melt, to take root?

I sit here with my blessed candle burning and I see my children's happy faces, and now I know what to say: Dory, Dory, the heart has reasons, for which reason has no knowledge.

*****

20 February, 1947

Letters make a certain impact on us in different ways. Mostly they cause a little tremor — I break the seal and I think of the people who have found it fit to write to me; it is wonderful, exciting, to receive a token that has breached the miles. I think of the feast-day greetings, the lovely Christmas cards. Yes, letters, wishes are like standing face to face with a warm hand-clasp and for a fraction, I hesitate to open the letter; this is how I feel while I say: I am so glad! But this afternoon what were my feelings to receive a letter that caused a real impact? I saw the name "Sussex Priory of Our Lady of Good Counsel" and there was no hesitation, no fraction of a second lost in opening the letter. And then, with eyes somewhat blurred, with the open letter in my hand, I walked straight to the chapel and knelt down to thank the Lord of Hosts. And now I hardly notice the icy corridors, the pain in my shoulder, or my stiff neck. I just say, "*Alles sal reg kom*" (all will come right).

Yes, this letter from a Reverend Mother — of what seems to be a large convent — reads:

I thank you for your letter... you will be welcomed by us... we have room for you in our large Communal house.... Regarding work in England, you will probably find a suitable occupation with us; there is also much offered in the village and in the vicinity that may attract you. However, that can be decided when you are with us. We look forward to your next letter telling us when to expect you at the Priory.

Yours faithfully in X, M.M Baptist, Prioress.

Forthwith, I am dispatching this letter to Prague to Consul Heynau, with the request for the Embassy to arrange our visas for England.

*****

This letter from Rev. Mother is soothing, like "winds that blow to the south" — or rather, to the South, taking us to South Africa.

*****

We go on a pilgrimage.

Crescenzia is a kind person, the sort that is often found under a rough exterior, — a useful person with a kind heart and a good sense of humor — and she tries to teach me Czech. She also finds time to assist me with my washing — when she can take the time off from assisting her brother Arnost, who is blind, by cutting and preparing the willow wands for his basket-making.

This morning after we had done the washing and hung it out in the orchard under the apple trees, Crescenzia said to me, "On Sunday, there will be a pilgrimage to Hrabin where, after High Mass, the cross on the church, that had been shot down when the church was partly destroyed by Russian artillery fire, will ceremoniously be replaced. Will you come with us?"

"I would love to go to Hrabin."

Among many other pilgrims, with my children and a basket of sandwiches, we started on our way on a beautiful Sunday morning. The wonder of spring was all about us, the light warm breeze, the calm blue sky, the springing green, and above all, the cuckoo call — loud and clear, no wonder we felt we walked on air. The six or so kilometers we walked seemed greatly diminished by the prayers led by old Illik, recited on the way together with many choruses sung as only Slav people know how to harmonize. Crescenzia taught us to sing a little cuckoo cantata: "Arise all little sparrows, the sun is out on high. Over the hills and valleys the cuckoo's call is clear. Arise! All arise! The cuckoo's calling you." By the time we got home, we were all singing in Czech: "*Kukazka vola ven!*" and we are not likely to forget it. Nor are we likely to forget the solemn High Mass and then the raising of the cross by the strong forceful men. St. Matthew 23:30 — Our Lord said: "And I, if I be lifted up from the earth, will draw all things to myself." This is why we venerate the cross and why the cross was lifted up again on the little church spire in Hrabin in Czecholovakia on that Sunday morning in spring. It is as simple as that; but it can be read with force.

This is not quite all. My son Petty did not return with us. I did not worry, thinking he was with the people of Kyjovice, but when it got late, and then later, I got very distressed and I intended going to the police. "No," said Crescenzia, "he has taken a long way round. He was seen with a good family on the way to Elgoth. He'll be here in the morning." I spent a sleepless night. Then, early in the morning, I saw Petty, walking up the chestnut avenue singing, "*Kukazka vola ven!*" "I am sorry, Mammie," he said, "it was too late to walk home, so after we had fried potatoes and bacon I slept with the other children in a big high bed and I dreamed of a silver cross."

*****

5 May, 1947

We are still in Kyjovice, chewing the cud of impatience. The trouble is the dance our Embassy is leading me with one promise after another of speeding up our visas. Last Saturday, I received a letter from Prague saying that permits for our stay in the United Kingdom may now be granted, providing I produce a valid passport. I immediately wrote a reply thanking His Excellency, but I asked him please to tell me how I can produce a "valid passport" when indeed I have been waiting for two years for the Visa Section to arrange a visa for me. And once more — all over again — I repeated all our difficulties to him and not least among them that they are acquainted with the fact that our money is in a frozen account. Perhaps this together with Reverend Mother's letter will induce some sort of action. (I would have liked to tell him to get a move on!)

If they do not notify me soon, I have decided to leave here with sack and pack for Prague, where I hope it will be possible to personally wind up our affairs. There has been no end to the palaver I have been through — taking our personal effects to the authorities in three different towns and *Vibos* and paying the fees. Our cases will still have to be sealed by the travel authorities in Prague. Well, while there's life there's hope, and there is nothing like looking forward to a feast, which will be next Sunday, May 14th.

Mother's Day is a feast that will always make me smile; it is celebrated on the 2nd Sunday in May — a lovely day! All children, young and old, prepare presents for "*Maminka.*" Verses are written, pots of flowers, cakes, cards, etc. All are taken to the village recreation hall, but what I find really beautiful is that the graveyard is not forgotten; people walk to and fro with flowers and candles for their mothers' graves.

Early on this Sabbath morning, we accompanied Milka and Crescenzia to the graveyard. A heavy dew sparkled on the grass, inviting the children to pull off their shoes and stockings. We found the graves all tidied up and the paths swept. Everywhere, splashes of colourful flowers bloomed:

peonies had burst their bounds and bloomed in gay abandon, violets and buttercups peeped from every creek and crevice.

When we arrived, there were many people busily lighting candles on their mothers' graves. Crescenzia lit her candles while we wandered among the lights and flowers on the graves. I felt in that peaceful atmosphere with incense-laden air — from the adjacent pine forest — with all the light and colour and those flickering candles, the graveyard was a veritable garden of memory and a good place to rest in.

My four had each made a pretty card at school for me. They were placed on the breakfast table with a vase of those beautiful little early spring blossoms. I thanked my children. I must not forget to congratulate the school teacher.

Early in the afternoon, we all repaired to the school, where "joy was unconfined" by an unfamiliar but infectious holiday spirit — much laughter and much talk (which, as I understand very little Czech, sounds to me rather as if people are having a heated argument!). In the schoolroom, a large picture of Our Lady with the Holy Babe was set up — the example of holiest, highest Motherhood. The priest now drew our attention to noble mothers. He told us of the suffering and martyrdom of the brave mother in Maccabees, who died together with her seven martyrs and deserves a crown immortal. The children then presented their pots of flowers and recited suitable poems and now the fun began!

A long crocodile march was started to the sports ground. It was headed by the priest in his long, flowing black robes with two boys, one on each side — one carried a large flag of the Republic (very important) and the other, a tall cross. Behind them walked the schoolmaster; after him marched the girls and maidens, looking very picturesque in Czech national costumes; after them marched the boys and the young men, proud as prosperous peacocks in their richly embroidered shirts and waistcoats; behind them followed the village brass-band, playing one of the latest hits, "Your Blue Eyes." Behind the band, stepping high, marched us — proud mothers; after us marched a solid squadron of fathers; then followed the spinsters and bachelors; after them, in surging rows, came a noble commando of perambulators; and last but not least, on a low one-horse cart, sitting astride two large barrels of pilsner beer came Mr. Staffin and his son Maxel from the local guest house. This march to the village green was altogether a most comical and colourful sight and gave me a childish feeling of extravagant hilarity, which by no means diminished when we arrived at the Green, where the young people had games and sports. The older people settled in groups under the trees, glasses were freely passed round to more lusty music and songs, chiefly "Your Blue Eyes," and "The Black Gypsy Baby." Until it was time to wend our steps homeward — for supper must be prepared and cows must be milked... even on Mother's Day.

*****

Whit-Sunday, 25 May, 1947

Meanwhile, we are in good health and in good spirits and today — Sunday — has been another colourful holiday. I have indulged myself together with the children by letting the warm spring sunshine sink right deep into our hearts. With our frying pan and with eggs and bread and coffee we spent a long afternoon in the forest. Peter carried the pet hedgehog, Lieutenant Pinkerton, rolled in a tight ball in a little bag on his back. Mr. Ripka's dog also accompanied us. When the lieutenant was put down in the green wood, his "tension" relaxed and while we made fire and prepared lunch, he dug for grubs and nosed about. Some of his antics were so amusing that the children said the lieutenant has spring fever, and spring fever can be catching when the lilacs are in bloom — we all felt a bit heady! It is not possible for anyone who has not actually experienced the change to have an idea of how wonderful spring is here in the Northland. Only a few weeks ago an icy wind was still blowing over the frozen snow banks and now, like the descent of the baton of the village brass band master, the magical rays of the sun have transformed the land into light and life and verdure and green — far greener than any picture in my young days! We listen to the voice of the gentle lark, the cuckoo's call, and a host of other bird voices together with the fragrant scents of spring; chief among these are the scents that Kyjovice is famous for — the scent of lilac and the incense of the pine forests. The meadows are white with daisies and starred with margueritas: last week, they were bright with butter-yellow primroses, dog violets, and drifts of snow-drops, while under the tulip trees, a sea of many-hued crocuses bloomed — like Auntie Mother had said, Aladdin has tripped along with his magic lamp.

Where the Austrian Empire held sway in Europe, the people continue to observe the Catholic way of life. Here in Czechoslovakia, not the least among the beautiful holidays are the feast days of the Saints together with all the other religious feasts. After Mass on Whit-Sunday morning, it is customary to spend the day simply with your family and with your frying pan in the forest, frying bacon and eggs for lunch and singing in harmony to the accompaniment of the brass band. It is a day to be remembered because The Holy Spirit unites and holds all things together, so we rejoice and are glad. The whole village, young and old, have packed their bacon and eggs and taken their pans to the forest, and now one can hear their merrymaking and the extravagant blasts from the band echoing far across the valleys! The children enjoyed their luncheon, and then found enough to amuse themselves for the rest of the afternoon by climbing trees and collecting gum and fir cones, until evening drowsily descended upon the hills. We packed up our frying pan and then we asked the Holy Spirit to grant that His gifts may not only be the first but also the last with us — and with all peoples. Alleluja!

*****

There is another of the feasts and it is one of the loveliest to which the Czech people are very staunch. It is the feast of the brothers, Saints Cyril and Methodius, who are the great Apostles of Moravia, Bohemia, Bulgaria, and Russia. These saints were sent out from Rome on a mission to evangelize the Slavonic peoples. These two brothers certainly led very active lives in their mission field; they are known as the "Slavonic Apostles." They are the originators of the Cyrillic (Russian) alphabet. The brothers travelled, taught and translated the scriptures, they brought peace and great happiness. Their feast day is on the 7th of July. It is a good day for feasting, and when the forest glades are inviting, a good day for picnicking.

Another important feast is that of "Good Saint Wenceslaus," who was a Czech Duke of Bohemia. St. Wenceslaus is said to have set a constant example of the great Christian virtues and marvellous events have been rewarded by his charity — it is good to cast one's bread upon the waters! Although he lived one thousand years ago, today he is still known throughout Christendom as "Good King Wenceslaus." His feast day is on the 28th of September.

Therefore, no matter whether the feasts are celebrated in summer or winter, a feast day in Czechoslovakia is nothing if not a day of social conviviality and the Czechs know how to make the most of them. I wonder for how long these simple homely feasts will be tolerated by the communist regime.

*****

20 May, 1947

Messrs. Thomas Cooke and sons have informed me that the best connection to Dover is by train: Prague — Nuremberg — Cologne — Dover. This will suit us admirably, as — do or die in the attempt — we must spend some days in the Gamburg. It will mean another permit which, notwithstanding the bad experience I had in Prague when trying to locate my boys from the American authorities, I still hope to get their permission to stop over in Germany when I am in Prague.

*****

Today! Friday, 30 May

Now I can dash off these beautiful words of happiness — our visas have arrived! They are here! My relief is sky high! They are nicely worded and should certainly be of great aid to me in getting our final arrangements made. I am eager to get on with the little odd jobs on hand — washing and packing and saying farewell to the good helpful people of Kyjovice.

*****

Princess Lobkowicz has written to say she can reserve rooms for us in the Pension Carl IV where she lives; terms reasonable, select, quiet. For more than two years, Kyjovice has been a breakwater for us and now, I become saddened by the thought of leaving — like birds facing the call of migration. Back to Kyjovice our thoughts will often carry us... to the great white house... the peasant village, with the black slate roofs (that are sometimes white in winter). In looking back, there will be no winter in our thoughts, but only a glow of excellent warmth and a prayer for God to be good to them here.

I went to say farewell to the good village people. Zdenka said she will make many signs of the cross and say many Our Fathers for us. Ferdi her husband said, "You must excuse the warlike spirit of the Czech people; we must be remembered as having a mixture of Slav and Germanic blood that can be blamed for many of the present happenings. You can see that we will never accede to the Russians. We can't stand them, but there will always be sabotage and bloodshed. We will continue to fight." He went on: "The Czechs are a people to be respected and feared, and if it was not for the Communist influence, we would be the finest people in the world!"

"Do you know," I said, "I have told the Countess that the South Africans are among the best in the world, perhaps because we are also mostly cosmopolitan — we have lived for generations in wide open spaces under a high, free heaven; I think it has implanted in us that deeper knowledge of how (as one of our poets has said: God is greater in the open, little man is less) to respect and fear and be fearless. The world knows that we have had grand men in a small country."

We both felt a little sad, like true patriots who don't say much, but feel much.

*****

Our Last Night in Kyjovice
27 June, 1947

The children played outside until it grew dusk and then, after I lit the larger porcelain lamp and prepared supper, I called them in. Rye bread, lettuce leaves with a little bacon, and a gold brown egg for each of us. Usually the children are not serious for any length of time, but this evening it was different. They were sober, even solemn. I would like to keep a picture of them like this always in my mind, the boys vivid and upright, Ilona a little coy and sweet. In the soft lamp-light her hair is golden, curling prettily — it has been washed in water in which I brewed a handful of chamomile flowers, a last gift from good old Milka. Milka will take care of Auntie Daisy; we are distressed at the thought of leaving our poor kittie — she would not be so peacefully curled up if she knew what is in the wind for tomorrow.

"When we are far away," said Lekkie, stroking the cat, "I'll often think of this little kitchen, with the homely scent of coffee and herbs."

"And fried bacon," added Peter.

"*Weisst Du wass*," said Petty brightly, "It's a pity we did not have more bacon."

"My children," I said, "there was once a greedy boy, who wished he was a king, he said, then I could swing on a gate all day long and eat fat bacon. But my children consider how God has supplied every need, to this very night, even to the lamp, casting a pool of light on the table. Let us try never to become lazy and greedy. Our fare has been humble, but we are grateful and happy because we are together — it could have been so different. It is the united effort of our prayers that has kept us together, like a little strong tower."

"Yes," said Lekkie, "and if Petty does not stay with us on the journey, I am going to tie him onto my belt!" Petty protested loudly.

"Fritzl," I said, "now, no little storm. Just make up your mind that you will not wander off alone, because you'll surely get lost, or fall into the sea!"

It was quite late when I had done the final packing, ready to put out the lamp — I was loath to leave our humble kitchen, where our long winter evenings have been spent; where we have had our little storms — sorting out the grain from the chaff — to find the spirit of many things, always in the warmth of companionship and of standing closely-knit together. I like to think of the words of Thomas a Kempis: "How sweet and pleasant a thing it is to see brothers fervent and devout, well mannered and well disciplined. How sad and distressing a thing to see the disorderly goings-on of those who do not follow up to that which they are called...." And if one day a little *"Heinzel Maennlein"* could pass around a hat full of wishes, then let him grant me this wish of seeing my children growing up in harmony together, and to hear the voices of this kitchen: the brisk and bright voices of the children, their laughter, the lilting Czech songs and lovely old Christmas hymns; the cat purring contentedly; the fire hissing a whispering and the kettle singing; all the homely influences that banned the storms raging without. Tonight we only say, "Good night dear God, and thank you for every, ev-er-y-thing!

Criscenzia gallantly volunteered to travel with us to Prague. She says if we meet a Russian on the way, and if he has any designs on our baggage, she will use her fisticuffs! Criscenzia is capable and I am grateful to have her help with our great mound of baggage.

We arrived at the Masaryk station in the early morning. After telling the children to keep together and while Crescenzia saw to our luggage I went to call a taxi. Somehow, with baggage and all, we managed to pile in. There was Regina's case with silver — heavy! — Auntie Mother's dressing case; Papali's cabin trunk; Count Kuno's case; our trunks, baggage and *plumeaux* (feather blankets); and don't forget the lunchbasket, said the children — what a trek! We arrived at the Pension Carl IV. Crescenzia and the concierge stacked the baggage on the floor of the first of our two rooms, where we had a small breakfast.

Prague in July can be as hot as a summer's day in the Transvaal low-veld, and now after a sleepless night on the train, with thoughts of the multiple things to be arranged:, our cases sealed by the Custom authorities, I must see the British Consul. My friend Consul Heynau will be so pleased to see me (?) — about trying to get some money out. Must see Charles Des Fours, Count Kuno's nephew, must try to keep the children happy and quiet. Suddenly my head whirled — was I having a nightmare? a nervous breakdown? I was sick, sick — Mimi's brooch stitched in my shabby old bust-bodice, lay forgotten at the back of the dressing table drawer in Kyjovice!

The children came to ask me if they could go for a walk. "Just leave me for a few minutes."

"Are you sick?" they asked.

"I must just try to think."

I cannot get it posted to me here — letters and parcels are censored, it is sometimes dangerous even to write. What must I do? Eventually I wrote a carefully worded express letter to Milka. I asked her to take my old bust-bodice from the drawer, to wrap it up and to ask Papali's old forester please to take it to Potstat, to Countess Mimi. Then I felt better. Afterwards, I wrote a second letter to Milka.

Meanwhile, I have my son Lekkie, the big man of the family to depend upon. He has taken charge of the others and with the kronen he earned from *Pan* Drastik, the tub-maker in Kyjovice, he hired a little boat, so they spend most of their time on the River Moldau. I have hot and anxious moments, knowing that none of them can swim, and also about my own business.

I am always saying we must be brave, but during these trying days in Prague I pray for courage. There have just been a few bright spots: I visited the Mayr-Hartings, Leopoldine and some other friends — all anxious, but very charming to me. Where possible, people are leaving the country. Then a visit from Charles Des Fours; he has a dry sense of humour.

Looking somewhat disapprovingly at our stack of baggage piled upon the floor, he said: "How are you getting away?"

"It will be very difficult," I said.

"You'll have to hire a large sized taxi," he said, "but don't worry. If I don't come and help you at the station, who will?"

I just said, "Who will indeed!"

After fruitlessly walking the hot streets, in vain. Consul Heynau is not the man I had hoped he would be therefore I did not expect much more from the American authorities either. I have decided to pack up and leave for England.

*****

11 July, 1947
Pension Carl IV, Prague

Deo Gratias, at last our train tickets are bought. Everything is in readiness to leave. I have said farewell to the few remaining friends. The Mayr-Hartings, Kerssenbrocks, Czernins all are also preparing to leave.

Subject to our limited means, we have bought everything that we intended buying. Many fine things can be obtained in this city of laughter and of human tears. First, I bought some very necessary clothing for the children — a grey linen suit for Petty; for Ilona a white peasant blouse embroidered in many colours with two little matching aprons, a yellow "dirndl" and yellow hair ribbons; shirts and a tie each for Lekkie and Peter. Then we went to a little shop and bought an assortment of brightly coloured Czech post cards. Lekkie bought a pretty patriotic picture entitled "*Kde Domov Muj*" ("This is my home"), which is also the title of the Czech national anthem, and with the last of his earnings, having indulged himself and the others to many delicious ice creams, — he bought a little silvery image of the Divine Infant of Prague. Peter and Petty, having only a few pence between them, bought a small machine — its only merit, as far as I can see, is a small volume of smoke issuing from a small funnel when set in motion, which delights their childish hearts.

After this strenuous week in Prague, what relief it will be to be off. My eyes ache, I feel *ganz kaput*. I still must take the children for a final treat — no, two. I have told them that before leaving I'll take them to see something of the city. We'll see the bridges of Prague, the old stone St. Charles' Bridge where you pass between the line of gigantic old stone figures; one of the most beautiful is the antique cross of the suffering Christ. At this crucifix, the men-folk passing by lift their hats. They are also lifted at the statue of St. Jan Nepomuk, the priest who, in the days when intrigue played a great role, refused to reveal the Empress' Confession; from the palace window Jan was thrown into the Moldau beneath. The water flows by peacefully, but in winter, the Moldau is frozen to the depth of quite a few feet and here the athletic Czechs, in the isotherm of an Icelandic winter, have ample opportunity to indulge in their favourite fast and furious ice hockey games. I told the children after seeing the bridges, we'll climb the hill and see the *Hradcany*, the fortified imperial palace of the ancient Kings of Bohemia that the Czech people have every right to be proud of, with its thousand rooms. At the back of the palace is an old fortress, where the grim story is told that malefactors were let down into the vault with a last loaf of bread and a jug of water to find the corpse of the preceding inmate. We did not have time to investigate.

In close proximity to the palace stands the Cathedral of St. Vitus, or Guy, singularly like Westminster Abbey in elegant Gothic. The Cathedral was originally founded in the 10th century by the Saintly King Wenceslaus who is also the Patron Saint of Czechoslovakia. The Cathedral also has a cleverly built stained glass window, said to contain a million pieces of glass (certainly too many for us to count). It is in the form of an eight-pointed star — beautiful, like a great halo.

*****

When in spring I visited Prague, how pleasant it was to walk beside the river Moldau in the sweet month of May, when pink and white blossoms shower out over the water and when I saw a Gypsy — poor old *Zigeuner*, hurrying along the path from side to side — I thought perhaps it is not due so much to the vodka as to the lilac-scented air; I myself felt a bit heady.

One moonlit night, two barges of students passed swiftly down the river singing, "*Tece voda, tece.*..." They sang as only Czechs know how to harmonise their tuneful folk songs; "*Tece voda, tece*" — flow waters, gently flow past the gates of old Prague. I could well believe that this was Jan Masaryk's favourite song. You delve right deep into history and are the richer for it when you walk the crooked streets of the old city, with its courtyards and arches — old towers, old churches, pleasant waterways, universities, magnificent Baroque buildings, Gothic facades. It only requires a feeling of intimacy with the people to make this city one of the most beautiful and romantic in the world.

*****

We felt tired after our long walk, so as a special treat, we sat down in one of the busy cafes in the Vaclavske Nemesti and each had one of the lovely fruit ice-creams that are obtainable again, and as we have to get ready for the best treat before leaving Prague, we bundled into one of the old, clanking trams, back to the Pension Carl IV.

Some days ago I mentioned to Princess Leopoldine that we would very much like to visit the Church of the Miraculous Infant of Prague, as we would like to get his blessings for the journey and also see all his garments. Leopoldine has obtained the permission and we are due at the church this evening.

*****

The Infant of Prague

The children were dressed in their new clothes. At 8:00 sharp we were at the doors of the Church of the Divine Infant of Prague.

Leopoldine was there with a number of friends. After we entered the church, the doors were closed, because we were being accorded a special privilege, that of seeing the little Infant dressed. If this was known, crowds would come in. We saw the little image, with pretty rounded waxen face, taken out of the glass and silver security case above the high altar. This is a ritual performed by a grey nun who tends to his garments, usually changing them whenever the colour of the church vestments are changed.

The chaplain now led the way for us all. We mounted a flight of dark old stairs to a small room in which stands a large, heavily carved wooden chest. There is no visible lock, key or handle to the chest. The chaplain, invited the boys to open it. Inquisitively, they investigated but completely failed to find the way of opening it. The chaplain then banged on one of the ornate corners of the chest. The lid sprang up to disclose neat trays of exquisite little garments.

There are numbers of small collars and armlets, all made of precious old lace. Gold and silver embroideries and threads glitter on precious material. Altogether, the statue has about forty complete sets of vestments, some very ancient. Many are made from wedding-dress materials, brocades, satins, silks and laces, presented by royal brides from many lands. We thought that one of the loveliest garments came from China: pale silk, beautifully embroidered with pastel blossoms. Embroidered on the band round the garment from neck to hem, in Chinese letters, is written "Pity the Poor Children of China." When this inscription was translated to us it seemed to say to me: there are countless millions of poor children, but your four children are rich, they are among the privileged, rich in the promises of Christ, linked to his Holy Church by His Own Blood. May the assurance of possessing our Great Salvation remain with us now and always.

The devotion to the Divine Infant started a long time ago when, towards the middle of the seventeenth century, a young Spanish princess came to Prague to marry a Prince Lobkowicz, ancestor to Leopoldine. With her trousseau, she brought the lovely waxen figure of the Divine Infant. Hearing about some very poor Carmelite Fathers in Prague, and wishing them well, the young princess presented them with the little figure, assuring them that it was her most valuable possession, and if they would piously honour it, their difficulties would speedily cease. Her words to the Fathers were verified and from that date to this, innumerable miracles have been performed and graces showered on those who cherish a devotion to the real Lord Jesus up in Heaven and implore help here at his shrine.

King Gustavus Adolphus, although a Protestant, was among the many great ones who have visited the shrine.

Before the Russians entered Prague, the little figure, together with the silver angels, was taken to a place of safety and only lately brought back to the Church. After the *Jezulatko* was duly dressed and brought down to us, we all knelt in a long pew of the church. The chaplain came and gave each of us in turn the blessing of the Divine Infant, a gift of God for our very own to take with us on our long journey that lies ahead. When it came to Lekkie's turn to receive the blessing, I was touched to see his little hand reaching out, holding his own silver image, which he briefly allowed to touch the hem of the Divine Infant's garment. Then, with a radiant face, he put the little figure — which we now believe to have special virtues — back into his pocket.

Because of every prayer, and every good thought that is from the heart and is likewise a prayer, we ask the Infant of Prague to pity the Poor Children of China, of Prague, of our whole world.

###

CHAPTER THIRTEEN
FAREWELL TO PRAGUE

2 July, 1947

The children are ready and I have put on my grey hat with the green braid. Now a hurried breakfast and a farewell to Princesses Josl and Christl, and we shall be off and on our way to join the luxury train to Ostend — London. We are off!

Charles Des Fours and our taxi man handled our baggage as if it was a featherweight. Thanks to Messrs. Thomas Cook and Son, we had no difficulty with officials at the station. We were fortunate in having our own compartment — it was fairly stacked with baggage, and it also seemed loaded with destiny. I did not let Auntie Mother's dressing case and Regina's silver out of my hand, and my eyes were constantly on Kuno Des Fours' case. Thus we bade Prague a final farewell, forever. Some of these people have become very near and dear to me. Charles looked closely at me, his fair, distinguished face very serious. "Destiny," he said, "but it is sad to see the last scions of a noble house leaving the country forever." I felt as if I was being drawn and held fast by quicksand, and lest I be tempted to stay, a sudden strong urge came to me to be away, away — farewell Charles, farewell Prague!

Unless destiny takes a hand, Charles Des Fours will never come into his inheritance in Potstat. Maybe he will practice law in a foreign land, or perhaps find work on his stony goat farm in Sardinia, but most probably destiny has ensnared Charles in Prague. Maybe later on — not now — I could make Charles smile by saying: Carl, you must look for a handsome, rich, American woman.

It was most agreeable to sit back and be rocked in the spacious compartment of the fast train from Prague to Ostend. Our baggage was placed in a pile on the floor between us. We travelled all day and as twilight deepened, we were travelling through Germany. I looked out anxiously at every station and inquired if it was possible to leave the train. "No, on no account. You are in the American Zone." And the train would start up again. Anxiously I thought: what will I do with all the luggage at Ostend? Eventually I had to say, "Curl up children, we'll go to sleep."

At 4:00 AM sharp the train drew up and we were at Cologne. On the platform, people hurried to and fro and I heard the call of "*Koelnisches Wasser! Koelnisches Wasser!*" The war had not spared the poor of Cologne, who in the early, still, dark hours endeavoured to sell mugs of *aqua simple* from the River Rhine to travellers — counting on the fame of their Eau de Cologne.

I called to a porter and asked if we could leave the train. "*Ja wohl,*" he replied.

"Are there no guards or policemen to prevent us?"

"No, no," he said.

"Then please help us with our luggage."

"*Ja wohl,*" he said again, "but can you give me some bread?"

Yes, I could spare him one of our Czech loaves. We had brought several large round loaves with us. The porter loaded our baggage on his trolly and led us across to where the train to Wertheim would start. — We had to travel a long way back. Our German money was useful; we bought our tickets and booked most of our baggage — all except Auntie Mother's dressing case, the silver, Kuno's case and some of our most necessary items. Then we made sandwiches, while the friendly porter went off in triumph with his large round loaf.

When the train arrived, we were disappointed. We had to scramble into dirty, patched-up compartments, where we stood or sat, crammed together like sardines. Three times we had to change trains — always the same scramble into over-filled, dirty compartments, but I did not let the silver and other cases out of my sight. I was very sorry for the children, having to cope with the heavy rucksacks. At long last, in the evening at 9:00 PM, dirty, disheveled and famished, and minus a few coat buttons, we arrived at Gamburg. Our arrival was quite unexpected; it was therefore the occasion of spontaneous rejoicing and excitement, and between big mouthfuls of bread and fruit, many questions and answers passed between us.

For some days after our arrival I had sore eyes — I could scarcely open my eyes and look around. This was due to the glare on the streets of Prague and to fatigue. Then, after using Anna's ointment and a good lotion, I opened them very wide to see the old Burg in all its pristine splendour; I forgot the rush and crush on the trains between Koeln, Wiesbaden, Frankfurt, Wertheim — for Frankfurt, I have no good word, perhaps I should learn to know it better.

Now the journey was something in the past — here was Gamburg! Oh I wish it was my Burg! I could love it tenderly, but that is not the right word — "mightily" is more in place for this old stronghold, standing loftily on a rocky eminence of a range of mountains that rise above the River Tauber.

The Burg has withstood the storms and stresses of almost one thousand years, with stone walls six metres broad, with solid winding stairways, deep cellars and dungeons around which many stories are woven. One can read these stories in the names of many ancient Germanic families who were associated with the Burg in past centuries. There are numerous coats of arms of noble families engraved on stone slabs masoned in some of the unbelievable rooms — the Great Hall, the chapel and others.

One notable aristocrat was the Knight Berenger, who in 1157 built the oldest great rampart of the Burg. Berenger also accompanied the Emperor Friedrich I (called Barbarossa — of the red beard) on some of his jaunts. There are many poems and legends telling about Friedrich, who when he went on a Crusade, called his knights, men at arms, nobles — a great company all wearing a white cross on their armour — and set out for the Holy Land. All went well until they had to cross the River Saleph, in Asia Minor, where alas, Friedrich drowned. There is no telling by what means; history says he may have suffered a heart attack when taking a bath in the cold water, or more likely he was overcome by the current, being weighed down by his heavy armour. We shall never know.

Legend says that Friedrich never really died: he is sleeping in a cave in the Thuringian Mountains — over the centuries, his long red beard has grown through the rock table at which he is sitting, while outside, the ravens circle the peak. One day the ravens will stop flying and then the Emperor will awake; he will emerge from the mountain and make Germany the greatest of nations. I wonder if the Knight Berenger accompanied him to the Holy Land? And was Berenger fond of roses? Because on a terrace that is surmounted by a broad stone balustrade, I found a beautiful garden of roses. This is where you can stand and look across the Tauber valley, where surely, the ladies of the Burg must have stood and watched for the return of the Crusaders. Or was it only the wild Huns galloping their shaggy-coated ponies with the narrow hooves across the valleys? (Some of these narrow horse-shoes can be seen in a collection in Gamburg.)

*****

9 July, 1947

This morning I awoke with a keen sense of pleasure; the calm blue day was looking in at the high window, the air, just now, is a wonderfully rich mixture of newly-mown clover-scented hay and cow dung, the dung from the peasants' cow byres in the village. At present the hay fields along the Tauber valley are being mown, early and late the people are making hay. This morning after the rain the air is heavily scented and as clear as crystal. Hurriedly I splashed some cold water over my face, dressed, and called the children. The boys responded at once, but Ilona? I took a mother's look at her face and let her sleep. The boys were ready. I took Auntie Mother's walking stick and we went for a brisk walk along the valley.

The river still steamy while the first sunbeams chased the mist clouds over the hills. For pleasant walking the hillsides are too stony, but we did not envy Ilona — the lazybones, enveloped in her down quilt — fast asleep, while we were emboldened to shout, like the foresters who traverse these mountains: *Frisch auf zum froelichen Tage!* (Rise and shine!).

Anna had been busy, she had polished the silver and she also had breakfast ready.

We heartily fell to! Papali came in and said, "How nice it is to be together again, and how agreeable to see the table laid with silver!" A sparkle was reflected all round.

From the high, grated window where I am sitting, I can throw a stone down almost directly on to the church tower, some hundreds of metres below the Burg. In the village, the children are singing their Vespers; their voices, sweet and clear, float up the slanting hill and echo down the valley. Here in this old Burg at this quiet evening hour, you can meditate and you feel that you can grasp the stream of life as it flows past and we can say a silent *Deo Gratias* for this great peace — that we hear the wild Huns gallop no more... nor bombers flying.

Ilona was just a little disgruntled that she had overslept the morning walk and although the afternoon was inordinately sultry, we started off up the stony mountain and went for a long walk; that is, Auntie Mother, Ilona and I. We took a good breather, then seeing ominous looking rain clouds and distant flashes of lightning over the mountains, we hurried homewards. Before we entered the turreted portal gate, a sprinkling of rain fell. After we were safely indoors, the storm gathered and strengthened, rain and lightning swept the hills, the murmur of the Tauber was silenced in the noise of the storm as were also the chimes of the clock in the church tower. The swifts that constantly fly about and circle the Burg found their retreat in one of the towers: the rain beat down, but we were secure within the stone walls, secure from rain and weather...just like preceding generations of people who have sheltered here. We are reading something of what these people have thought and done, from an old book the forester has lent us.... And anon, like all the people who have sheltered here down the ages, we also must soon say *au revoir* to Gamburg.

*****

11 July, 1947

We are expecting a visit from Count Kuno this afternoon. After being evacuated from Czechoslovakia, he now stays with relatives in Bavaria. Poor independent Kuno, I can imagine how unhappy he is — perhaps he should do what many are doing: make a prolonged round of visits with relatives and friends, but Kuno is independent, and many people are indifferent about poorer relatives... don't I know it? Well, we shall be glad to see Kuno.

Our mutual friend Dr. Vodeska, the veterinarian from Potstat, now also established in Bavaria, brought Kuno across by car. There was no formality in the greeting between old comrades in distress — Kuno was as pleased to see us as we were to see him. Of course, there was much talk, many questions and many answers and much of mutual interest discussed. Kuno remarked on the small-mindedness, one can call it "meanness," of many well situated people.

He said, "When one has suffered a loss, where the very foundations have been torn from beneath one's feet, it verges upon the comical, when people come with petty stories of woe about their treatment by the Americans.

"One old uncle repeatedly complains to me about his dreadful loss: some miniature models of cannons from his collection have been stolen! Another one, from a neighbouring castle has also sustained a great loss — six verandah chairs taken! There are many complaints of things being requisitioned by the Americans, but," said Kuno, "it really does verge on the comical."

As for Dr. Vodeska, we told him something of what his home and premises looked like after the Russian invasion. How tubes of medicament lay everywhere, half squeezed out — it was said the Russians tried it on their black bread. And how in the cemetery of Potstat, there are a number of Russian graves; the inscription reads: "Died for his Fatherland." We were sorry to say their deaths had been caused by imbibing methyl alcohol from Dr. Vodeska's jars. He only shook his head and said, "What animals!"

Kuno looked into the case that Mimi had entrusted to me but he was disappointed, very disappointed. Many articles that he hoped to find were missing; among them an oval miniature of his mother in a golden frame set with pearls; his father's photo taken in Hussar uniform; 60 vermeille spoons; one small vermeille snuffbox (empire style); one emerald sealing ring; one coronet, black pearls; etc. Kuno concluded that, as the jewels had been hidden in two different holes in the turret — only one had been opened (it appeared) from the contents of the case I brought him. He added that only the

Padre knows of the hiding place. "I believe they remain hidden to this day, guarded by the moping owl that, from yonder ivy-mantled tower to the moon complains...."

I don't know. Sixty golden spoons — black pearls? I was glad that I had been able to restore to Kuno the heavy signet ring that he had entrusted to me in Potstat. The children had been asking questions about me and Kuno's ring.

*****

22 July, 1947

We can tarry no longer. We join the train to Ostend. Gamburg has been like an oasis in the desert, Papali and Auntie Mother the epitome of sheltering palm trees, my eyes are somewhat blurred as we leave the sheltering shade. Now we must just go on and wonder about the beauty of the trees and give thanks.

Ostend, afternoon

There was a salty tang in the air and gulls mewed overhead when we left our luxury train. All eyes were turned to the sea. As the greater part of our baggage had been destined for Gamburg, I did not require much effort to get from the train to the ship that was ready to take us across the English Channel. The preliminaries were soon over (thanks to some Belgian francs that Auntie Mother was able to give us). Soon we were sitting on the deck of the little white ship as she breasted the wavelets.

It is difficult to explain the atmosphere that seemed to surround me. I felt as if I was touching deep soft velvet. I knew it was not due to the pleasant motion of the little ship, not the sparkling sunshine on the waves, not the mewing of the gulls that trailed the ship splashing happily into the sea, not the anticipation of landing at the historical port of Dover. No, it was an inward glow, the wonderful knowledge that a Fatherly Hand had linked our littleness with His Greatness, our little hands in His Hand... all along the way, on the long road.

And now for the second time within a couple of weeks, I felt rich, inestimably rich, although I only had the price of two bananas in my pocket — all I could spare to buy when the steward brought round a delicious basket of fruit. The children were hungry, so we took out our bread and butter and each child had half a banana. Afterwards, we sat quietly and gave thanks. After our little *Te Deum*, being human, I still had wishes, but they were small; I could put them in a nutshell: I wished for a cup of tea, real tea, not balm, and for scented toilet soap — real toilet soap.

It was almost dusk when we sighted Albion's white cliffs. In the pale light they looked like a low mist cloud, not majestic, rampant cliffs, like some of our own kranses. I was somewhat disappointed.

The little ship anchored at 8:00 o'clock. The children shouldered their rucksacks and, carrying suitcases, we marched single file with the other passengers to the customs. After being told by the Czech customs that the British authorities were very "sticky," I did not have much faith in my visa, but I thought, well, in an emergency I still have my Antenuptual Contract. However, the two men behind the counter could not have been more helpful and obliging, especially about our immigration papers: They did not so much as ask to look into our suitcases, just took my word and kindly informed us about trains to London. I confided to them that I had no English money. They advised me to tell the official at the ticket counter what currency I had, and if it was not accepted to come back to them.

At the ticket counter, they made no bones about accepting our Czech money. As I was about to receive the tickets to London, one of the Customs men came and kindly inquired if I was alright and if I was able to manage. I appreciated this very much indeed and more so as they were very busy in their own department.

###

CHAPTER FOURTEEN
IN A GREAT CITY OF THREE DAYS' JOURNEY

23 July, 1947

We arrived at Victoria Station at 1:00 AM with the children half asleep. I inquired from one of London's tall bobbies if there was a room to be had at one of the hotels. He answered, "You'll hardly find a room anywhere and not at this hour of the night, and considering your baggage, why not sleep in the small waiting room at the station?" to which he escorted us. The room contained wash-basin and water, a table and some rather wide leather-covered benches.

We have no travel snobbery and with the children remarking, "How good it is that the Russians have not been in England to strip off the leather," we spread our pillows and *plumeaux* and fell asleep.

It is difficult to believe that we are in London, an exceeding great city of three days' journey. After an early start, first going to Westminster Cathedral for Mass, then we looked, just looked, into Westminster Abbey, where one should spend days to enjoy its riches. Now I said, "We are ready for that good cup of tea! And soap! However, our breakfast was delayed and poor Fritzl was starving until the banks opened and I was able to change some money, but here again I'm stuck with my German money, the banks give no credit.

We have enjoyed toast — lots of toast and a pot of real tea — but soap? No, not in London, not in all England: only obtainable on children's ration cards. Too bad! I am exceedingly disappointed! Two years after the war! The Continent has made a better recovery than Britain.

Again I had to appeal to a bobby to direct us to Hyde Park and to South Africa House at Trafalgar Square. Hyde Park is only a short distance from Victoria Station — so different from our old black-wattle plantation at home, where we children in our carefree days had loved to roam, that we had called Hyde Park, where we had romped and played hide and seek, climbed high trees and collected gum, or peeped into strange birds' nests. Where the thread of fantasy wove its own colourful pattern with home-made sunshine in healthy minds, not looking out for gloom — that was our Hyde Park

I left the children sitting on a sunny bench, where there was lots to keep them interested: a little pond with water plants and frogs, and nearby, a path where children trotted their ponies up and down. Telling the children to be sure not to move away — as I would lose them — I walked to Trafalgar Square to pay, as I thought, a speedy visit to South Africa House. I was detained, very happily, for an hour or more by all that I saw, including some beautiful pictures of birds and scenes from the Low Country, even one from Mokeetsi — home! I fell deeply in love with each and every one of my compatriots to whom I spoke. These included a black man wearing a high snow-white collar and an attache, a Mr. Jan van der Poel, who was most kind. He has promised to see what he can do so to help me arrange our booking to South Africa. He said he would write and advise me and I know he will.

Back at Hyde Park, the children were nowhere to be seen. It was getting late and we had to catch the afternoon train to Sussex. I walked up and down, looking to left and right. The sun was hot. Where could they be? I became distressed, then decided to look for a bobby again, but when rounding a little low hedge, there on the bench where I had left them — with all the rucksacks still tied to their backs — were the dear sweet lambs, all four lying fast asleep.

One hour's journey from Victoria Station found us in Hayward's Heath, Sussex. The Priory of Our Lady of Good Counsel is about a mile from the station. We took a bus and arrived in time for an unexpected real English high tea, which was served to us at the chaplain's house by Joan, a sweet Irish lassie. Among the other good things that we enjoyed were two plates of sweet biscuits, which I am ashamed to say just disappeared between us. I, like the children, love sweet biscuits with a touch of chocolate. Our lives indeed are made up of a mixture of trials and surprises, and some circumstances and coincidences.

We are to stay in the chaplain's house, with Father Dorman, a grey-haired priest who received us very kindly. It is a small elegant house adjoining the stately Convent building.

In front of Father's door stand two glossy-leaved holly trees, where English robins have their refuge.

*****

24 July, 1947

As it was late yesterday when we arrived, I think Reverend Mother wanted me first to have the chance of settling down before asking me to come and meet her. The Augustinian nuns, like the Carmelites, are among the enclosed orders that are not free to "come and go" or meet people beyond their *Gitter* (grille). Permission must first be granted by their bishop. This morning Reverend Mother Mary Baptist, to give her full name, was already waiting for me behind the grille in the parlour; she welcomed me kindly and took full interest in everything I had to relate. I see that, like all Superiors of Convents, Mother Baptist is sagacious, practical, and a kind person. I have often asked myself, from where do cloistered people get so much knowledge of the world, together with a real understanding of our human frailties? I think knowledge comes because the Catholic Church is universal — big — widespread — and very human, and because from A to Z we all must pray our *Mea Culpa* (It is through my fault). If our prayer is sincere then surely people must be more understanding and become better by looking into their own minds.

*****

25 July 1947
A Coincidence

It must take a special kind of courage and faith — or vice versa, you can't separate the two — to become the prioress of a large convent of nuns, some very old, and at the same time to be head of a finishing school for young ladies: this I learned when Mother Prioress asked me if I was related to Elisabeth Praschma. Elisabeth is my sister-in-law. Vaguely, I knew that she had been to a finishing school in England, but I was astonished to learn that she had been an inmate of the Priory, as were also some Stolberg cousins. I call this a heaven-sent coincidence, that in our time of need we should have found unexpected asylum in a Priory where we are not regarded as strangers.

From Kyjovice I had written to Reverend Mother, explaining that we had no money. I asked her, would it be possible to get work of one kind or another in England? Now I find that the practical nuns have already made inquiries for me round and about Hayward's Heath. Forthwith, I've been given a list of places where help is required: a shop, a chemist, a gardener, a fruit farm, and a carnation grower. The children are all eager for me to apply to the fruit farm. I shall first make inquiries at the carnation growers — the work will last longer. I have always had my heart set on carnation growing.

*****

26 July, 1947

We are now working, that is, Lekkie, Peter and I, at the largest specialized carnation nursery in England — perhaps one of the largest carnation farms under glass in the world. The name of Allwood Brothers is known all over the world to carnation lovers, but not many are personally acquainted with the stalwart brothers Edward, George, and Montagu Allwood.

For us to have been in England and not to have known Wivelsfield Green would have been a great misfortune. The Allwood brothers, after working at other branches of farming and gaining valuable experience, united, and with limited capital, had started their own carnation enterprise. Looking for a suitable site, they halted their caravan and pitched their tent at Wivelsfield Green in Sussex. And while brother George was in America buying seed and large quantities of plants, Montagu and Edward worked on the nursery, putting up the first glass house, which was hardly finished in time to receive the plants.

Mr. Montagu Allwood said, "The first six months were the most miserable I have ever spent, but also the most rewarding. We, my brother George and our excellent staff, worked like galley slaves. It now seems pleasant to recall our beginnings, the first really large glass house, the gradual expansion, and of course, our early triumphs: 'Wivelsfield

White', 'Mary Allwood,' and many *allwoodii*. They certainly helped us up the hill of life — so did *Dianthus allwoodii* and other types of *allwoodii*.... Yes, it behooves us all to serve Nature faithfully and honourably and to the best of our ability...." This is Mr. Montagu Allwood, a handsome man — the epitome of one born and nourished for many generations by the soil of England.

It was pleasant travelling on an early morning bus to Wivelsfield — a matter of some fifteen minutes from the priory, where a crowd of men, women, and school-going children find employment at the glass houses. We were fortunate to be there in holiday time. The children are given all manner of jobs: cleaning and refilling the clay pots, mixing up soils, carting sand and compost, and such like. The men attend to insect pests, food for carnations, white-washing the glass roofs to keep out the strong sun, or cleaning them. The women usually pot out the young plants with special care. Another work that requires special care is the propagation of plants by cuttings — of course, the natural way of increasing plants is by seed, but those that are propagated by cuttings are originally from outstanding plants. Success depends upon every detail, of which there are many — the cuttings selected from young plants, must be kept under wet sacks until placed in the soil, and don't bruise your cuttings, says Mr. Allwood. There are 101 things that can give bad results.

There is disbudding; stopping the plants; cutting blooms for shows; sales and marketing; collecting and packaging seed — for all these things, the summer months are quite too short! It is remarkable that Mr. Allwood finds time to speak to each of his individual workers, but as he says in his great carnation book: We horticulturalists can never suffer from that deadly disease depression — from having nothing to do!

My boys delight in travelling with me by bus, and of course they delight in receiving their pay packets at the end of the week. After working for four hours every day, they return for lunch at the priory. Lekkie has found work at the local chemist — bottle washing — in the afternoons. He is saving every penny to buy himself a push-bike. Peter, who earns less, spends his money on little childish fancies; Peter's chief delight is the glass-house work. Ilona spends her days with the nuns, and our Petty — he has now taken on his name of Fritzl again — pesters poor Father Dorman. They make match-box motor cars, and Father has asked me why he calls them "autos," and, I've just learned that Father gives him a bath every afternoon (he gets another from me in the evening). Well, when Father bathes him, he has all manner of antics in the bath. Father has told him to behave — but it was when he turned a summersault, splashing water everywhere, that Father gave him a sound smack on his behind. Fritzl turned round and looked at Father in surprise. "Father," he said, "I did not expect that from you!"

And I? I grow more empassioned, enslaved, enamoured by the work; and by Mr. Allwood and his carnations; it is a sheer joy to walk down these long "corridors of light," flanked by wide beds of, as Shakespeare says, "The fairest flowers of the season, our carnations." And I am not alone in my esteem. Bumblebees fly in and out of the open windows humming loudly in praise and appreciation, and together, we are offended by any sort of interruption.

Mr. Allwood writes about carnations in many lands, including South Africa — Durban. But does anyone in Durban know the perfectly beautiful Doris Allwood, Mr. Allwood's masterpiece? Or the George Allwood? Or the full-petalled reds and whites and yellows? All are beautiful, but in size, perfume, and colour combination, Doris Allwood surpasses any and every carnation I have ever seen. Fully petalled in a luminous mauvy-pink combination, with a perfect calyx and strong guard petals; she takes pride of place. My weekdays pass swiftly at Wivelsfield Green.

On Saturdays I take the children up to London to learn something of the city. They are hugely delighted by every new sight. I felt amused when they brightly commented that "London is the most beautiful city in the world!"And this coming after Prague! "And why do you think so?" "Oh Mammie, just look at the busses!" The great big double-deckers painted with many advertisements are something quite new to us!

We have been to St. Paul's — quite impressed by the white marble tombs of England's illustrious heroes: the whispering gallery. We have been to see our friend Mr. Jan van der Poel, but it is the Tower of London that has drawn our

interest. I wonder why many people in London have never
visited the Tower, that most historical spot in the world. We
did not visit the ghosts who must dwell there, where three
tragic queens were beheaded on the Green — among many
others. The gruesome axe, the great block and the place of
execution are still in evidence. When Queen Elizabeth I was
imprisoned in the Tower, she expressed the wish to die like her
mother (never despair, for you never know your luck.) But
how many passed through those Water Gates never to return.
Many of the Catholic martyrs now live in the pages of history.
Some of them are poignantly remembered by the little prayers
and verses scratched on the grim stone wall of their prison,
now protectively covered by glass. The boys of course
delighted in seeing the suits of armor and the weapons. Ilona
and I would have liked to see the Crown Jewels but they were
not on display. Then there is Tower Bridge, where one is
constrained to stop and listen to the hooting of vessels and
watch the pleasure and cargo boats passing to and fro on the
rippling water. And here on the side of the bridge, I saw a
shamrock leaf drawn — I think it must have been by a poor
Irish soldier. In the leaf he had written, "Erin for ever, Erin go
Bragh." I was not only constrained to stop and listen to the
hooting of the ships, but by the magic those words brought of
how soon we would be travelling, like the swallows, on our
homeward way.

It was that fascinating place, Billings Gate Fish Market
on the river — reeking to high heaven — that drew us again
and again. Ripe fish and horse-manure lying about the street;
men coming up from the river, dressed in black tarpaulins,
looking like some weird regiment, with baskets of fish straight
from the sea on their heads; at the corner of the warehouse,
piles of decayed matter — lobsters, horse manure, fish, clam
shells, and much more. Some of these clam shells have come
with us to South Africa — the children were not slow to collect
and put some in their rucksacks. If I was one of those petite
mothers, I would have stopped them, but, as it is, I thought,
hands can be washed, and so they were in the Thames River
and so they were again at the priory. Saturdays are quite
enjoyable and lovely!

I think it is due to the war that I realize that we must
carry a common yoke together, and therefore I do not feel a

stranger in England. I am quite touched by the kindness of the people, I feel a strong bond of unity when people look kindly at my children. The English names that I had never particularly noticed seem to draw me, and the English voices seem almost like a call of the blood! But it is in the train, when you sit with people, that you learn to know them better, and here people have invited me to their homes, one lady to Hastings, another to Brighton. I would like to visit these sea-side cities, but time and funds fail.

*****

Circumstances = All

Surely it is because of many happy circumstances that the children are taking long strides and are much more settled — learning English, up in the mornings to serve early Mass for Father Dorman — that the pains in my shoulder and arm are quite gone. The chapel is beautiful, especially when dozens of tall, slender candles are lit on the altar, and also when the nuns sing their matins and then, "when darkness descends on the wings of night," you hear them singing their vespers — voices from another world.... Another day has gone its way.... It is here you find: "Peace I give you, my peace... not as the world gives I give to you... it is my Commandment that you love one another. Otherwise there will be night over all the earth, people will grope in darkness and be lost." It is in this spirit that challenges are met and sacrifices made.

Our Sundays are spent very quietly. I write many letters, knowing that people are anxious about our welfare. I have asked Reverend Mother if the nuns would like the children to sing for them. They would like it very much. Sister Dorothy, a very dear person, has written a song for the children: "Bethlehem, hearest thou thy Lord?" She has also written a little play for Ilona and Fritzl. I only hope my Wild Flowers don't discredit themselves!

August 1947

I have written out a program of songs for the children:

Two native songs:
> A Sesutho greeting, and "Kerrie! Kerrie!"

both in native language — short and sweet.

Two German songs:
> "*Kommt ein Vogel geflogen.*" (A Bird Comes Flying).
>
> "*Der Mond ist auf gegangen.*" (The Moon Has Risen).

Two Czech songs:
> "*Tece Voda, Tece.*" (Flow Waters, gently flow by the gates of old Prague).
>
> Arise Little Sparrows,
> > The sun is out on high,
> > Over all the hills and valleys
> > The cuckoo's call is heard.
> > Arise! Arise! The sun is out on high!
> > Cuckoo! Cuckoo! Cuckoo! Cuckoo!-
>
> This is a lively little canon.

Two English songs:
> "Bethlehem, Hearest Thou Thy Lord?"
>
> "Good Night to you all."

As encore: "Evening Prayer" in German — Brahms.

Afterwards, back in the chaplain's house, we felt very pleased with ourselves — and especially when some plates of those lovely biscuits with a little chocolate icing were sent over to us!

*****

9 August, 1947

Shortly after this little feast, we celebrated another feast — Ilona's birthday. I suggested we go up to London, see some of the sights, and then have ice cream in one of the old-fashioned cafes. Reverend Mother, however, suggested that we spend our usual quiet Sunday. She added, "We have a present for Ilona and the kitchen staff will make her a cake; how would you like that? Of course, I thought it would be lovely, and so it was. After Mass when we returned to the Chaplain's house, the fairies had set the table, there were flowers and a large, beautiful cake, and next to the table, in a doll's cradle, curtained with lace and pink satin, was a sweet baby doll in a long robe. Ilona was speechless — her face beamed with happiness — until she could whisper to me: "I shall call her Monica." Father Dorman and the Irish lassie Joan sat down to join us for tea; Father was much surprised when I rummaged in my suitcase and brought out the blessed candle given to us by the people of Kyjovice, which we lit at the table. But first, before we have our tea. I asked Father if he would kindly cut up the cake, as I would like to send the nuns a portion. Father cut it up into neat little portions, like a wedding cake. Joan took the cake on a tray to the nuns and told them how our tall candle from the church in Czechoslovakia cast a light, like a blessing, on the table. Father was impressed by our candle and he was amused when Fritz, in his solemn way, said: "*Weisst Du was*, Father? I think we must often have a party with a b-i-g cake."

After the vespers, "The nuns are equal to some more sewing," I was told, and I was fitted for a frock. "No trouble," said the good little sister, "some material has been given to us." And with a smile, "Just for you."

"Sister," I said, "is that a little white one?"

"No, it is just right for you."

I did not see the dress until it was sewn, then I said enthusiastically, "How beautiful! How lovely!" A cream silk dress, with pale pink roses and a little short coat; I do not know myself in the dress! I only know that I am deeply grateful to Reverend Mother... in a hundred different ways, for a hundred different things.

September, 1947

Lekkie, earning more than Peter, has been saving for his push-bike, together with one of his friends at the chemists. After studying the newspaper adverts, he has seen a bicycle for sale. Together they went out, and as Lekkie says, "We have returned with a splendid bicycle!" I feel sorry for my Peter, especially when we see Lekkie speeding along on his bicycle, while he has to sit quietly beside me on our way to work. I try to smooth it over by saying how sorry I am for Fritz, having to stay at the Priory and build his automobiles with match-boxes and I add: "Just spend our few shillings carefully, when you receive your pay packet. There will be bonbons to buy on the ship," but I know the temptation is great at the tuck-shop.

At South Africa House I was told that it would take several months before we would be able to get a booking to S.A. Now our friend Mr. van der Poel has advised me that arrangements can be made for us to leave on the 12th on an old boat called *S.S. Llanstephan Castle* for Cape Town. We must hurry through with final arrangements and good-byes.

When I told Mr. Allwood that we intend making tracks for home, he said he was sorry to hear it, but if it was not that he is getting on in years and that he is bound up in England, he would like to venture out and start a carnation farm in South Africa. He said carnations should do splendidly in S.A. in winter; with sufficient quantities of water and a light overhead covering of reeds or grass, they should also do well in summer. The flowers should retain their depth of colour.

With our last pay packets and a few farewell handshakes, Mr. Allwood handed me three of his books that he has autographed for me. I was deeply touched by this kind act, and more so when I sat in the bus and looked back at the magnificent rows of glass houses peacefully reflecting the late afternoon sunshine. The gauge of man's labour and industry — I should say of three men, the Allwood brothers, who have laboured shoulder to shoulder and who have not shirked duty's demands and their country's call. During the war, the glass houses were filled with potatoes, beans, onions, etc., hereby catering to the country's needs and putting aside the endeavours and dreams of a lifetime. This is where Montagu Allwood has reversed Lord Balfour's little saying, "The English race, it never forgives, but it always forgets." "Forgive and forget," says Mr. Allwood, and it has brought a rich reward: the glass houses have come into their own again — after two years of war — with a wealth that is beautiful to look upon.

11 September, 1947

Thursday morning. Felt very tired after several days of washing and packing and answering the Sisters' bell, etc. — the bell sounding very frequently for the children and me to come for farewell wishes and all the little holy pictures, chocolates and other gifts the dear nuns can possibly think of to speed us on our way. The boys have each received an especially beautiful gift for serving Mass, from Reverend Mother and community.

Lekkie has a beautiful cross such as one can find in a chapel — a carved ivory Redeemer on a black cross; in looking at it, the immediate response is to fold one's hands because you feel that there have been earnest and humble prayers said before it to God in heaven. Peter received a carving, done by a master's hand in Oberammergau, of our Redeemer's thorn-crowned head in a wooden security. Fritz has two pictures, framed in blue leather, of Our Lady and the Babe. These are greatly cherished gifts to take with us across the sea.

Mass was specially arranged early so that the boys could serve. They looked very sweet in their Mass vestments and very earnest as we all five went to communion.

Friday, 12 September, 1947

Breakfast was hurried: more goodbyes. Father Dorman gave us his blessing — "Goodbye," he said, "and may God help you to make a success of your lives."

Homeward bound. A taxi threaded its way through the busy traffic en route for the Royal Albert Docks. Perched on top of the taxi was a bicycle — practically all the parts of the machine were carefully wrapped about with newspaper. Among the occupants of the taxi sat the owner of the bicycle, proudly wearing a tropical helmet — we were nearing our goal! Already the first broad glimpses of the Thames with boats and barges and high bridges came into sight. The children were hugely enjoying this new adventure — delighted by every sight, delighted by the buses on the streets, strings and strings of London's early morning double deckers. They chatted animatedly, they commented on the number plates, they took stock of the advertisements and passed amusing comments about the drivers. "*Und weisst Du was?*" said Fritz innocently. "This is better than swinging on a gate!"

The taxi was taking us swiftly to the docks, we were passing along many interesting streets and I felt that here, right

now, we were irrevocably passing the most important mile-
stone of our lives, for what had seemed but darkly remote had
now become reality. This morning, in this great city, when the
Morning Star had dimmed, all the uncertainty, the turmoil of
the past, was pushed away — as if under a darkened veil, the
way was bright and clear... we were heading South — to the
Royal Albert Dock... to Cape Town!

Henceforth, if I look back, it will be to cast lingering
glances over my shoulder, to those places where I have been
graciously led and received: Hamburg, Falkenberg, Kyjovice,
Breslau, Gamburg, and so on, on to the still waters and
pasturelands of England — to Hayward's Heath. How good
God is; how good and gracious His people are! My prayers are
heard, my face is set to the south with my children by my side:
Lekkie very manly, wearing the tropical suit — and of course
the helmet! — gifts from the nuns; my dear Peter, cool in a blue
Palm Beach suit and white shirt; Ilona wears a dirndl with
white, braided yellow apron, above the white peter-pan collar,
her face, slightly tanned by the English sun, is very sweet —
she looks swell, her long braids tied with yellow ribbons; Fritzl,
"*mein froelicher Junge*," to me looks like a demure rose in the
light grey linen suit I bought for him in Prague.

We are taking long strides home. All eyes are bright,
the children nudge each other and they laugh. "Just look at
Mother," they say. "And what a song!" Mother's heart was
brimming over with feeling too strong for expression; she was
also swinging the gates of paradise, so she sang an old South
African song: "Sarie Marais."

###

CHAPTER FIFTEEN
JOURNEY'S END: WE RETURN WITH THE SWALLOWS

13 September, 1947

Our first day on the *Llanstephan* was comparatively restful. After getting ensconced in our cabins, we had nothing to do but sit on deck, watch the traffic on the busy Thames, have meals, and try to become acquainted with our fellow passengers. It seemed a long day — we had been up early and it was a relief when at 8:00 PM the anchor was weighed. The lights of London, of the Royal Albert Dock, of buildings and bridges beamed over the darkening waters of the river, when to the immense pleasure of the children, two tugs started moving the liner out to the open sea! When the last lights dimmed and then disappeared from view, we were ready to roll up and fall asleep.

After our first night at sea, nobody seemed to feel very bright, like the sea that was clouded over; many were absent from breakfast, myself included. However, I think we all felt that we had to try to make the best of the things we had to face for the next three weeks.

As the old *Llanstephan* ploughed the waves, many amenities were provided and the passengers were encouraged to give a helping hand with regard to arranging games, sports, musical evenings, concerts, and soon we were absorbed in the new life around us. The children hugely enjoyed every moment, they each won a couple of prizes at games: I was surprised at the effort Ilona put into a relay race, which in her quiet way and with the encouragement of her brothers, she won outright. The children continually call for my attention, "Now look at this Mammie!" "Now look at that!" "Look at the fish leaping in the sea!" "Come, come quick and see how the whale is spouting water, far out in the sea!" "Look at the birds, how high they are flying!" The birds were flying at such a height that only sharp little eyes could detect them; and an old sailor told the children that they were wild duck, they fly the highest of all birds. One of the highlights of the voyage was when I took the children up to the bridge and one of the engineers permitted each child, in turn, to steer the ship for a few minutes. Then they had to run to the back of the deck to look at the wavering course that had been steered clearly showing in the foam, in the wake of the ship.

We sighted Las Palmas early in the morning, lying like a mirage on the horizon that gradually turned from pale grey to varying shades of green; pale mountains rolled back from the coast to lose themselves in mystical heights — it looked a very interesting island. The town was also a pleasing sight, with pastel-coloured houses, and beautiful gardens with lush tropical flowers that I had not seen for many years: bright oleanders, hibiscus, masses of bougainvillea and many shady trees. Standing guard over the town is the age-old Cathedral, with twin spires and Gothic arches, built in the fifteenth century. Even before the liner moored in the impressive harbour, a swarm of boats surrounded us with tempting wares — fresh fruits and vegetables, and beautiful Madeira work: table cloths with matching embroidered napkins, handkerchiefs, and blouses, fetching very low prices. What really fascinated the children were the singing birds — full-throated canaries that rivalled each other in keeping up the reputation of their islands — we must buy a canary, yes, two canaries! And so, ultimately two canaries were bought with the assurance that they were very precious songsters. Alas, our canaries never sang a note. Who can blame them if they left their voices at Las Palmas? But perhaps we had just been cheated.

To stretch our legs, we went for a walk among the foothills, where there was much to admire. Then we visited the chapel of San Antonio, where Christopher Columbus prayed for guidance before voyaging into the unknown. But the children had much more amusement in the pleasant courtyard of the casino with its carved dogs of Spain set up along the wall. They each chose a dog, and then wanted to sit on them! No, no, I said, Saint Rochus will object, he is the patron saint of dogs. We'll get into big trouble!

Then once again out on the open sea, the ship churning its way through unlimited, dark-green, troubled waters; all was dismal and dark, there was no lone star — "*Kein Stern!*" I

called out in my sleep. Now I was fully awake. "*Kein Stern....*"
How often did I have this dream in the tumultuous days of the
war; and what doleful fears had been in my dream? How I had
prayed for just one star! The star that we unconsciously follow.
I know what had, in a measure, influenced the dreams: the
tragic Volga song by Franz Lehar from the Czarevitch so often
heard during the war. It still haunted me, a song that echoed in
how many broken homes? "No star.... Have you forgotten me,
up there? You have so many angels with you. Send just one
down here to me. The night is so dark.... No star! Have you
forgotten me?"

Memories will remain with us; sometimes they will
follow like a bogeyman. I tried to push the dream away and
turned round on my narrow bunk. We were safe; the
Llanstephan was churning its way through the waves. I turned
my pillow — no good, the faces of the vanquished people, the
blameless children, pitiful faces followed me and looked
accusingly at me. It was only when the grey light began to
spread over the ocean and I said, "*Mea culpa*: I also am at fault,"
that they began to disperse. It behooves each one in his own
sphere to serve man and beast faithfully, thus following our
Star that leads to God in all his trailing clouds of glory.

The children thumped at the door. "Are you sick?" they
asked. "Don't you know, the sailors say there is going to be
great commotion on the ship, today we run the gauntlet of
Father Neptune and his assistants!"

(This mock initiation is performed whenever a ship
crosses the equator, into "the realm of King Neptune.") There
was much fun and the children took great pride in their big
certificates.

A concert was arranged among the passengers, and it
was a nice diversion. Members of the sports committee came
round looking for talent. The children joined in by singing a
few of their Czech and German songs. They dressed up in so-
called Czech national costume, the boys in their ancient leather
pants, wearing my embroidered blouses. They looked rather
cute, although Fritzl's blouse was a few sizes too large. "Never
mind," said Ilona, as she tied a kerchief round his head, "they
can look at my dirndl," of which she is very proud. After the
concert, several passengers came to compliment and

congratulate us, saying the children's songs were the best and most enjoyable part of the programme.

And so the days speed by. I could scarcely see them pass swiftly enough in anticipation of our arrival in Cape Town. And then we had a little delay, only about one hour, but it was packed with suspense! After dinner and drinks with only the ship's lights on the dark waves, there was a loud call of "Man overboard!" with a blast of the ship's siren, she stopped in her track.

Everybody had something to say and everybody had something to think about and when we all stood along the rails and peered into the dark surging water, touched only here and there with little wreaths of foam, we hoped to see a form, a head, a hand stretched out for help! Then someone thought they had seen a hand and then everybody thought they had seen a head — even I thought I saw something dark! Suddenly I thought of the children. Are they all safely asleep? I rushed to the cabins. Ilona was soundly asleep and so were Peter and Fritz. Engelbert, who slept some distance away on a high bunk, was not to be seen. I became frantic. He was certainly not on deck! I groped for the light and stood on tiptoe to look into the bunk and there sleeping like a cherub, tightly rolled in his blanket, was my son Engelbert, in the far corner of the bunk. Meanwhile, a list of passengers and crew was taken and the *Llanstephan* started on a grinding course again — no one was missing. Apparently it was only a lark played by some of the R.A.F. soldiers who had been celebrating.

I had taken quite a lot of pride in the *Llanstephan*, until — well, until I became acquainted with the fact that she had landed the first consignment of Spitfires ever sent to Russia, and she had been accorded a tremendously enthusiastic ovation by their civil and military authorities! That was surely enough for the old ship. And if those Spitfires are the only weapons of war sent to Russia, then the "Free World" will perhaps continue as a free world.

*****

3 October, 1947

All was bustle aboard the ship as we glided into the harbour — Cape Town! The portal gate to the hard road that leads on to future endeavour; but this was not the question concerning us now. How good it was to be back! This precious moment will never entirely fade! I was impatient to set my feet on African soil, but had to wait until all the preliminaries were arranged and then we were still delayed by a reporter from the Argus Company who insisted upon hearing our "full story." At long last our baggage was booked to Pietersburg. This included the precious bike and accordion, also bought by Lekkie.

The children looked at the Cape Coloureds (a dark-skinned mixed race unique to Cape Province) rather fearfully; Fritzl spoke in whispers and kept close to my side. I reassured them, saying, "You can speak any language and no one will harm you and you are free to come and go." This was bad policy, and it was just enough, after being cooped up for three weeks, to rouse their curiosity for sightseeing in a new city and perhaps be up to mischief. "Not now, just *wag en bietjie* (wait a little) — I am going to buy some lunch, which we'll have on the mountain. But first, we must offer a *Te Deum*." This we did at St. Mary's Cathedral. Afterwards, with a few mixed thoughts, I stood and looked at the nearby statues of Queen Victoria and Cecil Rhodes

"Well, you two, now did you ever think," I said, "when you British conspired with Fate and triumphed over us Boers — could you have thought that one day, an old Boer Backvelder would look kindly at you and say like a little child, "The nations that are great must stand together, otherwise they will be great and free no more.'"

As I stood chatting to the old statues, an old lady got out of a big car and nodded at me. With a friendly smile, she said, "I saw you at the Cathedral; can we give you a lift anywhere?" I thanked her and said after three weeks at sea, we intend taking a walk and having a picnic somewhere on the mountain. We introduced ourselves and stood talking for a short while. Then the kindly couple — Mr. and Mrs. Stuart-Coe (an old Irish name) — inquired what time our train would be leaving for the North. Then they took us for a drive up Table Mountain and dropped us at a suitable little picnic spot.

Here we sat and admired the craggy mountains and the deep blue sea and sky, and I told the children about Cape Town and our ancestors. How the Huguenots, after having been persecuted in France by their countrymen, had taken refuge in foreign countries — some had settled in the Cape, where the leader Baron Pierre du Plessis had gained a broad valley from the Dutch East India Company. He had named the beautiful valley, "Franschhoek," the name it still bears today.

Some years later other members were added to the Huguenots by our ancestor Commodore Ferreira and officers, and this is how it happened. In 1691, Ignatius Ferreira, in command of a Man-o'-War, sailed from Lisbon to China and Japan to take ambassadors from Portugal for the purpose of making a Treaty of Commerce and peace with both nations.

However, in a great storm which raged for a whole week, the *Sarpine*, as the vessel was called, was driven on to the rocks near Hottentot's Holland. An old seaman named Simon saw the ship lying between the rocks. He at once went with two boats to save the crew, but he found only five men clinging to the mast. With great difficulty, he managed to rescue them. He sent a message to the Governor of the Dutch East India Company, Simon van der Stel, who at once drove down in his carriage and took the commodore and the others to his residence. On their arrival, the poor sufferers were so weak, the doctor had to order warm baths and hot wine for them, and it took a whole week before they were able to walk again.

The governor was obliged to tell the commodore that he regretted that he would have to send them away, as he had strict orders from Holland not to allow foreigners to remain in the town. So Ignatius was packed off to the Huguenot settlement of Franschhoek, where the Huguenots, knowing what adversity meant, made him feel as comfortable as they possibly could. It did not take long for Ignatius to learn French and soon this dark-eyed young man endeared himself to his benefactors.

Like my grandparents had related to us, I told the children how these grand old people had faced the hardships of this untamed country with courage and fortitude, fought wild beasts, poisonous snakes, droughts and storms and dangerous *assegai* (spear) wounds; then came tomorrow — a brand new day, held out like a shining silver bowl, filled with the rose of hope — made strong by the hardy experiences of their lives.

So they toiled on to carve a home for themselves and their descendants in the beautiful valley. Incidentally, I much doubt that the commodore knew how to handle a gun. "An Admiral, not knowing how to handle a gun?" they said. Well, I don't know, but he managed alright, because he married Countess Almine du Pre, granddaughter of Baron Pierre du Plessis, and they settled in a home he built for her in the Cape. Today, it is owing to that tragic storm, to that course of events and to the courage of the people who left their homelands in a sailing ship so long ago — that we sit here on Table Mountain and with pride can recall our ancestors.

We arrived at the station in good time before the train left and were getting ready to settle for the night when we had a very pleasant surprise — to see Mr. and Mrs. Stuart-Coe coming along the platform. "We've come to see if you are nicely settled and to say *au revoir*," they said. We were delighted. Then, handing us a basket, they said, "Here is something for the journey." The basket contained fruit, drawing paper and pencils for the boys, and a prettily-dressed Japanese doll for Ilona. "And this," said Mrs. Stuart-Coe, "is for mother, as I don't think you could get make-up during the war." She handed me a pouch; it contained lipstick, powder, etc. I could not express my thanks to these beautiful people (and good-bye to beautiful Cape Town) who had received us with such open arms.

We are at the last stages of our journey — flying with the swallows. This third day of October, with warm spring breezes and with good people, is our Thanksgiving Day. The train takes the ups and downs steadily. Onward, always onward, in long steps — we go.

We arrived at Bloemfontein Station. There stood my *Oom* Victor to welcome us. How wonderful, after all the eventful years, to meet my own people again. Here was Jackie, his wife, whom I love, and their two daughters — now grown into beautiful young ladies. They said, "Marvellous to see you back after the tumultuous years in Europe," and we could not keep our eyes off each other. "Yes," was all I could say, and we laughed and laughed, all joining in together, in sheer happiness. I kept thinking, "Blood is thicker than water... we are one family!" And then I said, "I feel like old Rip van Winkle after his long sleep — grown old in years, but warmer and nearer." *Oom* Vic said, "Yes, things have changed and yet they are the same."

There was much to relate and many questions. The children were also invited to relate their experiences, some of them causing wonder and amusement (in their broken English-German expressions), so much so that I heard one of the girls saying, "Just listen to this... I am tickled pink!" The children of course enjoyed this new expression. It took some minutes for them to settle down to the evening meal, before which each child made the sign of the cross — this again caused wide-eyed interest from my Protestant family.

After dinner came an absorbingly quiet evening when *Oom* Vic took up his violin and the old tunes — that he played after returning from the conservatoire where he studied in Brussels — reached out. As I always thought, only *Oom* Vic can make the violin speak. Looking into the past, I seemed to gaze at the portraits as in an album. My mother in a new flowery dress sitting at the piano playing accompaniments; my father sitting in his weighty old armchair listening appreciatively. I turn the page: we don't wait for an invitation to crowd round my grandmother, she comes in with a large ladle which she has forgotten to leave in the kitchen, and a plate of *tamaletjis* (home-made toffees) for us. Again I turn a page, I see my benign grandfather — like a patriarch of old, tall and lithe and tanned with a flowing white beard; we walk in the late afternoon sun together and while we sit in the shade of the bouldered kopje. Granddad turns to me, his blue eyes are very kind as he takes my hand that is small again in his, and I echo the words that he slowly says: "To the red aloes that cling to the rocks, forever ageless; to the little living creatures that scurry by; to God and man, my love, my thanks...."

*****

9 October, 1947

Another night on the train and we arrived at the rather dreary station of Pietersburg, but it was quickly enlivened when we saw my sister Clemence and Herbert and their two offspring, Errol and Dolores, waving a welcome to us on the platform. This time we did not laugh and laugh like we did at Bloemfontein. All that Clem could say was, "*Mei ou Sissie!*" (My old sister!) and we all — even Herbert; the generous white haired man, as I call him — wiped a few tears from our eyes, and the children shyly made the acquaintance of each other. After all preliminaries were arranged, Clem said we made an early start this morning, thinking that we'll travel straight back and have a picnic breakfast on our way, under some mimosa trees on the veld. We all piled into the light delivery lorry and after travelling for some miles reached the mimosa trees — the long-spiked, white thorns that are the prominent feature of the trees were almost hidden by the tufts of fragrant, yellow pompom flowers. It was while we unpacked the lunch basket and the kettle was boiling that Clem recited: "Dear little flowers I loved of old, sweet little curly heads of gold." Lekkie looked at her and then said to Uncle Herbert, "She is like my mother; in Pretoria she kept reciting about 'Jacaranda, Jacaranda...'." And so I think these two, uncle and nephew, seemed to have made a little pact; but I dare not write what Herbert said. Meanwhile, we had so much to say to each other that the sixty kilometres from Pietersburg to Olyfberg seemed all too short. Then, as we travelled down the mountain road, on the opposite side of the deep valley ran a parallel mountain, Herbert pointed across the valley and said: "There is our farm, Avon!" In the distance, the house and garden looked like a neat postage stamp; on the lawn I could clearly read "Avon" marked out in purple Japanese verbena. A friendly welcome.

*****

And so, good-night.

We have arrived at our journey's end: We are at Avon. Like the Wise Men of Old, we have followed the Star — we have reached our Mecca... our striving... our dreams... our beautiful Homeland! What gifts have we to offer? All are inadequate. We have no frankincense, we have no myrrh, no gold. What does one offer when you reach your Mecca?

You bow very low and then you kneel, very solemnly, you offer what you owe to your God and to your fellow man: love and honour and a high regard, gifts to present with a little child's simplicity — gifts that are counted far beyond the price of rubies. Never mind — as you go on your way, the tears that stand in your eyes. Those little bright tears, they are also scooped up and counted in heaven.

And the swallows? A day or two after our arrival, they also reached their journey's end. We sat under the wild fig trees in the late afternoon when they arrived, flying low and without ceremony they flew through the open doors and windows into the house, they settled on the beams in the lounge — never worrying about the other rooms — they settled on the furniture, on anything where they could perch, they just flopped down. We did not disturb them. We wondered if they had been flying through a great storm. If they had been sprayed with insecticide? They reminded me of the prisoners of war I had seen: utterly weary, dejected, exhausted. What had happened to them? It is a question for The Voice of Nature. Why did they fly into the house when in the vicinity there are so many indigenous trees where they could have settled? At the crack of dawn, they left as unobtrusively as they had arrived.

Poor swallows, we wished them well; to also arrive at their journey's end.

But what a cleaning up we had!

###

Epilogue

Dorothy, Countess Praschma

My mother's life was not easy after her return to South Africa. As she had no formal training, she struggled to find employment but made every effort to have her children well-educated. We were all four admitted to boarding schools and eventually led successful lives.

While supervising the nurse's residence at a Johannesburg hospital she wrote short articles which were published in the *Rand Daily Mail*. Among others, she took under her wing a poor, lost waif, also a refugee from war-torn Europe, named Heidi Herzog, who eventually became a well-known artist.

Today, Dorothy lies buried in her beloved Transvaal, at her request, under a granite boulder which reads, "She Gave a Dog a Bone."

Castles
Falkenberg

Now called Niemodlin, this estate has had a checkered history since war's end.

In May 1945, when the Russian armies poured into Eastern Europe, looting and destroying whatever they came across, the vault under the chapel where the Praschma ancestors were laid to rest was broken into. Ancient caskets were pried open and dry bones exposed to search for anything of value. The remains of Engelbert, the last family member to be placed in the vault, were dragged through the streets of Falkenberg and publicly humiliated.

After the Red Army left the castle was used for a time as a school for troubled boys, then fell into neglect. A wealthy Polish gentleman bought the property and began restoring it to its former glory but when his financial empire crumbled the castle once again also crumbled. A movie, *Jasminum*, was filmed in the castle in 2006.

Currently it is owned by the Polish authorities and has become a popular tourist attraction.

Figures of the four house saints, Florian, Johannes Nepomuk, Donatius and Wendelin, have been partially restored and still guard the entrance to the castle on the bridge over the moat.

Kyjovice

After the war ended, Kyjovice was briefly occupied by the Caritas as a home for orphaned and abandoned children. Now, the lovely white castle on the hill, at the end of an avenue of stately chestnut trees, is an old age home. The chapel, once reverently maintained as a sacred place, is used as the mortuary.

Old people from the village fondly remember how the castle proudly stood surrounded by its park, among the botanically richest in all of Silesia, where rare and exotic trees collected over the years by the Stolberg ancestors flourished. During the final months of the war, when fierce fighting raged all around, trees and shrubs were uprooted by German tanks and destroyed by Allied air attacks. The park has since been restored, and has become a popular place for relaxation by the local population. The Czech government laid claims to the lands, forests and farms which were once a part of the estate.

Count and Countess Stolberg and their daughter Regina are buried in the village cemetery, their graves lovingly tended by the people of Kyjovice.

— IPB

###

GLOSSARY

Andenken — Keepsake

Antenuptial contract — Prenup or marriage contract

Assegai — Long-bladed spear said to have been invented by Chaka Zulu

Babushka — Grandmother

Backvelder — Simple Boer farmer, someone from the country

Benes, Edvard — President of Czechoslovakia

Beschluss — Conclusion, decision

Biltong — Jerky

Braai — A cookout, a barbecue

Britzka — An open horse drawn carriage

Bruin oog — Brown eye

Cape Coloureds — Mixed race people of the western cape

Caritas — Charity organization

Cerna kava — Black coffee

Champignons — Mushrooms

Chasy — Watches

Coupe — Train compartment

D-Zug — Express train

Dirndl — Embroidered dress worn by Austrians, Germans and Czechs

Dobre — Good

Dobre den — Good day

Dobre noc — Good night

Dobre vecer — Good evening

Donner wetter — Thunder, or an expression of surprise

Dritte Reich — The Third Empire, so named by the Nazis, supposed to last 1,000 years

Du lieber Gott — Dear Lord

Duivelskloof — A small town in the northern Transvaal

Eintopf — Stew

En jolie compagnie — In good company

Fransch Hoek — Small town in the western Cape Province

Gasse — Alley, lane

Goetterdaemmerung — The turbulent ending of a regime

Haken-Kreuz — Hook-cross; a swastika

Haus Heilege — House saints

Haushelferin — House helper; a servant

Heller — Penny

Himmel — Heaven

Harde beskuit — Rusks

Hottentots Holland — An area in the western Cape province of South Africa

Hrabenka — Countess

Indaba — Meeting, conference

Kaput — Broken, exhausted

Kleinod – Jewel, precious little thing

Kolace — Czech pastries, sweet rolls

Kommissar — Commissioner

Kopjes — Small hills

Krans — Rocky ridge, cliff

lager — Camp

Lazarett — Field hospital

Lorry — Truck or vehicle

Low Veld — Low country

Luft Waffe — Air Force

Masaryk, Jan — Prominent Czech diplomat

Meine guete — My goodness

Militsiya, Militz — Police

M.V.D. — Russian Military Police

Nacht Quartier — lodging

Narodne Vibo — Czech Military Police

Nun ade Du mein lieb Heimatland — Farewell my Homeland

Oberstabsarzt — Senior military surgeon

Okresni Vibo — District Police

Oom — Uncle

Osthilfe — Policy of the German government to give financial support to bankrupt estates in East Prussia

Padkos — Food for the journey

Palaver — Discussion

Pan — Mister, sir

Pani — Woman, lady

Panzer — Tank (literally, "armor")

Plumeau — Comforter, duvet, coverlet

Portmanteau — Traveling case

P.O.W. — Prisoner of War

Pryc — Go away, shoo

Quo vadis — Whither goest thou

Rapunzel — Lamb's lettuce, salad

Rucksack — Backpack

Sarie Marais — A traditional Afrikaner folk song

Sobirayem — Collecting (as a levy or tribute), stealing

Stara maminko — Old mother

Tameletjies — South African homemade toffees

Tece voda — The water flows

Togal powder — A brand-name analgesic

Transvaal — Northern province of South Africa

Ticho — Silence, be quiet

U.N.R.R.A. — United Nations Relief and Rehabilitation Administration, an organization founded to give aid to areas liberated from the Axis

Veldt or *Veld* — Open grassland

Vertrag — Agreement

Vibo — Police

Voetsek — Shoo, scram, hoof it

Voortrekker — Pioneer

Waldmeister — "Forest-master"; the flowering herb woodruff

Weide — Meadow

###

PHOTOGRAPHS

Wedding of Dorothy Ferreira and Engelbert, Count Praschma, Baron von Bilkau, June 1930

Dorothy Ferreira riding an ox while trekking in the veld

As a countess with her children: Englebert, Fritz, Ilona and Peter

*Dorothy, Countess
Praschma, c. 1935*

*Englebert, Count
Praschma, c. 1935*

Dorothy's parents-in-law, Marie and Johannes Graf Praschma, and an early woodcut of Castle Falkenberg

The Stolberg-Stolbergs of Kyjovice: Antonia ("Toto"), Fritz and Regina (below)

Kyjovice, "the white house on the hill"

The Stolberg family, with Dorothy and Ilona (right), 1941

Kyjovice household staff in their Sunday best

Dorothy and her sons

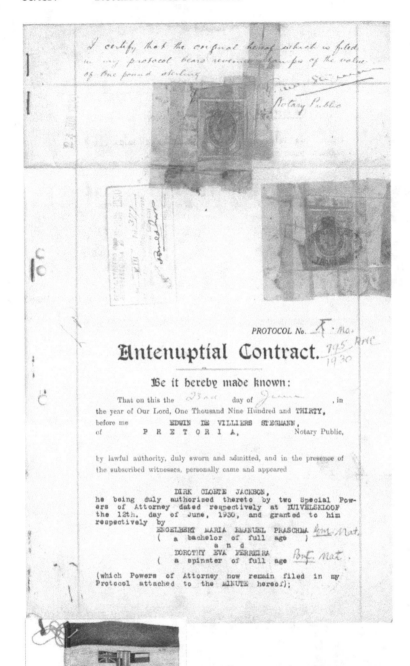

PROTOCOL No.

Antenuptial Contract.

Be it hereby made known:

That on this the   day of   , in
the year of Our Lord, One Thousand Nine Hundred and **THIRTY,**
before me   **EDWIN DE VILLIERS STEGMANN,**
of   **P R E T O R I A,**   Notary Public,

by lawful authority, duly sworn and admitted, and in the presence of
the subscribed witnesses, personally came and appeared

          DIRK CLOETE JACKSON,
he being duly authorised thereto by two Special Powers of Attorney dated respectively at **DUIVELSKLOOF**
the 12th. day of June, 1930, and granted to him
respectively by
        ENGELBERT MARIA EMANUEL PRASCHMA
     (a bachelor of full age   )
               a n d
        DOROTHY EVA FERREIRA
     (a spinster of full age   ).

(which Powers of Attorney now remain filed in my
Protocol attached to the MINUTE hereof);

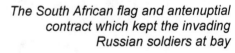

*The South African flag and antenuptial
contract which kept the invading
Russian soldiers at bay*

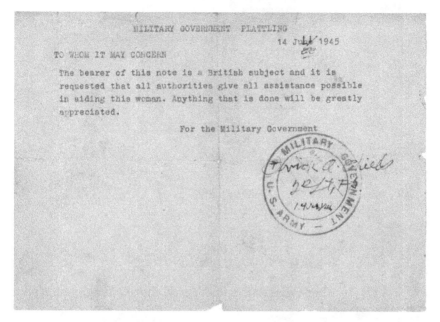

Travel permits from British and American authorities after the war's end

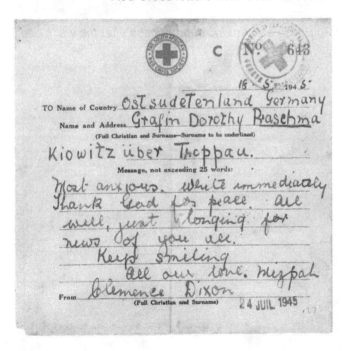

Red Cross letters from South Africa after the war's end

Gamburg a. d. Tauber

The Castle Gamburg

THE UNION-CASTLE MAIL STEAMSHIP COMPANY, LIMITED.

(Registered in England.)

Head Offices:—3, Fenchurch Street, London, E.C.3.

Royal Mail Service.

TOURIST CLASS PASSENGER'S TICKET.

This Ticket is not transferable, and its acceptance by the holder will be considered as binding him to the terms and conditions specified on the inside covers containing this ticket.

TOURIST CLASS.

Ticket No. AK 144   Date of issue 1 9 197

BERTH No. 427/1/2 762 INDEX No.
435/1/2 G3
M 439/1 G3 Countess DE Raschwa

and four children (three boys and one girl) have secured Passage from England to Capetown

by the "Llanstephan Castle" intended to sail on
(or other Vessel)

the 12th day of September 1947

To embark at See notice before m. on the day of sailing. Passage Money in full £ 160.10

for THE UNION-CASTLE MAIL STEAMSHIP COMPANY, LIMITED.

This ticket is issued subject to the terms and conditions specified on the inside covers containing this ticket.

THIS PART OF THE PASSAGE TICKET TO BE RETAINED BY THE PASSENGER AND PRODUCED TO THE OFFICERS OF THE COMPANY WHEN REQUIRED.

Tickets for the family's return on Llanstephan Castle, *October 1947*

RMS Llanstephan Castle *of the Union-Castle Line*

Dorothy's headstone, a granite boulder from her beloved low veld, inscribed as she requested with the words, "She Gave a Dog a Bone."